RECORD APART

Record Apart

The Very Reverend
ANDREW HERRON
M.A., B.D., LL.B.

Moderator of the General Assembly
of the Church of Scotland 1971–1972

1974
SCOTTISH ACADEMIC PRESS
EDINBURGH AND LONDON

Published by
Scottish Academic Press Ltd
25 Perth Street, Edinburgh EH3 5DW
and distributed by
Chatto & Windus Ltd
40 William IV Street
London WC2N 4DF

SBN 7011 2044 4

© Andrew Herron 1974

Printed in Great Britain by R. & R. Clark Ltd, Edinburgh

Contents

To all who by their hospitality, their arrangements, their prayers, made it possible for my wife and myself to travel so far and to do so much, these Irrelevant and Irreverent Recollections of a Right Reverend are humbly dedicated.

Prologue

'To keep the ordinary records of the courts . . . free from the presence of undesirable matter . . . the principle of a Record Apart shall be adopted in all cases where moral delinquency is alleged'—so reads the relevant section of the Act of Assembly dealing with the keeping of Church records.

Somewhere in the 'ordinary records' of the Church of Scotland there is reference to the fact that from May 1971 until May 1972 one Andrew Herron, Clerk to the Presbytery of Glasgow, acted as Moderator of the General Assembly, presiding in that capacity over the deliberations of the court and travelling extensively in Scotland and farther afield to represent the Kirk in divers places and in a wide variety of contexts.

I should be the last to wish to see 'undesirable matter' intruded into such a record (even if, as I trust in the present case, there were no faintest whiff of moral delinquency); and so it has seemed good to me to avail myself of the opportunity which the Record Apart provides for setting forth some of the less formal, less factual, less fossilised features of that year as Moderator; and it has seemed good to me to present them as seen, not as in the Record Proper from the point of view of the recording angel but from that of the suffering agent—as the recollections of a Right Rev.

Irrelevant these recollections often are, irreverent in many cases they may well be—but for that very reason they are probably of greater interest. In any case it would appear from the Act that you're not entitled to keep a Record Apart unless you have some 'undesirable matter' to report. And what more undesirable than the irrelevant and irreverent—particularly when associated with a Right Rev.

It is said—rightly I think—that the telephone has killed the once highly-prized art of correspondence. It could be said that television is fast killing the delightful art of conversation. Even the pastime—I should not dream of elevating it into an art—even the pastime of fireside chatter is fast withering and shrivelling before the onset of central heating. It seems a great tragedy.

In keeping the formal records of the Presbytery I find myself in bondage to a most formal and foostie style of language, peppering my sentences with whereunto's, heretofore's, thereupon's and the like; I find myself writing in fine ecclesiastical journalese of how we (I always describe us as 'the brethren present') have met pursuant to resolution within some hall from which we repair to the Church where someone who has compeared is forthwith enjoined to await an order and to give due heed thereunto as he shall be answerable . . . and so on.

For the purposes of a Record Apart, it seems to me, one is entitled not only to introduce 'undesirable matter' into the text but also to deal with it in an undesirable literary style, in a slightly modified form of the fast-withering fireside chatter—what might be described as fireside chatter suitable for a smokeless zone. At least that is how this Record Apart is written.

CHAPTER I

The Last Day

'Moderator!'

In stentorian tones he bellowed the word, emphasising the first syllable, giving a grand drum-roll to the final 'r'. He was the Assembly Officer, and in morning-coat and white bow-tie he stood just inside the east doorway of the Assembly Hall. I stood immediately at his back, unseen beyond the doorway, while behind me in turn stood my two chaplains. It was precisely 11.30 in the morning and the day was Tuesday 23rd May 1972.

The business part of the proceedings of that year's General Assembly of the Church of Scotland with all its traditional formality and splendour was about to begin in the Assembly Hall on Edinburgh's Mound.

Already the fifteen-hundred-odd commissioners were in their places, most of them talking animatedly, some waiting expectantly, some waving to friends in faraway corners, some standing resignedly inside the doors, for the seats seemed all to be taken. The East Gallery above our heads was, I knew, filled to capacity with ticket-holding members of congregations—only those who had applied months in advance were ever fortunate enough to secure tickets for the opening day. To our left in the Public Gallery were those who for the past couple of hours or more had queued outside in the Lawnmarket. The procession of officials had moved in a few minutes before and were in their places—Principal Clerk, Junior Clerk and Procurator sitting in a row beneath the Moderator's desk, and the Business Convener ('leader of the house' he's sometimes called) on the far side of the table within the general enclosure around the desk.

Standing there we were far enough away from the main entrance to the Hall from the Mound, yet I was intensely conscious of the fact that at this very moment the Lord High Commissioner and his party would be there, in process of being received. The time-honoured custom is that two ministers and one elder (chosen, I fear, because of their possession of frock-coats and silk hats rather than on ecclesiastical grounds) are on parade each day, shake the hands of the Lord High Commissioner and of his lady, and, in name of the Assembly, cordially welcome them. In the vulgar tongue they're known, these three-a-day, as 'shakers'. The idea that they have some connection with the Quakers is understandable but erroneous.

The Commissioner would, I knew, be accompanied by Her Grace Lady Clydesmuir and her entourage. There would also be the Lord Provost of Edinburgh, the Purse Bearer, the Lord Advocate (normally the Solicitor-General, but in this Parliament he happens to be a Roman Catholic so Mr Norman Wyllie was acting in his stead), the Secretary of State for Scotland, the Lord Lyon King of Arms with his retinue of Heralds in all the resplendent glory of their brightly coloured tabards, the Hereditary Standard-Bearers, Dundee with the Royal Standard, the red lion rampant on a cloth of gold, and Lauderdale with the Saltire Flag, the blue St Andrew's Cross of Scotland.

All of them—I could envisage it so clearly—would be getting out of cars and forming in procession in the quadrangle beneath the statue of John Knox. So busy would they be preparing to make their grand entry into the Gallery set apart for the Lord High Commissioner and his suite that none of them, I felt sure, would spare a moment to wonder what the great Reformer up there on his plinth was making of it all. When he had envisaged a General Assembly had he had any pre-vision of this?

The Lord High Commissioner's Gallery is not strictly a part of the Assembly any more than is the Public Gallery which confronts it. There's a long and intensely interesting historical tale here—good and sufficient reasons why the Queen's accredited representative, though he 'represents Our Sacred Person and Royal Authority', though he is warmly welcomed by 'the shakers', though he is treated always with all the honour and deference due to the monarch, should not have access to the Assembly proper but should be confined in a gallery whence he can keep a watching brief. This gallery I could just glimpse through the doorway—on my right and immediately behind and above the seat I should shortly be occupying.

I could picture the gallery already filled with its colourful complement, for I knew all about the Lord High Commissioner and his party, having seen them all just under an hour before at the Service in the ancient Church of St Giles, a quarter of a mile down the High Street.

Each year the Assembly opens with a Service of Public Worship in St Giles' Cathedral, attended by commissioners and others, conducted by the Moderator's Chaplains, the sermon being preached by the retiring Moderator—his last major official utterance. Before the service I had stood, along with the Minister of St Giles, at the West Door of the Church while the party from the Palace arrived and while the Lord High Commissioner inspected a guard of honour. Thereafter I had been formally presented.

'Moderator!' Again the Officer's voice rang out, ending with its drum-roll. For upon the general clamour and confusion in the hall his first bellow had made little impact. This time the message got across, and commissioners throughout the hall and the public in the galleries having risen to their feet we set off upon the journey that would take me to the dais—for my last time as Moderator. When I reached the desk I would bow thrice with great formality, first to the front, then to my right and then to my left. Then together we would sit down and await the arrival of the Lord High Commissioner and his party. For while the constitution allows the Assembly to ignore him once he's there, courtesy—not to say loyalty—demands that the official representative of the Queen, the person who is 'supplying Our Presence and holding Our place' should be received with all due honour and respect. So each morning the Assembly, with their Moderator, await the arrival of the royal representative before they constitute for the day.

It's not a very long journey from the East Door to the Moderator's platform—if it's twenty yards that must be all—and even at the stately pace set by the Officer it cannot occupy more than a few seconds. It's amazing how many and how varied thoughts can in that brief space flash through the mind, how long a journey one can travel down the lane of memory, how many vivid pictures, like a cartridge of coloured transparencies, can project themselves on the mental screen. We are told that the walk to the scaffold in olden days was very much like that. My journey was of a less ominous nature, and I enjoyed the great advantage, not shared by Sydney Carton, that

I should be able afterwards to recall some of the memories that came to me.

I had contrived a quick glance to the Gallery on the left of the Lord High's Gallery as I approached it, to see my wife and the wives of my two chaplains along with three of our four daughters ranged along the second front seat. That took me back right away to the first time I had made the trip just a year before. On that occasion they had occupied the front pew and our second daughter had been able to come home from Rhodesia for the occasion. Vividly I recalled with what misgiving and trepidation and shaking at the knees I had walked the distance then and how the kindly smile of Hugh Douglas, the retiring Moderator, had reassured me. And, remembering that, I resolved I must be sure to have the same kind of welcoming and understanding smile for my successor when, in a few minutes' time, he would be arriving at the rostrum, looking, doubtless, utterly composed, feeling, doubtless, completely bewildered.

The Lord High Commissioner's Gallery looked particularly desolate in its emptiness against all the other areas of the hall packed to suffocation. And 'suffocation' was the right word, for before long the powerful television lights (so much brighter and stronger since we've switched to colour) will have generated an almost unbearable heat. For the moment, though, the only effect of the lights is to accentuate the emptiness. It would be but a couple of minutes till they came filing in and took their places. Lord Clydesmuir himself, flanked by the Lord Provost of Edinburgh on his right and the Purse Bearer on his left, with the Lord Advocate and the Secretary of State for Scotland somewhere around. Immediately behind him his own Domestic Chaplain, Minister of St Mary's Biggar, the congregation of which he is a member. At the rear the College of Heralds, and the Standard Bearers, and the Duke of Hamilton, Hereditary Keeper of the Palace of Holyroodhouse. Then in the seats to his left his lady and her suite, and behind her the Chiefs of the three Armed Services with their ladies.

I was able to picture them all very clearly for my wife and I had spent the previous evening at the Palace of Holyroodhouse as the guests of Their Graces. To most people, I imagine, the name 'Holyrood' brings to mind a picture of the tragic Mary Queen of Scots, of insolent Darnley slouching about its apartments, of the murder of Davie Rizzio, of jaunty buccaneering Bothwell hijacking a royal bride, of shadowy spiral-stair intrigue, of cloak and dagger drama at its most dramatic. All very dark and dismal, all very tragic. Or perchance there are those for whom the Palace is associated with that other romantic figure of Scottish history, Bonnie Prince Charlie—for it was here in 1745, during his triumphal journey south, that the Jacobite aspirant to the British throne held glittering court. All very bright and glamorous, all very romantic. In either case the reference is to what are now prosaically called 'The Historical Apartments'.

The main part of today's Palace of Holyroodhouse is a most attractive modern—or at least reasonably modern—palace of three storeys, built around an open square and looking out to the south on Arthur's Seat and Salisbury Crags. It is the residence of the Queen when she visits Scotland's capital and it is here that Her Majesty's representative is housed during his stay in Edinburgh for the Assembly. Within its fine banqueting hall and beautifully proportioned reception rooms are held gatherings of Churchmen and others prominent in the life of Scotland. And on its smooth green lawns is held that most popular event of the Assembly's social calendar, the Garden Party.

To Holyroodhouse my wife and I had been bidden for the Monday evening. To facilitate our admittance to the Palace Yard and our movement generally during Assembly time I had been given for display on the car windscreen a diamond-shaped blue sticker bearing the mystic message 'Special Police Pass'. Armed with our sticker—or should it be stuck with our sticker—to Holyroodhouse in the course of the afternoon we had betaken ourselves. In the evening a small and intimate dinner party was held, and this was followed by an interesting little event called 'the Ceremony of the Keys'. In presence of a small company in one of the reception rooms the Lord Provost of Edinburgh handed over to the Lord High Commissioner—as he would have done to Her Majesty in person—the keys of his City, and the Lord High, having expressed his utmost confidence in the Provost and Magistrates as fitting custodiers of these instruments, had, with great solemnity—and, I thought, with some little relief—handed them back again.

Well could I understand his anxiety to be quit of them. I cannot conceive what kind of doors they might have opened, these monstrous keys. One thing about which I'm quite sure is that you couldn't have dropped them inadvertently. Far more effective than all the keys of the city was that little blue sticker with which my windscreen was bedecked. That, I knew, would open for me doors whose locks the keys would not have fitted. At the same time I suppose that from the strictly ceremonial point of view it would look a bit odd were the Lord Provost solemnly to hand over to the Lord High Commissioner a blue windscreen-sticker.

The Ceremony of the Keys had been followed by a full-scale reception attended by a large company of people connected in one way or other with the Assembly itself, or with the life of Scotland generally—officials of the Church, Lords of Council and Session, members of the armed forces, and a great number of what might be called 'ordinary Church people'. Many of these latter were known to me personally, and it had been my job to present to Her Grace as many of them as possible. The guests having departed it was no surprise to me, considering the enormous strain to which both must have been subjected in two solid hours of introductions, and considering what lay before them next day, to find Their Graces indicating that for them 'straight to bed' was the plan.

On Tuesday morning we had all breakfasted together, after prayers conducted by the Domestic Chaplain and then I had set off, accompanied by my wife, for the Assembly Hall, there to forgather with my two chaplains and their wives. All of us then proceeded to St Giles' in preparation for the Service.

So, you see, I knew very well all the personalities who would so soon be filing into the gallery at my back. In the few moments of waiting there was quite a splash of colour to occupy my attention. For the front seats on either side of the table enclosure were occupied, as the custom is, by the Provosts, Town Clerks and Bailies of the Cities of Edinburgh, Glasgow, Aberdeen, Dundee and Perth (with the exception of the Lord Provost of Edinburgh who—no doubt weighed down with his keys— would be marching with the Lord High's party). All of them were in their robes of office, and such a splash of scarlet and ermine and sable and wigs is rarely to be seen in this sober land of ours. I found myself wondering how the proposals of the Wheatley Commission for local government reform were likely to affect this parade, and hoping they would not deprive us of one of the few remaining touches of symbolism and tradition. And then I realised that the Clerk and others had now turned and were facing my way. So I too turned around to acknowledge the greeting of the Lord High Commissioner when he would make his three bows to the Assembly.

And so began the General Assembly of 1972—began as should in my opinion begin every solemn assembly within the Kirk, with a call to praise God—'Let us worship God; let us sing to His praise and glory in the words of . . .' I had chosen the opening verses of the Metrical Psalm 147, 'Praise ye the Lord. For it is good praise to our God to sing', and we were taking it to the fine old tune 'Huddersfield'. Up stepped James Ross, the Precentor (at other times Minister at Paisley Abbey), who gave us the note, and we were off.

There's something unique in the singing of the opening praise at our General Assembly. The sound of more than two thousand voices, mostly male, singing words which they've known and loved since childhood to these old Scottish tunes, as grand as they are simple, is something that has to be heard to be believed. There are dangers, of course. I remember once the Precentor had it in mind we should sing a particular tune; the Assembly took it in their head they would sing a different tune; the Assembly won. No shame to the Precentor—the odds were too heavily against him. Probably the Assembly's tune was a better tune anyway.

I clearly recall one evening in my own Presbytery of Glasgow when we found ourselves unexpectedly confronted with something of a musical crisis. We were meeting in Glasgow's ancient Church of St Mungo, that most magnificent example of Gothic architecture, for the licensing as Preachers of the Gospel of the twenty-or-so students who had completed their course at University and College. All Cathedral services are held in the Choir, which seats about six hundred people. As in procession the Presbytery moved out of the sacristy I noticed that every seat appeared to be occupied, but I was conscious too that there was something unusual which I could not at first identify. Then it dawned on me. There was no organ accompaniment

for our procession, only an ominous—what might even be called
an audible—silence. As the person responsible for the arrangements I found myself immediately wondering what I had done
or failed to do to achieve this unprecedented result. As a matter
of interest it transpired that a letter to the organist had been
forwarded to him at an address in England he had left some time
before, had been held for a fortnight in a mistaken hope he
might return, and then readdressed to him in Glasgow to arrive
the day after our Service.

By this time I had given up wondering what had happened
in favour of the more urgent question of what was going to
happen when we reached our places in the Sanctuary. I need
not have worried, for our Moderator, Hamish MacKenzie of
Giffnock, completely unflurried, in full command of the situation, announced the singing, gave the note, and led off, to be
taken up by the whole congregation with a zest and enthusiasm they would never have shown in trying to compete with
an organ which they well knew had the edge on them anyway. The grandest praise we've had at a Licensing Service in
years.

Talking of the Assembly's ability to sing brings back to mind
one of the really great and memorable moments of all the
Assemblies I've attended. The Cameronians, that old Scottish
regiment so closely associated with the Covenants and the hill-
preachings in a day when the Kirk was sore harried and
persecuted—the Cameronians were being disbanded as part of
a major scheme of Army reorganisation. They had asked to lay
up their Communion Silver in the custody of the Kirk with
which they had such close historic ties. The silver had no great
commercial value, but its sentimental worth was considerable.
So we arranged what the television people call a 'slot' in our
agenda one day, and a few representative officers and men
came along from the regiment to do the handing over. As a
prelude we sang what must surely be the most aggressive of all
the Psalms, the 135th, 'Now Israel may say and that truly . . .
If that the Lord had not our cause sustained . . . When cruel
men against us furiously rose up in wrath to make of us their
prey . . . But blest be God who doth us safely keep. . . .' What
singing! I just can't imagine how, after the last note had died
away, the Commanding Officer contrived to say his piece. In

that packed Assembly there was scarcely an eye without a tear. Assembly singing is always great; that day it was superb.

To return, though, to our opening praise. When it was ended and the brethren had resumed their seats the Principal Clerk read a passage of Scripture, and I said an opening prayer in which was invoked the aid of the Holy Spirit to guide and uphold and direct us in all the multifarious concerns that would engage our attention. It is what is called 'constituting the Assembly' and every court in the Church—Kirk Session, Presbytery and Synod as well as Assembly—before it can engage in any business must be constituted with prayer by its Moderator. Indeed an extract minute of its proceedings will be accepted as valid only if it bears testimony to the fact that the court at a certain place and on a certain date 'being met and constituted' did such and such.

So we constituted the first sederunt of the General Assembly of 1972.

That done, I called for commissions to be laid on the table and the Principal Clerk promptly complied with my request. For those who attend the Assembly are not, as is sometimes supposed, delegates but commissioners. They are appointed by Presbyteries—roughly one to every four members of Presbytery—and they are enjoined 'to repair thereto, and there to attend all the diets of the same and there to consult, vote and determine, to the glory of God and the good of His Church, according to the Word of God, the Confession of Faith and the Constitution of the Church'. In other words each is to be guided by his own conscience.

Most Presbyteries work on some kind of rota system, sending an equal number of ministers and elders, and trying to ensure that the former have an opportunity of regular four-yearly attendance. But always they reserve the right to scrap the rota and send whom they will. Circumstances could well arise when it was important to have reserved that right. If a major issue were to confront the Church on which opinion was bitterly divided, Presbyteries would be in no position to instruct commissioners how to vote—they are to vote according to the guiding of their conscience—but they could always arrange to send people with the right kind of conscience. No difficulties of that kind presented themselves this year, and the commissions

B

were quietly enough laid on the table—symbolically, I imagine, for I didn't see any bulky mass of papers suddenly appearing there.

My second-last Moderatorial task had been duly performed. For me there remained only to introduce and to instal my successor.

But first I had the opportunity to say a word or two about my year in office—a year of which only a few brief moments remained. I began by pointing out this very fact. 'You are beholding at this moment', I said, 'that most interesting ecclesiastical specimen, an expiring Moderator'. Lest anyone with a particularly literal turn of mind should have fears for my health I hurried on to remark that I was shortly to join the all-too-fast-swelling ranks of the redundant in Scotland, mentioning as an aside that I had been asking the Lord Advocate the previous evening whether he thought I might qualify for any kind of benefit under the Act, but that he had been as depressing as solicitors normally are.

That one rather blew up in my face, as I later discovered. Part of the proceedings had, apparently, been recorded and put over on BBC news at 6 o'clock. The following afternoon a minister friend in Edinburgh was being collected by a taxi to attend a wedding and the driver regaled him with the remark, 'It's a richt dirty shame that auld fella Herron gettin' made redundant.' My friend was delighted. My own horror at realising that I appeared as an aged patriarch was somewhat mollified by the thought that my redundancy appealed as 'a richt dirty shame' rather than as a long overdue deliverance.

I went on to thank various people—and they had been much in my mind in that last hour—people to whom I was indebted for many things in the year that was fast closing. First, naturally, I thanked the Kirk as a whole for the confidence they had shown in me in making me Moderator—a choice about whose wisdom I myself had entertained serious doubts. I went on to tell the story of a day early in my ministry when a special congregational anniversary having come around I had invited one of my professors to be guest preacher. I had been young, enthusiastic and inexperienced enough to think this was a good idea. Visiting, in the course of the following week, an old farmer, a devoted church-goer, an experienced sermon-taster and a remarkably shrewd character, I asked him, 'And what did you think of the Professor on Sunday?' 'Oh', he said, 'he was verra guid—verra learned, ye ken—oh ay, verra learned. But dae ye ken what I'm goin' to tell ye; ye're every bit as guid yersel'.' And then hastened to add—'in yer ain ignorant kind o' way'. It had, of necessity, been in my ain ignorant kind o' way that I had discharged the duties of Moderator. For myself I had found a great measure of satisfaction in the performance of them and I only hoped the Church had not been unduly embarrassed.

And then I thanked all those who had arranged my tours, and all the vast company who had extended hospitality to us, all who had invited us to functions of one kind and another; my own Presbytery that had granted me leave of absence for the year; an often-maligned Press for the courtesy with which they had invariably interviewed me and the fairness with which they had reported me; and last and by no means least I thanked all those who throughout the year had supported us in their prayers. I told of how one day in the midst of an almost intolerably heavy programme a man had asked me, 'And how are you bearing up?' and that with utter sincerity I had replied, 'I'm not; I'm being borne up'. That feeling had been with me far too often and I had felt it far too deeply for it to be other than the literal truth.

All that remained for me now was to enquire whether the Assembly accepted the nomination of The Reverend Ronald Selby Wright, Minister at Edinburgh's ancient Kirk of the Canongate, as their Moderator. The question was essentially a rhetorical one, and it elicited the hearty acclaim I had expected. Away went the Clerks and the two senior ex-Moderators—Lord Macleod of Fuinary and Dr John A. Fraser—to break the news, and a few moments later, while the Assembly stood to receive them, they returned leading the new Moderator, followed by his chaplains. I remembered about the welcoming smile, and I hope it helped. In traditional fashion I welcomed Dr Selby Wright in name of the Assembly, placed on his finger the Moderatorial Ring, and in prayer installed him in his high office.

And so I stepped down from being a leading figure in the life of Scotland, entitled to take his place at official functions next after the Royal Family and the Lord Chancellor and

before the Prime Minister and the Dukes—back down to my
normal condition of nonentity.

And the evening and the morning were the last day—my last
day as Moderator of the General Assembly of the Church of
Scotland.

CHAPTER 2

'That's What It's All About'

Everyone, I imagine, knows the chestnut about the man who on learning that his mother-in-law had just driven his new Daimler over a cliff remarked that he received the news with mixed feelings.

It was with mixed feelings, inevitably, that I had passed on the ring of office and in so doing brought to an end my year as Moderator. On the one side there was a feeling of relief at shedding an unusual and not inconsiderable burden, a profound sense of satisfaction at having reached the tape without major disaster, a deep-set pleasure at the thought of returning to my normal way of life, which if unspectacular is not without its own interests and rewards. On the other side it was difficult to say farewell to this exciting pattern of living—it's pleasant to be feted and fussed-over wherever one goes, reassuring to discover that one's views on all sorts of subjects are much sought after and regarded as of great significance, comforting to think that one counts for something not only in the Kirk but in the wider community beyond. I'm quite sure, though, that it's just when you're getting to that stage of satisfaction with yourself as Moderator that the time has arrived for your spell in office to be over, and for you to be back once more at the proverbial kitchen-sink, whatever the precise nature of the chores you there have to perform.

It is an admirable provision this by which our Moderators 'last' for only one year. People sometimes say it's far too short a period—you're only learning the tricks of the trade when your time is up. This is as it should be. A Moderator who was well versed in all the tricks of the trade would be to that extent a bad Moderator—the element of naïvety is no small part of his charm. Besides, at the pace at which we take it a year is long enough. There's this too, that so long as we're going to appoint men from parishes and other normal forms of ministry a year is as long as a man can afford to be away from his regular post. Otherwise he would feel obliged to resign and then have to look for another appointment when his period was over. This would probably mean making it a five-year stint, which is far too long.

Most important consideration, though, in my view, is just that at the end of a year most men are coming rather to enjoy the experience of being somebody. In other words, delusions of grandeur are setting in—a most dangerous state of affairs in any man's life, and made all the more menacing because one of its chief symptoms is an inability to recognise the condition. In any system this kind of thing is unfortunate; in a Presbyterian system which believes the parish ministry to be its highest office it could be particularly dangerous.

In his sermon 'A Step Forward in Church Relations' preached at Cambridge in 1946 the Archbishop of Canterbury (Lord Fisher) spoke of how in his view it was nothing less than essential that episcopacy should be a feature of any united Church of the future, and went on to suggest that as 'a step forward' towards more profitable discussion of Church union with Anglicans those of other communions should consider 'taking episcopacy into their system'. At least there was an honesty here that hasn't always characterised the ecumenical debate. The phrase, torn out of its context, became a popular one. To me it has always seemed that this would be a most lamentably retrograde step, an attempt to turn back the hands of the clock (which never does the mechanism any good), and I have wanted to urge rather that others should consider taking Moderators into their system. For I am sure that we in Presbyterianism have here discovered something that is worth sharing. I am sure too that a Church that is designed for the future rather than patterned on the past will include something comparable to our Moderator and will have done with Bishops in the Apostolic Succession.

What exactly is a Moderator? It's a good question and one with which in the course of my year in office I have from time to time been confronted. Usually I have taken refuge in the reply that most good dictionaries give a variety of definitions, but that the one which most appeals to me is 'a mechanical contrivance to regulate and control the flow of gas'. That, I have explained, if you will substitute 'human' for 'mechanical', is a fair enough description of the functions of the Moderator during the sittings of the General Assembly.

To regulate and control the flow of gas, yes. To ensure that the opportunity is provided for all the important issues to be fully and adequately discussed, and at the same time to be constantly on guard against allowing mere talk for its own sake; to see to it that anyone who has something original or significant to say, however diffident he may be, gets the chance and the encouragement to say it, and to be no less firm in restricting equestrian displays on pet hobby-horses by professional riders; to sense when the Assembly has had enough and is prepared to vote, and on the other hand to hold an impatient Assembly in check while an issue, if the need arise, is still further explored in debate—all these form part of the duties of the Moderator occupying the chair on any of the eight days when the Assembly is engaged in the discharge of regular business.

It's quite a tricky assignment, and it's important that it should be done reasonably well. Practice provides you with a certain expertise, and experience gives you some knowledge of your people. You get to know them—to know the man who, spreading a few closely-typed sheets on the rostrum, says, 'I hadn't really intended to take any part in this debate, but . . .'; to know the man who only wants to ask a simple question, 'Does the Convener not think his proposal is a very stupid one?' (as if he'd have made it if he had thought that); to know the man who wants to ask 'for information' a complicated question to which obviously he's the only person in the hall who knows the answer; to know the man who in all good faith comes forward to the microphone to say a couple of sentences, but to whom the sight of so vast a congregation without a preacher presents a challenge he cannot resist. Yes, you get to know them, if not always how to deal with them.

To cope with points of order raised from the floor—and it's amazing how often a man thinks he's raised a point of order when all he's done has been to express a point of exasperation. To know something of the Standing Orders as they apply to the conduct of the business and to apply them with that degree of common sense that can sometimes mean turning a blind eye on their provisions. To know about voting, to be able to spot an amendment when you hear one and not to confuse it with a counter-motion, to remember who has the right of reply to the debate—and so on. All this is the business of the Moderator—

all fairly enough characterised as regulating and controlling the flow of gas.

Then there are the occasions when the Assembly sits as a judicial court—the supreme and ultimate justiciary within the Church—when parties go to the bar, there to plead their cause. There are very clear and specific rules governing the procedure in this field, rules determining how and when and how often parties are to be heard, when they may be questioned, when they are to be withdrawn, what kinds of motions are in order, how they must be put to the vote. At least the rules appear very simple and straightforward when you examine them in the peace of your study the night before; they're never quite so clear in the heat of battle. And here, of course, it's desperately important that things be done properly and in order, for parties have rights to claim or to defend. It is essential, therefore, that justice be done, and it is most desirable that it also be seen to be done. Against a final judgment of the Assembly there can be no redress—not to a Church court, for there is no higher court to which to appeal, and not to a civil court, for it is well-established law that the courts of the Church in dealing with matters that fall properly within their domain cannot have their judgments reviewed in the civil courts. Here again it's a matter of regulating the flow of gas, but gas under considerable pressure with a real danger of a big explosion if carelessly handled.

It is, I think, most important, whether for judicial causes or for ordinary affairs, that the Moderator should contrive to give the impression of being very much in command of the business. Let him display the least hesitancy or seem to be in the slightest doubt on a procedural point and there will be a dozen commissioners (ministers are the worst offenders) qualified and anxious to put him on the right lines—usually, unhappily, on different lines. Let the trumpet speak with an uncertain voice and there are normally plenty of clarinets and trombones ready to sound a steady blast. The Chair should always give a clear, emphatic ruling. It's very desirable it should be the right ruling, but it's much more important that it should be clear and emphatic.

In my first Presbytery, before I had been very long in the ministry, one night at the close of a meeting I remarked to the

Clerk—for whom I had already formed a great regard that, as the years passed, was to grow to a deep affection—that I thought he was the perfect Presbytery Clerk. Looking a trifle startled he wondered why that should be. 'Well,' I said, 'if you're asked for guidance in the course of a meeting you give a clear and convincing exposition of your view and your reasons for holding it, and then when you get home you check it against the authorities and if you had been wrong you correct it in the minutes.' He gave the sickly smile of one caught with sticky fingers near the jampot.

For the very reason that the Assembly represents the end of the road in any matter of litigation it is especially important to ensure that the business is properly conducted. Unfortunately the Assembly is not a court well designed for performing this kind of function. A bench of fifteen hundred judges is a bad starting-point. There is no provision for leading evidence, in the sense of examining or cross-examining witnesses. There are no written pleadings. And always over the business there hangs a consciousness that we haven't all the time in the world. So different from the civil courts where one gets the impression that only the decision of the case really matters, when it is reached is quite inconsequential—even if the litigants are dead and gone the profession will be grateful for a *cause célèbre*. They tell the story of a couple of lawyers discussing a vast fortune disposed of in a will of doubtful validity and of the hope expressed by one of them that whatever happened to the fortune it would at least not be frittered away among the beneficiaries.

No, the Assembly is, on the face of things, not well suited to sit as a court of justiciary. At the same time it is very jealous of its position in this field and would not, in my opinion, agree to hand this function over to any kind of select judicial commission. In the long run justice probably gets done, even if it is in a somewhat rough and ready fashion. Indeed I think justice is more often done than it is seen to be done. Understandably not every Moderator enjoys being in the chair when a case is due to be heard.

Over and above all these exercises in the regulating and controlling of gas there are times when it is the Moderator himself who has to provide the gas. Retiring Conveners, officials, and so on have to be thanked; new professors, new secretaries have to be welcomed; missionaries setting off for the field have to be sent forth with a blessing; to returning field-scarred veterans the gratitude of the Kirk has to be expressed. Normally a certain amount of warning is given of such occasions and it's possible to do a bit of home-work. It is in fact not uncommon for the Committee which has the responsibility of presenting the person for welcome or thanks to supply the Moderator with some notes (of varying adequacy be it said) on the victim's curriculum vitae. All that remains then is to cull from this the necessary material for making a small speech with suitable allusions. As the recipient of the address stands invariably at your side you have either to speak directly to him from memory or read your notes into outer space, ignoring his presence. The latter course has always seemed to me an unfortunate one. Hence the need for adequate preparation.

Yet even the best preparation has its inadequacies. One afternoon I was to be thanking three retiring professors and welcoming two newly-appointed ones. None of the five was particularly well known to me, and two of them I would actually be seeing for the first time in my life. You can imagine how happy I was to be supplied the previous evening with a neat, compact little factual statement about each one of them. You can imagine, too, how utterly nonplussed I was when in presenting them to me and inviting me to address them the Convener of the Committee concerned read over word for word the material I had been given. To make bricks without straw is bad enough—but to make bricks while before your very eyes someone has just stolen your straw! One of the occasions when it was far from easy to arrange for a flow of gas.

From all of which it must be clear that the Moderator is just a kind of glorified chairman, and not very glorified at that. A chairman is at least accorded the dignity of being addressed as 'Mr Chairman'. It is frowned upon to address the chair in the Assembly as 'Mr Moderator'—oh no, just 'Moderator'. There have been times when I have claimed that the Moderator is the least influential man in the whole Church, for while every other commissioner at the Assembly has a deliberative vote the Moderator has only a casting-vote, and with a court the size of the Assembly you would think there would be few opportunities for using that. I can remember only two occasions when a casting-vote has been called for—and one of them had to fall to my lot—in a judicial case at that.

It was getting very late in the evening and we were involved in a number of appeals concerned with congregational readjustment. The house had thinned down to about a couple of hundred. The particular case before us had to do with the town of Buckhaven in Fife, where there were three congregations all vacant at the one time. The Presbytery of Kirkcaldy had resolved to unite all three into one. An appeal had been taken to the Synod, asking in effect that there be two congregations in the town. The Synod dismissed the appeal and sustained the judgment of the Presbytery. Again an appeal was taken, this time to the Assembly.

This, then, was the issue before us. After parties had been heard, questions had been directed to them and answered, and generally the issue had been fully and fairly explored, I asked for motions and got two. First a motion to sustain the appeal and direct the Presbytery to proceed accordingly; and secondly a counter-motion to uphold the judgment of the Synod. The voting resulted in a dead-heat. I cast my vote for the counter-motion and explained that in so doing I was following the accepted practice whereby a casting-vote is given in favour of the *status quo*—you don't make a change unless there's a clear majority in favour of it. There were those, I understand, who found serious fault with my decision. The *status quo*, they argued, was three congregations in the town, and I, by casting my vote as I did, was ensuring there was to be but one. Two would have been nearer the *status quo*. This, of course, was nonsense. For our purpose the *status quo* was the position at that moment of time when the appeal was taken—that is, a decision had been duly reached by the Presbytery of Kirkcaldy and sustained by the Synod of Fife that the three congregations be united to form one. That was the status which the appeal wanted to see changed. But, you see, you can be faulted even in trying to apply what must seem a simple enough principle. Moderators have this much in common with Gilbert's policemen—their lot is not an 'appy one.

Before engaging in this orgy of self-pity I had been commenting upon the fact that so far as the Assembly meetings are concerned the Moderator is just a kind of chairman. He is *primus inter pares*, having all the authority in the matter of keeping good order normally vested in a chairman, but having no power at all outside the meetings or beyond the business of the court. Constitutionally and traditionally it is after the Assembly has actually met that he ought to be chosen, and when he has pronounced the benediction that brings the last sederunt to a close he should quietly retire to the obscurity from which he came. At that end—the close of the Assembly— the situation is not now so simple, and for that reason it has been inevitable that the other end—the beginning—should also have become more complicated.

In October of each year there meets in Edinburgh a body known as the Committee to Nominate the Moderator—a committee consisting of all ex-Moderators and about fifty others, ministers and elders, appointed by Synods (that is, on a geographical basis) under the chairmanship of one of the ex-Moderators. This body having been convened, the chairman indicates he is prepared to receive nominations, and any person present may put forward a name. Always it has been a minister, although I am not aware of any sufficient constitutional reason why an elder should not be chosen. But there is much to be said for the Church being represented by one of its full-time servants.

The only other requirement is that the proposer should be able to state that his nominee if elected will be prepared to accept office. This I dislike, for it seems to me to introduce an element of candidature, which I regard as undesirable. On two occasions to my knowledge Mr A, when approached, has said he is not prepared to have his name go forward if Mr B's name is also being considered, for, he feels, Mr B deserves it more than he. All very modest and very proper. But is it? As I see it, it is for the Committee and not for one of the possible nominees to determine the relative merits of Messrs A and B. Further, we're getting perilously near to candidature when a man says whether or not he's prepared to contest the position. I feel too that there are good men who if asked 'to stand' would un-hesitatingly refuse, but who if told they had been unanimously chosen could not so light-heartedly turn aside.

Some years ago I managed to persuade the Committee that

this was so, and got their agreement to depart from the requirement. As luck—bad luck—would have it, the person unanimously elected, when approached, felt compelled for reasons
of health to decline. Until the nominee could be approached
disclosure of the name had been withheld and members of the
committee had been put under an obligation of confidence. A
second meeting had to be convened, but in the meantime one
of the newspapers discovered what was afoot and gave it some
publicity—with most unfortunate results. And that, I fear, was
the last—as well as the first—year that nominations were
allowed in the absence of an assurance that the nominee was
agreeable.

Having got all the nominations made and spoken to—there
may be two and there may be ten—a vote is taken and repeated
until one person has a clear majority of all votes cast. The
invariable practice has then been for the meeting to make the
choice a unanimous one. It is generally accepted as desirable
that every area of the country and every aspect of the work of
the ministry should from time to time be represented—a parish
minister, a Gaelic-speaking minister, a professor, a missionary,
an administrator—but this is the kind of consideration that is
put forward in support of a particular candidate rather than a
principle to guide the final choice.

The choice having been made the news is immediately
passed to the media, and the nation learns who is to be next
year's Moderator. The meeting being held at 4 o'clock in the
afternoon the information goes out on the BBC Scottish News
programme at 6 o'clock, and the morning papers get busy with
preparation of a potted biography enlivened with 'quotes' from
people within the Church and further afield.

In my own case I had been in Edinburgh that very Tuesday
afternoon attending a meeting which finished in time to let me
catch the 4 o'clock train back to Glasgow. I had reason to
believe that my name was likely to be put forward, but that
was all; and I hadn't mentioned the matter to my wife far less
to the family, for I thought it a pity to involve them in an issue
which surely wouldn't come to anything anyway. I got home
just after 5 o'clock to be greeted with the question, 'What's
this you've been up to?' It appeared that a few minutes earlier
someone from *The Scotsman* had phoned and asked to come out

and photograph the pair of us. 'Of course,' Queenie said, 'but what do you want our photos for?' 'Don't you know,' the caller asked, 'that your husband is to be next Moderator.' To which she replied, 'Look, you must have got the wrong number. That's not my husband.' Thus it was that I first heard of my nomination. The Principal Clerk was on the line a few minutes later with the official intimation and invitation.

It was in the newspapers the following morning that I learned—to my own no small surprise—just how well fitted and how excellently suited I was in every way for the appointment. Reminded me of a bus driver I knew who got himself involved in a collision of a not very serious nature but who found himself charged with careless driving. He was satisfied it was his fault and wanted to plead Guilty, but was persuaded that since his licence was at stake he should deny the charge and engage counsel for his defence. He was duly acquitted. 'You know,' he said to me afterwards, 'I was quite sure I was in the wrong, but when I heard yon fella in the wig explainin' it a' to the judge I could see clearly enough it wasna' my fault at all. A clever fella yon in the wig.' By the same process of reasoning I concluded that the newspaper-writers must be 'clever fellas'.

A couple of days after the choice has been made there falls the regular meeting of the Commission of Assembly and the nomination of Moderator is always reported there for information. It is the Assembly itself which in due course has to ratify the choice. There was one occasion in my knowledge when a nomination was made the subject of challenge. It was that supremely controversial personality George MacLeod who was the unanimous choice of the Committee, and the retiring Moderator enquired whether it was the will of the Assembly that he be appointed. Amid general consternation a commissioner moved that Dr MacLeod be not so appointed, going on to criticise his views on a variety of subjects. This, of course, was not really a competent motion at all, since the only way in which Dr MacLeod's nomination could be effectively challenged was by putting up someone else. The business before the court was the appointment of a Moderator, not the acceptability to the Church at large of Dr MacLeod's views on this topic or on that. The challenge had little effect and the nomination was approved with loud acclaim. It was, though, perhaps a salutary reminder that the last word in this matter, as in all others, lies with the General Assembly.

In the States, I understand, half a dozen nominees are paraded at the opening of the Assembly, each makes a speech about his policy for the Church and answers questions from the floor. Then a vote is taken. I am not surprised to hear complaints that they are not getting the best men for Moderators.

From October to May can seem a long time, but it is not by any means too long for all that has got to be done by the Moderator-designate. He's got to make arrangements to be freed from his parish or other duties for at least the year involved, and if at all possible for a couple of months in advance to allow for some preparation, and even for a brief holiday. For while it is still the constitutional position that the end of the Assembly sees the end of the Moderator the fact is that the end of the Assembly marks only the beginning of a hectic year of travelling and speaking and representing.

It was, I believe, Professor W. M. Macgregor, Principal of Glasgow's Trinity College (known affectionately to his students as Williemac) who in the year that he was Moderator of the then United Free Church Assembly, put forward a plan that he should visit some of the areas in the north and west of the country where people were a bit isolated from the main stream of the life of the Kirk, and that he should convey to them a word of greeting and cheer and encouragement from the General Assembly. This, as was to be expected, proved an overwhelming success, and the following year it was extended and elaborated, and so on until now each Moderator visits six Presbyteries during his year and accordingly each Presbytery of the Church enjoys a Moderatorial visit of this kind once in ten years. Odd that Williemac should have been the originator of a plan that has come thus to magnify the office of Moderator, for none hated more bitterly than he any succumbing to delusions of grandeur, none was more devoted than he to the principle of the equality of the ministry.

As well as visiting the home Presbyteries there's always a trip abroad—and that occupies most of two months. For administrative purposes the overseas work of our Kirk is split into three sections involved respectively with Africa, India and Europe, Israel and the Americas. Each Moderator undertakes to visit, usually in the spring, in some part of one of these areas.

Ex officio the Moderator of the General Assembly is frequently an Honorary Vice-President, or Patron, or what-you-will of a great variety of organisations, and on occasion he has to attend meetings, dinners and other functions connected with these. This too can be a time-consuming and travel-involving business. So what with one thing and another you find that by the Christmas that precedes the May of your installation your diary is getting relentlessly filled and you are grateful for the adequate warning you have been given by being nominated in October.

The length of warning also makes it possible for you to get yourself fitted out and robed in the traditional garb of a Moderator. It's a controversial subject this of the Moderator's 'rig'. By long-established custom he wears the court dress of a Scottish gentleman of the seventeenth century—cut-away coat with vest and breeches all in black, black stockings and silver-buckled shoes, with jabot and cuffs of lace made in India— the jabot worn on the left side only. There is a legend about the dress, and though I cannot vouch for—indeed would gravely doubt—its authenticity I pass it on. On one occasion during the reign of King James VI and I (difficult days for the Kirk) the Assembly resolved that someone should wait upon His Majesty and confront him directly with some important issue. The emissary rode off to the palace where the king was at the time and arrived bespattered from head to foot from his fast riding. The king, glad of any excuse to avoid a confrontation, ordained that no-one was to be allowed to see him who was not properly dressed for the occasion. The messenger, understandably not having had the forethought to bring a change of raiment, had to return, his mission unfulfilled. To prevent a recurrence of such a misadventure the Assembly ordained that its Moderator should always be in court dress, ready at a moment's notice to wait upon Royalty. It's an interesting story.

There is certainly some advantage in being constantly dressed in a fashion suitable for every function and for every type of occasion. Many a time throughout the year, as my wife wrestled with the question, 'I wonder what I should wear?

Exactly what kind of function is this anyway?' I have rejoiced
to think that for me there was no problem.

At the same time I admit to a certain feeling of incongruity
about stepping in full Moderatorial gear into a motor-car, and
still more about climbing into a plane, let alone sitting in the
cockpit of a modern supersonic fighter. A coach and pair
would so much better fit the part. Or even, perhaps, a sedan
chair. Which reminds me of the tale of the man who was being
transported in such a vehicle—is it a vehicle?—when the floor
fell out and he found himself trudging through the mud
between the bearers. Explaining his unhappy plight to a friend
later he remarked, 'If it hadn't been for the look of the thing
I'd have been as well walking.'

As I have said, the garb has given rise to considerable
controversy. Not long after my nomination it was suggested to
me that since I had a great reputation for unorthodoxy—the
reference was to the fact that I prefer a bow-tie to a clerical
collar—I ought to be the first to break with the court-dress
tradition, which was ridiculous anyway and served merely to
make the Moderator a laughing-stock. Were I to give the cost
of the outfit (a considerable sum) to some worth-while Christian
project I would do myself and the Kirk generally an inestimable
service. To this idea I gave some serious thought, but in the
end decided quite heartily against it. If, I decided, I am
equipped with any reforming zeal I should reserve it for
attacking some of the things that really matter. In any case,
for a distinctive office a distinctive dress seems desirable if not
essential. This traditional dress of ours, as I was to discover, is
nothing if not distinctive—a crowd outside a football ground
will disperse before you more quickly than if you had someone
going in front with a bell shouting 'Unclean! Unclean!' It looks
dignified. It is reasonably comfortable to wear and—once
you've conquered your first enthusiasm for putting your
fingers through your silk stockings—easy to don and to discard.
The Inverness cape which is worn with the dress for outdoor
occasions is a quite wonderfully useful garment.

But I do wish something could be done about the hat. The
proper model is a tricorn affair which, with the cape and the
black stockings, immediately conjures up the caption—which
no newspaper-man could resist—'Dick Turpin Rides Again'.

With a view to keeping the journalists out of the way of temptation I have consistently refrained from appearing in the headgear. I haven't worn it—or even carried it—once during my year and I don't expect to do so now. And I don't expect it'll fetch much at a jumble sale.

One advantage of the distinctive dress is that it provided you with a wonderful starting-off point for speaking to children —they're sitting gazing at you open-mouthed, thinking clearly enough that you're something left over from Hallowe'en. The fact that the garb is so old gives an opportunity to refer to the continuity of a Kirk that runs so far back in history; the fact that the lace is made in India by girls on our mission-station in Chingleput is a reminder of our world-wide commitment; and the signet-ring with its amethyst carved with the crest of the Kirk, the burning bush, can speak to us of the obligation to stand only for what is genuine and true.

I love the story which Dr T. M. Murchison tells of how during his tour in 1969 he stepped out of a little motor-boat on to a slipway on one of the Outer Isles, complete in all the splendour of his Moderatorial outfit, and was accosted by a little girl who enquired in round-eyed wonder, 'Have you just come out of the ancient past?'—by motor-boat, presumably.

There you have him, then, this figure in the dress of three hundred years ago, presiding over the deliberations of the Assembly, representing the Scottish Kirk on all sorts of formal occasions at home and abroad, visiting congregations and schools and hospitals and factories at home and mission stations overseas, conveying the greetings of the kirk to all and sundry— that is the Moderator. In the words of the popular old song, 'That's what it's all about'.

CHAPTER 3

The Flight of the Herron

It was the last day of June, a pleasant day at that, with a touch of sunshine and a fine fresh breeze, and we were in the BEA Viscount that links Abbotsinch with the Northern Isles. It was the return journey we were making from Kirkwall, having spent rather more than a fortnight between the Orkneys and the Shetlands. We were crossing the Grampians and from the window of the plane it was easy to identify the River Spey, and the railway and the road intercrossing one another as they zigzagged along through the river valley. Immediately beneath us was Aviemore, that resort on which so much has been spent and is being spent to make it attractive to the dollar-spending tourist and valuable to the native Scot as an all-the-year-round conference centre. It seemed no time since we had been at Aviemore at a week-end conference of the Law Society of Scotland, though it must have been a couple of months before— incident-packed months.

It's interesting how as Moderator-designate I had come to be invited, along with my wife, to this event. The fact is that against the possibility of my wanting to appear in court to plead a cause I keep (at very modest cost) my name on the Law Society's list and can take out a practising certificate without difficulty. Someone had thought it significant that a name from the list of members of the Law Society of Scotland should appear as Moderator of the General Assembly of the Church of Scotland. It was the first time it had occurred. Hence the invitation.

I suppose the really interesting story, though, and one which I don't think would be generally known, was how my name came to be on the Society's list in the first place. It's a simple enough story. Since 1940 I had been minister of the ancient parish of Houston and Killellan, a quiet rural area in the Renfrewshire uplands, the village of Houston situated some seven miles west of Paisley and five east of Kilmacolm, equi-distant (thirteen miles either way) between Glasgow and

Greenock. For countless years the parish had enjoyed a quiet rustic way of life, too far from a railway station to become a dormitory suburb and with nothing to attract industry to its doors. And so it seemed likely to continue. Until suddenly— on 4th January 1950—we learned from the Press that we had had the distinction of being chosen by the Secretary of State for Scotland as the site of a new town that was to house a population of some twenty-thousand souls, overspill from Renfrew, Greenock and Port Glasgow. Confusion broke loose in a big way. There was the army of reporters and photographers that descended upon us, causing confusion enough. But there was, too, the general sense of bewilderment among farmers likely to lose land their fathers had ploughed, and villagers whose whole pattern of living was likely to be disturbed. What was to be done?

Not unnaturally I'm sure—for the Kirk still stands for something in the life of any rural community and the manse is an inevitable rallying-point at any moment of danger—not unnaturally I found myself very deeply involved in the resistance that was organised to halt the big guns in their advance. We were very conscious of just how big the enemy guns were, and of how light and primitive were our weapons by comparison. But we believed we had a just cause and we were undaunted. Not to make too long a story of it, we managed one way and another to stave off the attack and at the end of the day that particular project was shelved. It was twenty years later, when the position had considerably changed in any case, that development on a significant scale finally came to the parish. Our victory at the time was certainly well won and had been worth fighting for.

Over and above its main effect in preserving our parish the battle had as one of its side effects that I became a solicitor. It was all very accidental and unpremeditated. In the course of preparing our defences in the matter of the new town I found myself constantly confronted with legal questions, more and more dependent upon my lawyer friend John Clyde for advice, information and assistance. I discovered that even to write a letter in this kind of situation represents an exercise in legal skill. I found I had to read up quite a bit of legal precedent, I had to follow the case of Stevenage through all the English courts to the House of Lords itself, I had to follow up the many cases referred to in the pleadings. It was my first inroad into the volumes of reported cases and I found myself deeply intrigued and inclined often to stray from the case for which I had got out the book to read other cases having not the slightest connection with new-town legislation. Reading the judgments was to me a real delight. The neat, tidy kind of argument used by their Lordships appealed to me intensely. It took me back a long way to first learning Euclid under a teacher, Campbell Stephen, who was later one of the four famous Clydeside MP's of the early 'twenties—and of how much I enjoyed it. I just happen to have that kind of mind.

I remember how after the publication of the results of the Honours examinations in Philosophy in which I was a candidate I was talking to Professor H. J. Paton, then in the Chair of Logic in Glasgow, and he mentioned to me in his best Oxford accent that the external examiners had commented upon the fact that 'you have a very neat and tidy mind'. Not a little pleased about this I went home and reported the matter to my mother, who snorted and remarked, 'They should see your bedroom.' What's called a home truth, the kind you get at home, the kind that goes right home. It would be relevant to this day to point to my study at home or to my desk at the office. And yet I do have a mind that likes to get things neat and tidy. Just goes to show you can't judge by appearances.

Inspired to some extent by all this reading, with a feeling that I would enjoy it, and with a vague notion that I might even be able to derive from it some help in our battle against authority, I decided to attend the class in Scots Law at the University. This class met in the morning at 8.30, an hour not likely to interfere overmuch with my pastoral activities, and I could fairly easily cycle up to town—motor if conditions were unfavourable. I discovered on enquiry that to take three classes was considerably better value than to take one, and so, being a good Scot, I enrolled for the three—Forensic Medicine and Public International Law as the extras. Early on in the session I found that unless I had an objective in view I was unlikely to work very hard, so I decided to enter for the degree examinations, which I could sit in September—though at that time without any thought of graduating. I'd have something to keep

my nose to the legal grindstone during the winter and I'd
have the comparative quiet of the summer to prepare for the
exams.

It was at this time that I formed a lasting friendship with
Oswaldo Franchi, then a somewhat diffident student though
now a prominent solicitor in Glasgow and in Italy. He was a
member of that colony of Italians, first generation to be born
in Scotland, whose parents of solid Italian peasant stock had
come to these parts and had set up in the fish-frying and ice-
cream businesses—in both of which they excelled—and who by
dint of sheer hard work and old-fashioned thrift had weathered
the hard times of the 'twenties and early 'thirties and now were
established as an integral part of the Glasgow scene.

I just happened to find myself sitting next to Valdo in the
Scots Law class and we got talking. He was a very diligent
attender and a copious note-taker. I was neither. Other com-
mitments arose from time to time that prevented my getting
up to town for the lectures, and when I was there I found
Professor Dewar Gibb so interesting I was content to listen and
not to write. My very good friend the late Dr Tom Honeyman
in *Art and Audacity*, published just before his death, quotes the
definition of lecturing as a process whereby the notes of the
reader become the notes of the hearer without passing through
the mind of either—which I accept as a perfect picture of a
process I have often observed. I certainly found that allowing
the material of the lectures to filter through my mind greatly
impeded the note-taking.

Valdo, while a prolific scribbler, was anything but a good
writer and so his notes for all their fullness lost something by
being all but illegible. We made an accommodation. I took
home his notes, studied them along with my own scraps of
writing and my recollections—vivid usually if not always
accurate—and was able to reconstruct something fairly comprehensive, of which I typed out two good clear copies. In this
way two negatives did add together to make a positive.

By the following year I had come to think that the class on
Evidence and Procedure, which at that time was under the
care of Robert M'Donald, Procurator Fiscal at Glasgow, a
most interesting and entertaining lecturer as well as a very fine
fiscal—I had come to think this was a class it would really be

worth my while attending. Once again I found that the principle of three more or less for the price of one to be quite irresistible, so I took also the class in Conveyancing, along with one in Jurisprudence which I much enjoyed but was rarely able to attend because it met in the late afternoon. Had I known that I was to become Clerk to the Presbytery of Glasgow I should certainly have paid more heed to the erudite and painstaking lectures of that most conscientious of teachers, Donald M'Leish; for a good knowledge of property-tenure would have been a great asset in my present post. When I had at length finished this second year I had actually completed all I had set out to do, but having now six out of eight subjects necessary for an LL.B. degree I felt it would be a pity not to have something to show for my labours. An apprenticeship of sorts served with my friends John Clyde and Andrew Ralston in their Paisley office and I found myself with an LL.B. and a Practising Certificate. All very much the result of an accident in the first place.

That was how we came to be attending the weekend conference of the Law Society of Scotland at Aviemore. A most intensely interesting weekend it had proved. The principal guest of honour was the Lord Chancellor, Lord Hailsham. I was to have the opportunity of meeting him on many occasions in the following months, but this was our first encounter and I was considerably impressed. On the Saturday he made the long walk through the Larig Ghru, a pass linking Deeside with Speyside, a long and difficult journey calling for plenty of grit and endurance. It occurred to me he must have thought often of that walk of his when some months later questions were being asked in the House of Commons about a party of Edinburgh school-children tragically lost in that very part in a wild November blizzard. But even in April it's quite a walk. On the Sunday afternoon when he read a paper to us he looked as though 'his feet were killing him'—but he made the trip and all honour to him for it.

Incidentally, I had had a disconcerting, if somewhat amusing, experience earlier that Sunday when in the course of the morning I conducted a well-attended service in the great theatre hall. I had been assured that an organist was laid on and that the words of the hymns were stencilled and would be handed out, so I could rid my mind of worry on the praise part of the proceedings. There were, however—as I was to discover too late to do anything about it—two snags. One was that the opening singing was meant to be the Metrical Version of Psalm 121, 'I to the hills will lift mine eyes', but they had stencilled the Prose Version, 'I will lift up mine eyes unto the hills'. Secondly, they had provided the organist with a sol-fa edition of the hymn-book and he, reasonably enough for an instrumentalist, read staff. What with the organist vamping something which, whatever its musical excellence, bore no resemblance to the tune French, and the congregation struggling to fit in words which didn't belong—this item of praise was certainly not up to the standard of Assembly singing. We fared better, much better, when at a later stage we abandoned both print and organ and sang the Hundredth Psalm unaccompanied.

And now here was I in the Viscount looking down upon the mountains this lovely afternoon and remembering very vividly our attempt to sing 'I to the hills'.

I remembered too another recent occasion when my wife and I had taken to the air. We had not that time been looking down on the mountains of Speyside, but had literally been looking down the lums of Leith, for from a helicopter we got what might be called a sweep's-eye-view of the town. A great gala had been organised on Leith Links by the local Churches' Council for the afternoon of the Saturday immediately after the close of the Assembly. We had been asked to appear— indeed to stage an appearance. It had been a lovely afternoon and thousands turned out for the occasion. As part of the programme a helicopter was to give a demonstration of air-sea-rescue operations, and it was thought a good idea that in the middle of the park in the middle of the afternoon my wife and I should be delivered by helicopter.

So we were picked up in the Queen's Park just outside Holyroodhouse, rigged up in crash helmets, and carefully strapped in (wouldn't do to lose a Moderator *en route*) and so skimmed over the rooftops, and out into the Forth estuary and back and down into the field. Here, as was to be expected, we were surrounded by press photographers vying for a shot of the Moderator in full official dress with crash helmet. One of these made its appearance next day under the caption 'The Flight of the Herron'.

The helicopter trip had been exciting enough, but the most alarming part of the proceedings was still to come; for it was envisaged that I—Queenie, mercifully, was excused this one—would leave the field in the basket of a hot-air balloon. The man in charge was, I had been assured, the top man in Britain in hot-air balloons, and the journey would be pleasant and without incident. This I was prepared to accept without wishing to put it to the test.

I just couldn't get out of my mind the silly story of the jet-liner heading for the States, and of how just west of Ireland a voice came on the intercom, 'Good afternoon, ladies and gentlemen; we have just passed over Shannon. At this point it is customary for the crew to introduce themselves, but that is not possible on this trip since there is no crew. This plane is being completely directed by remote control from an office at Heathrow and will continue to be so until precisely five hours and fifty minutes from now it touches down at Kennedy Air-field, New York. Ladies and gentlemen, it is your privilege to be making history. Nothing so ambitious as this has ever before been attempted. So sit back, unfasten your seat-belts, light your cigarette if you care, and prepare to enjoy your flight for nothing can possibly go wrong possibly go wrong possibly go wrong possibly go . . .' I was prepared from the security of terra firma to believe that nothing could possibly go wrong with the hot-air balloon.

If our arrival in the helicopter had been well named 'The Flight of the Herron' the sequel seemed to me to deserve to follow D. K. Broster's trilogy and be called 'The Dark Mile'.

I was got into the basket which was held, none too securely, by an army of volunteers, while above my head an oxy-acetylene flame leapt into space, heating the air captured in the great blue-and-white silk dome and threatening at any moment —or so it seemed to me—to set the silk alight. The police, it appeared, were taking an interest in our affairs and now inter-vened to say that the wind had risen to such an extent that it would be quite unsafe for us to take off. I have no reason to believe that they were referring to the wind which I personally had contrived to generate at the thought of our journey. But having ascertained beyond a shadow of doubt that we were not to be allowed to go, I was able to express a deep sense of frustration at being denied the enjoyment of a trip to which I had been looking forward with such keen anticipation.

I was much amused later when a friend who had seen me in the basket remarked that he would very much have liked a picture, for he felt the scene to be symbolic of a debate in the Assembly earlier that week—the Moderator struggling to keep his feet on the ground while all around him people were generating hot air. Unhappily on that earlier occasion I hadn't had the advantage of the police coming to my rescue.

Strange the thoughts that crowd into your mind as you fly over the Grampians.

CHAPTER 4

The Gleam in the North

Of all our ventures into the air, none had been more exciting than the trip we made to Foula near the end of our spell in Shetland. Foula is a little island off the west coast of the mainland of Shetland, separated from it by twenty miles of the roughest kind of sea—few claim to have made the three-hour crossing without being seasick most of the way. It has a western cliff-face that rises thirteen hundred sheer feet out of the sea. It has a population of thirty-two souls. Its main link with the outside world is a mail-boat which sails fairly regularly to Walls on the Shetland mainland, though there are times in the winter when for weeks on end not even these hardy seamen would dream of putting to sea. There is, of course, no road on the island but only a series of tracks, and the wheeled transport consists of barrows, there being no horse. The principal source of income is manning the mail-boat, but there is also, of course, a certain amount of fishing (for local consumption), a measure of agriculture of the most primitive kind, and a deal of knitting. There is a school attended by five of the children—the three others are under school age—and the Schoolmaster, John Vernal, is also the Missionary in the service of our Church, while his wife is the District Nurse in the employ of the local authority.

The creation of the air-strip must have made a considerable difference to Foula. I hesitate to call it an air-strip, and the word creation has been used because I can't think of any verb that accurately describes what has happened. It's not the kind of thing any normal person would readily identify as an air-strip, for it had been just a flat stretch of heather until the islanders, with great labour and much sweat, had pulled out the tufts and divots. They have done little to fill in the holes, and nothing to provide a smooth surface. It's like a dirt track, only more so, and when the little Islander plane taxis to a standstill you wonder whether it could possibly have been any rougher had you come by boat. Still, it's an air-strip and with skilled handling and good nerves it's possible for the plane in reasonable conditions to land and to take off. Even under ideal conditions the eight-seater Islander will carry only four passengers, the number decreasing as the wind-velocity increases. There are times when the plane can make it and the boat could not, so it's a valuable life-line.

Captain Whitfield is an Englishman from the crowded south-east corner, brought up to the bustle and the bright lights, who came up to Shetland to fly the Loganair Islander that links the air-field at Sumburgh with the many Shetland islands and with Orkney. He has fallen completely under the spell of the land and has no thought of ever returning south. The facilities which his plane provide are much in demand. Sumburgh, the Shetland airfield, is a little strip of level land at the southern tip of the mainland, enclosed on every side but one by hills, constantly liable to be enshrouded in mist, unapproachable in many winds—altogether a most unreliable place for an airfield. Thus the Viscounts that link Shetland with Inverness and Glasgow, and with Aberdeen and Edinburgh, often get no farther than Orkney. Indeed, having gone on to Shetland they may well have to turn back and land at Kirkwall. This is when the little Loganair plane comes into its own—ferrying between Orkney and Shetland. It's also in constant demand for connection with Unst in the far north, with Fetlar and with other remote islands. So Captain Whitfield is kept busy. He has, of course, no regular service to Foula but will go when chartered—weather permitting.

He told me that at a time when for some reason Foula had hit the headlines and become 'good copy' he received a phone-call from a television company in the south booking a flight to the island. The lady explained that they were just taking out a single camera and a small crew and all they wanted was one or two shots here and there and an odd interview. She went on to ask if he could arrange, please, for a taxi to meet them and take them around. He explained something of the character of Foula and in particular that it had no taxi. 'Don't try to kid me,' said the lady, 'if there's an air terminal there's bound to be a taxi.' In fairness it has to be remembered that she hadn't had the advantage of seeing, much less of jolting along, the air-strip. 'Air-striptease' might be a better name for it.

The day proved an excellent one from the landing point of view, so four of us duly boarded the plane—Bruce Cannon, the Church's Press Officer, John Firth the minister of Walls in whose parish the island lies, and my wife and myself. We had a pleasant flight and an uneventful landing. There wasn't a taxi to meet us, but, next best thing, John Vernal, the teacher-cum-missionary, was there with his schoolboy son wheeling a barrow containing a wide selection of gumboots. We were warned to get into a pair of these before venturing off the air-strip. It was only about a hundred yards to the road, but damp heathery bog all the way. The greatest danger, though, was not of sinking in the bog but of treading upon the nests of the Arctic tern with which the area was literally peppered. Many had hatched out, and the fluffy little fledglings were scurrying about: others were still just clutches of eggs set in the heather. Each footstep had to be the subject of the most deliberate consideration.

Just across 'the road' from where we had landed was the little Church, and to it already the islanders were making their way. I was interested, and mildly amused, to learn that it was in fact the Congregational Church, the Parish Church being at the other end of the island; but they were all one flock now. They had no need of a church bell, the noise of the Islander's engine being sufficient indication that the service would shortly begin. Since the mail-boat was at sea we did not have a chance to meet the younger, able-bodied male popula-tion, for which I was sorry; but everyone else was present, including a girl from Essex, on Foula for a holiday (she had accidentally discovered the island the previous year). In a way I was making history, for I understand I am the first Moderator to have visited Foula, and I strongly suspect that when the time comes round for the Moderator to be in Shetland again there won't be on Foula a population for him to visit.

It's called The Edge of the World because of its great cliff bastion to the west—nothing after that till America—but as our missionary shrewdly remarked, 'For the people here it's the centre of the world, and for the bairns here it's the whole of the world.' Yes, it's all in your point of view—a principle that was brought very clearly to my mind one day in a Glasgow street where two women were gossiping on the pavement while

a small boy jumped trampoline-wise on the bonnet of a parked
car. He had wearied of the jumping and was kneeling on the
bonnet, drawing his sticky fingers down the windscreen when
one of the women turned, caught sight of him, and said, 'Och,
come doon oot o' there, son; ye'll get yersel' a' dirty afore ever
we start.' Yes, how things appear to you depends largely upon
where you happen to be standing at the time.

Inevitably one wonders what the future of such a community
can possibly be—whether, in fact, it has a future. Naturally one
thinks of St Kilda, now abandoned to the sea-birds. Enquiries
which I made in the course of a lunch given for us by the
County Council at Sumburgh immediately on our return from
Foula elicited no definite figure of what it costs the County to
maintain the community, but it seemed clear they could have
afforded to pay each inhabitant a tidy sum to get off and to
stay off, and have been left with a fair credit balance. Not that
the inhabitants would have agreed to take their money.
Furthermore, you may say, there is an obligation on a local
authority to make it possible for such an independent little
group to maintain their own peculiar way of life. As a way of
life it may not much appeal to us, but it is a way to which they
have been born and bred and they ask no other, so why should
they not be allowed to continue? But it's not so simple as that,
and quite honestly it's not an independent community at all.

For all its contempt for the big outside world it wouldn't be
able to survive for any length of time without that outside
world—otherwise why work so hard on the airstrip. It's funny
too, when you think of it, that the principal money-spinner
should be manning the maritime link. Nor will the community
just die out in time or perish through in-breeding. There's
always the odd person joining the fellowship—that lassie from
Essex might well come to do so. The mother of most of the
children is the daughter of a former missionary there, herself a
graduate, who was drawn to go back and who told me that
now she just couldn't contemplate any other kind of life. There
is, though, the problem of health. Outward seeming a robust
race, they go in constant terror of contamination and possible
infection with some epidemic. Not without cause, I imagine,
for it could well be that just because they've never known the
need to equip themselves with antibodies a simple affliction

like common 'flu' could rage through the island with deadly effect. An odd thing that their greatest health hazard should be their robust health.

The last thing the good folk of Foula want is our sympathy. They are content with their lot, and you can't expect people to lead a normal life on the edge of the world. I am sure, though, that they need our understanding, for, if I mistake not, they themselves are perilously near the edge of a cliff.

It had been a very different flight we had taken with Captain Whitfield some days earlier when we had flown to Unst, the most northerly of the group of islands that constitutes the Shetlands, passing, on the way, over Fetlar, the home of the snowy owl. Arrived at Baltasound, as the guests of the parish minister, Douglas Lamb, and his wife we had visited schools, seen Shetland spinning and knitting and other handiwork in progress, had been shown around the RAF early-warning radar system at Saxavoerd, and had viewed from afar the Lighthouse on the Muckle Flugga away at the northernmost tip of the island. I was due to conduct a service on the neighbouring island of Yell at 8 o'clock in the evening, so it had been arranged that I would preach in the Church at Baltasound on Unst at 5.15. That hour on a week-day seemed to me an ill-chosen one, though I recognised the difficulty that had led to its choice. Before the Service there was laid on in the Church Hall what was modestly referred to as a Buffet Tea—tables groaning with savouries, sandwiches, sausage rolls, cakes, biscuits, scones and what have you, all of the most luscious home-made variety.

As the time of the service approached the hall steadily filled up, and a large and representative gathering did full justice to, if they made little impression upon, the Buffet Tea. Immediately at the close of the service we had to make a hurried departure, for we were being driven to a ferry that would take us across to Yell where we were to be collected and driven on to Mid Yell, the scene of our next assignment. As my wife and I left the Church to walk the few yards to the car we found our path on both sides lined three-deep with children in uniform, boys on one side, girls on the other, waving and cheering in the most heart-warming fashion. A few yards down the road as the car made a right-hand turn I leaned out for a

last wave, only to find the area deserted—not a child was to
be seen, it was as though some mighty atom bomb had swept
them into oblivion. Later I discovered that the kids had been
instructed, 'After the Moderator's car drives away you can go
round to the Hall and clear up what's left of the eats'. With so
big a job on hand there was obviously no time to be lost.

On the occasion of an earlier visit to Shetland Gordon
Riddell had invited me to preach at the re-dedication of the
kirk at Lunna, which had been extensively redecorated. I had
been pleased and proud to take part in the Service at that
little sanctuary in the lonely bay looking out towards Europe.
For Lunna had been the Scottish terminus of what came to be
known as the Shetland Bus—the route by which during the
war a vast number of Norwegians made the journey across
the North Sea in little boats to train here, returning later by
parachute to perform the most daring acts of sabotage in their
own country. The grave-yard bears testimony to the memory
of many who failed to complete the journey.

Waiting one day some years ago for a ferry near the Norwegian port of Aalesund I was accosted by a local traveller
who had just parked his car behind mine in the queue. 'You
English?' he enquired. 'No, Scottish,' I replied. I fear we Scots
are far too sensitive about the identification of England with
Britain. He all but threw his arms around my neck. 'But from
Scotland!' he cried. There was a tear in his eye—and before
long in mine too. He, along with another twenty-six young men,
had set off from Aalesund in the dark of a winter's night in
what was little more than a rowing-boat and had successfully
made the crossing to Lunna. He had been trained in many
parts of the country and in many strange skills like mountain
warfare, sabotage, parachute-jumping. But the time that stood
out supreme in his recollection was the stint he did in Scotland
with the Black Watch. Then and there he wanted us to come
with him and his family to his hunting-place somewhere in
the hills so he could in some way return the hospitality he
owed to our land and people. Scarce would he take No for an
answer; but declining his offer the best way I could I tried to
get some guidance from him about the route we were supposed
to follow. He explained in great detail. For a spell I would be
on a straight wide road and then I was to veer off into one

that was 'turny and thin'. He had learned many things from
'the Jocks', but not that surely!

Whalsay also had a visit from us. Willie Glencross, the
minister, had been a mining engineer in Ayrshire before
turning to the ministry, and Whalsay must have proved a
mighty change from Kirkconnel. Among many places to
which he took me was the school. An interesting story centres
around the building. A laird of yester-year decided he wanted
a magnificent house of granite built on the hill at the top of
the village street. The labour and sweat and—a commodity
not so plentiful—the 'siller' that went into the shipping of all
that granite and the building of that fortress just don't bear
contemplation. But a laird was a laird in those days and his
whim was law. Today the great mansion belongs to the Education Committee, and it's been converted into a very splendid
modern school. The top floor has made a lovely penthouse
flat for the headmaster, who with his wife—a delightful Clydeside couple—entertained us to coffee and a view, and it's no
slight on the quality of the coffee to say, 'What a view!' He
must surely be one of the most exalted schoolmasters in
Scotland.

Shetland is at present enjoying a wave of prosperity. It has
not always been so. The fishing is doing well, as are its ancillary
industries; knitting—'the hosiery' as they call it—is booming,
having captured a number of continental markets; Lerwick,
the capital, is a cosmopolitan city serving Norse, Danes,
Swedes, Laps, Russians from the great fishing-fleets and
factory-ships in the North Sea. Whalsay itself, as an important
fishing centre, has come in for a fair measure of the prosperity.
At least it's about a Whalsay man that they tell a very unkind
story. One day, it is said, this Whalsay man stepped into a
bank in Lerwick lugging an enormous chest which he hoisted
on to the counter. Of late, he explained to the Manager, what
with the improvement in the fishing and plenty of work on the
hosiery, he and his wife had been able to lay by an odd shilling
against a rainy day. According to long-established tradition
they had put it in a 'kist' under the bed. Having read a lot in
the papers about robberies, however, it had occurred to him
that his money might be safer in the bank. So he had brought
along the chest with its contents—£4000 exactly. The banker

duly had the contents of the 'kist' checked. 'I'm sorry,' he said, 'we can only make it out at £3850.' 'Dammit,' said the fisherman, 'have I no' been and brocht the wrang kist!'

There were no obvious 'kists' of savings but plenty of boxes of fish on the quay on the Saturday morning when we came to board the *Earl of Zetland* for the return journey to Lerwick. My wife had been most diligent the previous evening in making enquiries as to when exactly the boat was due to call. Oh, she had been told, it wouldn't likely be before 10 o'clock, might even be the half-hour; sometimes, in fact, it might be nearer 11. But when was it due? Queenie persisted. 'You can look from the window and see her coming and that leaves you plenty of time.' It appeared that the *Earl of Zetland* came when she was ready to come—neither before nor after.

Sure enough, from the Manse window we saw her rounding the headland and off we set. But no-one had told us of the twelve tons of fish that had to be loaded or we needn't have hurried. Captain Sinclair, the master of the hardy little craft, insisted that we have coffee with him while the loading was in progress, and that we spend the remainder of the journey as his guests on the bridge. One of the most enlightening journeys I've ever made, in which we learned a lot about geography, about seamanship, and about life in general. An amazing man who contrives to maintain the life-line of the regular boat linking all these islands right through the dirtiest days of winter. Loganair may supplement, it can never supplant, the *Earl of Zetland*.

What wonderful days these were that we spent in Shetland among a company of ministers and ladies-of-the-manse who for all the central heating and double-glazing and mini-cars must still find the life a strange and isolated one; and among a people so different from our own and of such gentleness and generosity. For the Shetlander, however little gear he may possess to enable him to maintain the position, is always and essentially a gentleman. An old lady would lead you to the chair beside her peat fire with all the grace and dignity of the Queen receiving you at Balmoral—but then her grannie had probably come to that very house many years ago as a bride, her great-grandfather had maybe built it with his own hands. A gracious, kindly people, they've left us with many happy memories and they loaded us with gifts to the point of embarrassment.

By comparison with Shetland's constant travelling and living out of suit-cases our days in Orkney, where we were stationed in Kirkwall and established in an hotel there, were somewhat quiet. The land here is so much more fertile than in Shetland. It's sometimes said that while the Shetlander is a fisherman with a croft the Orcadian is a farmer with a boat. Probably that sums up the position fairly enough.

It had been very pleasant to be centred on Kirkwall. For one thing our hotel bedroom overlooked the harbour, where the constant movement of vessels and the coming and going of little craft provided an unceasing source of interest. And just around the corner was the paved shopping precinct along which the cars drive and where something of interest is always to be seen or heard. St Magnus Cathedral, that wonderful mass of many-coloured spendour, was unhappily in a condition where repairs—and vast sums to pay for them—were called for, and the Sunday Service at which in normal circumstances I should have been preaching had to be moved to the other Church.

A particularly vivid memory is of a woman's meeting held in Twatt Kirk, a sanctuary, like the light of scripture, set on a hill, without another building in sight. The women had come in cars and buses and boats from all parts of the islands, and it was a packed audience I had to address. So much it reminded me, if on a somewhat reduced scale, of the Women's Meetings in the Usher Hall in Edinburgh during the time of the Assembly. There are usually four of these, beginning on the opening day with the great Guild Rally, for which tickets are as precious as for a Cup Final—though I don't think they rise to a black market. The Moderator is expected to visit the Rally and one other of the meetings, but with the kind of luck I invariably enjoy I found I had to give a major address at three out of the four. Not that I'm complaining, for I found them the most delightful and responsive of audiences. Though as you step from the green-room straight out on to the platform and get that first glimpse of the serried ranks of women it can be a quite terrifying experience—you realise how the Colosseum lions must have felt when they entered the arena and looked around them.

Then there had been that evening meeting of office-bearers in Kirkwall, held in the Town Hall when more and more

chairs had had to be carried in, and at which, as well as giving
a talk, I had the privilege of handing over long-service certifi-
cates to men from many parishes who had given faithful
service in the eldership over long periods. Plain men, all of
them, fishermen, farmers, tradesmen, boat-builders, postmen,
men with gnarled hands, men with weather-beaten faces, men
clearly who had known life where it was hardest, but men who
had known the Lord Jesus and His power and goodness and
who had sought to serve Him and His Church.

It was not, mercifully, a typical day, but it was a most
memorable one that time we visited the island of Hoy. The
early part of the forenoon had been left 'free'—which meant I
had spent a couple of hours catching up on arrears of correspondence—and then at 11 o'clock we were collected and
driven over to Stromness where we lunched as guests of the
County Convener and his wife in their lovely house with its
magnificent outlook high above the town. Leaving there we
spent some time in an Eventide Home, and then on to the
school where we had the chance of seeing something of the
scope of the teaching, and concluded with 'afternoon tea' in
the staff room and an informal meeting and chat with the
teachers. The 'afternoon tea' was equal to any normal 'square
meal'. From here we made straight for the harbour whence,
joined by the Moderator of Presbytery and his wife, we set off
under the care of one, Ginger Brown, for the sail to Hoy—
just under an hour in his little launch. Arrived at the slipway
at the north end of the island we were collected by Ewen
Traill, the local minister, who drove us first to the north-
western tip to see The Old Man of Hoy, the climbing of which
has more than once been the breath-holding subject of a
television programme. Then on to several other parts of the
island, ending up by paying our silent tribute to selfless courage
and devotion to duty as we stood by the memorial in the local
grave-yard to the life-boatmen of Longhope, seven of whom
lost their lives when their boat capsized on an occasion when
they should never have been called out. The new boat had
been delivered just a few days before, and a new crew instantly
enrolled. Such is their courage.

By this time it was 7 o'clock and I was due to conduct a
service in the Church at Longhope at 8, so we made for the

Manse to wash and freshen up and sit for a minute or two to
collect my thoughts—or so I fondly imagined. How desperately
far wrong I was, for Mrs Traill had a full-scale dinner awaiting
us. It need scarcely be said that we did rather less than justice
to this before hurrying off to the Church. After the service we
were ushered in to the village hall, where we were to meet and
chat informally with the local people. Need I explain that a
'cup of tea' had been laid on, and that this again was the kind
of snack on the strength of which you could have done a day's
work. I contrived to do the maximum of meeting and chatting
and the minimum of eating, until in due course we bade farewell to the good folk and set off to be driven back the thirty or
so miles to where Ginger Brown awaited us with his boat. Or
at least *had* awaited us, for it was clear he had wearied of much
waiting and now only the boat awaited us. The minister's local
knowledge was equal to the occasion, however, and Ginger was
quickly found and we set off. The wind had freshened considerably since our coming, so that, while our boatman thought
the crossing a quite straightforward affair, neither my wife nor
I was wholly sorry when around 11.30 we sailed into Stromness harbour. Then the forty-mile drive back to Kirkwall, our
hotel, and our bed—and another Moderatorial day was over.
In these northern regions and in the month of June it was, of
course, still broad daylight when we got back to Kirkwall, but
we were ready to call it a day for all that. You can see what I
mean when I say there are only two kinds of Moderators—
tough Moderators and late Moderators.

Orkney and Shetland—I had heard a lot about them in geography lessons at school and read about them from time to time,
and had seen the relevant entries about them in our Church
lists. I had never imagined I should visit them, least of all in
the capacity of Moderator. They talk up there about crossing
over to 'Scotland'—for each group of islands reserves the term
'mainland' to denote its own principal island. I suppose this is
fair enough, for it all depends, once more, on your point of
view. As in the case of the famous minister of Millport (a little
village on the tiny Isle of Cumbrae in the Firth of Clyde) who
in his Sunday intercessions invoked the divine blessing on 'the
Greater and Lesser Cumbraes and the adjoining islands of
Great Britain and Ireland'. There's more than this, though, in

the reference to 'Scotland' as 'way out there', for, you see, they are not very sure whether or not they are part of Scotland—with, I think, a distinct preference for the 'or not'.

There are historical reasons—the islands came to Scotland as part of a Queen's dowry. There are obvious geographical reasons. It's said that a Shetland farmer, filling up a form for delivery of feeding-stuffs, found himself confronted with the question 'nearest Railway Station'. Getting out the atlas and a ruler he hopefully wrote in 'Bergen'. I suppose too there are ethnic reasons. Besides, independent people like to think of themselves as an independent people. I imagine, though, that the principal reason is that communities which are essentially different and apart bitterly resent being swallowed up in a larger unit which doesn't understand their problems, which adopts the attitude that if only people would be reasonable the problems would go away, and which always insists on trying to make everything conform to its general patterns. The 'nearest railway station' query is typical. There was the effort recently to establish one single water authority for Caithness and everything north thereof. As if the business of providing a water supply on the mainland and in a group of islands had anything at all in common, apart from the water. In fact it's the very same thing as we Scots are always fighting in our relations with our neighbours south of the Border. How completely divorced from reality can the bureaucratic mentality of government become!

It's significant from the Kirk's point of view that these island parishes are staffed almost wholly with 'Scotsmen'. Only one Shetland minister is a local man, and two, I think, Orkney ministers are Orcadians. They have their problems, all of them, but the Kirk is still a very vital institution in the life of the community, and the minister is accorded a status he may not enjoy elsewhere. Not that they are still at the stage represented by the small boy walking down the street of a Scottish village, his hand linked in that of his grannie, who found his arm suddenly jerked nearly out of its socket, 'Strachten yer bunnet, Wullie, here's the minister's dug'.

Certainly at least they gave the Moderator and his wife a wonderful time—in spite of their coming from Scotland—'ferry-loupers' as the Orcadians call them.

CHAPTER 5

'Meet the Bishops'

'The Lord Mayor of London and Lady Studd request the pleasure of the company of the Moderator of the General Assembly and Mrs Herron to meet the Archbishops and the Bishops at Dinner in the Mansion House on . . .' It was a very magnificently engrossed card and conveyed a very gracious invitation. As I was later to learn, it came from a very gracious personality—Sir Percy Studd, one of London's really great Lord Mayors.

For many years, it seems, on the evening before the Convocation of Canterbury is due to convene, the Lord Mayor has been in the habit of giving a Dinner in the Mansion House 'to meet the Archbishops and the Bishops'. This particular year had seen a change, for instead of the Convocation it was the Synod that was to be held, and in York instead of London; but Sir Percy had decided to continue the function. He had, apparently, decided also to include the Moderator of our Assembly as the one outsider—I hesitate to say rank outsider—in the company. I had already undertaken another engagement in the Metropolis for the following day, so it was very convenient for us to accept.

A most notable, interesting, and enjoyable occasion it proved. I had not expected to know many of so august a company, but as I looked around I found that in fact I had met quite a few in one ecumenical context or another. There was the Bishop of Bristol, Convener of an Episcopal-Presbyterian Liaison Committee with whom from time to time I had crossed swords; the Bishop of Sodor and Man, encountered in the same context; the recently appointed Bishop of Oxford, Kenneth Woolcombe, who had until recently been Principal of the Episcopal College in Edinburgh and my chief sparring-partner in many a punch-up in a Scottish discussion group; the Suffragan Bishop of Kingston-upon-Thames with whom while he was still Canon Montefiore of Great St Mary's in Cambridge I had argued about Church unity on a television programme; and Bishop

Sansbury, General Secretary of the British Council of Churches, of whose Administrative Committee I had recently become a member.

It seemed strange, in a way, that I should be there. I began to feel a little as Daniel must have done when he heard the gates of the lions' den clanging-to behind him. Lions are all right, but you don't want to take on too many at the one time. Suddenly it dawned on me that with all these people whom I recognised, and with whom we had been exchanging greetings, I had been at serious variance on every previous meeting. For all my days I have been violently 'agin Bishops'. For myself I believe they represent what is essentially an anachronism, but if Anglicans want it that way that is a matter for them to decide. What I resent and object to so bitterly is the thesis that their presence is a 'must' if an institution is to be a Church, and I would contest with all the power at my command any proposal that the future Kirk in Scotland must of necessity be an Episcopal Church. I have always been convinced that, despite the vehemence of the protestations to the contrary, what is at stake is not the principle of episkope exercised as a personal oversight rather than a conciliar oversight, but is the question whether it is necessary for someone in the Apostolic Succession to take part in the conferring of orders that are to be effective orders, the question whether a Bishop in the Apostolic Succession must be present at all ordinations of ministers. It is not just that I don't much like this idea, it is that I find it repugnant, in flagrant contradiction to all that the faith means for me.

It was as long ago as 1932 that Principal Macgregor (the Williemac already referred to) pleaded with the Assembly not at that stage to accept an invitation to engage in conversations with the Episcopal Church. 'We know our own position,' he said. 'We know the position of the others in so far as they have one—or at least we know several of their positions. We shall not learn a great deal. We may come back and report progress; and so time will drift on and on and nothing will be achieved. The really fundamental thing is what our friends do not wish to be touched upon. Are they prepared to recognise us as in some full sense constituent members of the Catholic Church of the Lord Jesus Christ? They doggedly and continuously refuse or evade that decision.' No-one listened very earnestly to his plea and discussion was begun and continued in a desultory kind of way and without any very spectacular results.

The new wave of ecumenical fervour of the early 'fifties gave a fresh impetus to this debate and resulted in there being brought to the Assembly in 1957 a document that came to be known as 'The Bishops Report', a document destined to figure largely in much popular debate in Scotland for many a day. I've often wondered—and sometimes thought it was significant —that the document didn't seem to make any comparable impression south of the Border. The clergy appeared to know of its existence and to feel they ought to be mildly interested. Members, good members, of the Church of England to whom I have spoken hadn't heard of it, or if they had they thought it was something that was happening in Scotland. There was nobody in Scotland who hadn't heard of it!

The document—it was the report of the lengthy discussions of a top-ranking committee representing four bodies, the Episcopal and Presbyterian Churches north and south of the border—covered a very large field and contained a number of proposals of a most interesting kind. Chief of these was the suggestion that the best hope of finding a way towards a new unity lay in the devising of a system of Church government wherein Bishops would act as Presidents of Presbyteries.

Bishops, chosen by each Presbytery, from its own membership or otherwise, would initially be consecrated by prayer with the laying on of hands by Bishops from one or more of the Episcopal Churches and by the Presbytery acting through appointed representatives. Thus consecrated each Bishop would be within the apostolic succession as acknowledged by Anglicans on the one hand and as required by Presbyterians on the other. He would be the President of the Presbytery and would act as its principal minister in every ordination and in the consecration of other Bishops.

The Report went into no kind of detail as to how the respective powers of Bishop and Presbytery were to be balanced, seeming to suggest that once we got down seriously to it this would present no very serious difficulty. Make it vague and it will sound simple.

The Presbytery would still retain its full and essential place in the life and government of the Church, except that a permanent

Bishop-in-Presbytery would take the place of the changing Moderator. The General Assembly would retain its full existing authority
in doctrine, administration, legislation and judicature. Bishops
would be members of the General Assembly, without constituting
an Upper House within it, although decisions on doctrinal and
constitutional matters might well have to require their consent.

In straightforward terms this seems to say that the Presbytery
would continue as before except that it would be essentially
different, and that the Assembly would retain all its powers
except that it might well have to relinquish them.

There seems to have been a feeling that a good deal was
being required of the Presbyterians and that some kind of
quid pro quo would not come amiss.

Lay persons would be solemnly 'set apart' for some measure of
pastoral responsibility towards their fellow-Christians, in an office
akin to the Presbyterian eldership. . . . Efforts would be made to
procure a wider and more effective lay representation in the Church
Assembly and to revise the relationship between the Convocations
and the Church Assembly viewed as a National Synod.

Never during my lifetime has any ecclesiastical issue caused
so widespread a furore, not only within the Church but
throughout the country as a whole as did the Bishops Report.
The fact that the *Scottish Daily Express* reported the matter
so fully, produced special features on it, and came down so
heavily against it, no doubt played a part in bringing the
matter before the public and keeping it there, but apart from
that altogether the Report certainly did make the big-time
news. It probably wasn't true, but it could well have been
true, the story of the man who was vituperating against the idea
of bishops in the Kirk when his friend challenged him, 'But
Willie, I ay thocht you were an agnostic.' 'That's right,'
Willie replied, 'So I am. But I'm a Presbyterian agnostic.'

It was some years later during a conference at Holland House
in Edinburgh that once again the *Scottish Daily Express* was
very critical of some of the proposals being discussed—particularly of the idea of 'Covenanting for Unity' which it was
later claimed had not been discussed at the conference at all.
At one of the sederunts a good deal had been said, some of
it pretty bitter, about this publicity. Leaving the hall I was
discussing the matter with a distinguished Anglican layman

from Oxford, and had been saying that for my part I thought
in the long run it was good for these matters to be made the
subject of critical public scrutiny, to which he replied, 'What
amazes me coming here to Scotland is to find that anything
connected with the Church can make front-page news in a
national newspaper. With us, if this were reported at all it
would be found in a little paragraph in an out-of-the-way
corner.' 'Oh but,' I rejoined, 'the Kirk still counts for something in Scotland. We may not have enough life to start a
revival: we've certainly enough life to start a fight.' And when
you stop to think of it there's not so much difference between
the two. Looked at from one angle the Reformation was a
fight, from another it was the greatest religious revival Europe
has ever known; Methodism was born of a quarrel that was
no less a great spiritual awakening; our own Scottish Disruption
was the result of ten years' conflict or of ten years' evangelism
according to how you look at it.

I was minister at Houston at the time when the Bishops
Report appeared, and, indeed, had just become Clerk of the
Presbytery of Paisley, a part-time appointment. We in Paisley,
in common with many throughout the Church, were much
opposed to the proposals and took a fairly strong line towards
having them rejected by the following Assembly, going so far
as to table an Overture to this effect. The anti-Bishops group
was strong numerically but lacking leadership and for a time
it looked as though those who supported the Report were going
to carry the day. One of them had even got around to referring
to his opponents as 'the lunatic fringe'; while another, commending the Report at a meeting of a Presbytery, went on to
say that when the Holy Spirit is leading the Church towards
something new that is the moment when the forces of anti-
Christ band themselves together to impede Him. I had not, I
admit, thought of myself as the forces of anti-Christ, but I was
certainly prepared to do my best to overturn the proposals of
the Report. And I have a deep-seated dislike of the man who
claims a monopoly of the Holy Spirit. Blackmail is always a
nasty business; spiritual blackmail is especially despicable.

In the event, after the matter had been fully debated in
Presbyteries, the proposals were rejected by the following
Assembly. A new Committee of Fifty was appointed to enter

upon a fresh series of exploratory discussions with representatives of the other three denominations involved, the object this time being to seek clarification of a number of specific areas of difference rather than to seek a solution of differences in general. Some little time later I was myself nominated to fill a vacancy among the fifty, but I was able to take little part in the deliberations—indeed my attendance at Holland House (in January 1965) to which I have already referred was the first appearance I was able to make.

It has always seemed to me that Principal Macgregor was right in his claim in 1932 that in this field of ecumenical debate we tend to avoid the basic issues about which we are seriously divided. There are things precious and essential to you which I in conscience just cannot accept. No doubt things that matter intensely for me are in like manner repugnant to you. This, to me, represents the heart of our disagreement and until we have taken some steps to resolve these differences little progress towards unity seems possible. By forgetting these issues and bringing our fringe practices together we may achieve a degree of uniformity, but surely that is precisely what is meant by the phrase 'papering over the cracks'. I remember once in my office being surprised by an application for a Property Grant which explained, 'There is dryrot in the floor of the vestibule and we want to put down new linoleum.'

Rather than face up to the big issues on which we differ radically we find it more comforting to discover how many things there are about which we are agreed. If we've reached an absolute impasse in your attempt to sell me your motor-car it must comfort us greatly to know that we are completely at one in thinking it's a nice day.

There's always the temptation, too, to make statuesque pronouncements that don't require anything to be done about them. We talk a lot, for example, about 'the sin of our divisions'. I've never been quite clear what this means. It could mean that our fathers were difficult, thrawn people from whom we've inherited a deplorable situation—'the fathers have eaten sour grapes and the children's teeth are set on edge'. The strange thing, though, as I hinted elsewhere, is that the divisions came out of times of acute spiritual awareness—strange that so good a tree as the Reformation-revival should bear so bitter a fruit

as our sinful divisions. Or it could mean simply that the fact
that we are divided is evidence that we are sinners—else we
should have patched up our differences long ago. To me this
is not a self-evident proposition. If you and I differ on some
important aspect of the faith and if that is inevitably a sign of
sin then manifestly there must be something we can do about
it, for we cannot have sinned unless there had been another
course open to us. What was that other course? Should I have
twisted your arm and forced you to come with me, or should
I have meekly gone with you against all the dictates of heart
and mind and conscience, or should we perchance have tossed
a coin to see which way we'd go, or, by splitting the difference,
should we have followed a route that neither of us believed led
anywhere? What should we have done to avoid sin? There
must be an answer.

May not there come a time when righteousness compels us
to differ—to agree to differ perhaps, but certainly to differ?
May it not be a time could come when it would be true to
speak of 'the sin of our alliances'? What should Martin Luther
have done with his Articles? There can come a time when in
the name of truth and righteousness, no less than of Christian
love and charity, one is entitled—if not actually compelled—
to say, 'Here I stand. So help me, God, I can no other.'

All of this is based upon a belief in responsible individual
human freedom. Now one must recognise there are dangers in
too great a degree of freedom being accorded to everyman to
accept only what appears to him reasonable and proper and
to reject as false whatever does not commend itself to him.
Ultimately the doctrine that everyman is the judge of what is
truth could lead to the situation where everyman had his own
truth since no-one else's came quite up to the mark. One
thinks of the proliferation of sects within some denominations
today, or indeed of that which occurred within Scottish Presbyterianism in the late eighteenth century. The Auld-Licht Anti-
burgher Non-lifter must, I often think, have been a most
intensely interesting, if somewhat negative, specimen, worthy
of a place in any ecclesiastical museum. And that kind of
thing, it must be conceded, is where complete individual
freedom can lead when carried to its *reductio ad absurdum*. The
alternative, however, is no less extreme and very much more

terrifying. For the doctrine that the Church itself is alone the guardian of the truth, that you must leave to wise mother-Church to decide, and that there only remains for you to conform—this led to the Inquisition and to the Fires of Smithfield. These, after all, were the contemporary means of purging us of 'the sin of our divisions'. Conformity no less than freedom has its *reductio ad absurdum.*

I think too there has been a great tendency to confuse unity with union and to equate the visible unity of the Church with the unity of the visible Church.

I've never understood why we should not as a first step towards a fuller unity try to introduce some form of federation. It seems, however, to be universally agreed that this must not be countenanced and that the only objective worth aiming for is organic unity. This term as applied to the Church's situation I frankly conceive to be irrelevant. To me the term 'organic unity' is one which is properly applied to the uniting principle that binds together a number of utterly different and disparate things because they all play their part in the life of one organism. Obvious example would be, say, heart and liver. See them lying side by side on a mortuary slab there is no resemblance and no obvious connection between them. But there is a bond of essential unity because of the respective parts they play in the functioning of the one human body. This to me is organic unity. Completely different in character, utterly separate in function, but each making the life of the other possible because together they serve one common organic purpose.

What I cannot understand is how this analogy can be applied to a union of denominations. I am certain that when Churchmen speak about organic unity what they mean is organisational unity, that the various denominations, without losing their individual character, without sacrificing their distinctive witness, are to be bound together to form one organisation.

Even this may sound fine and worth working for, until you face up to the question of how the individual characteristics and the differing patterns are to be combined within the one organisation. For the trouble about the differences is that in most cases they are mutually contradictory and exclusive. You cannot have the dignity and splendour of the Service in the Cathedral and the heartiness and spontaneity of the meeting

in the Salvation Army Citadel both at once. You pays your
money and you takes your choice, and not even by paying a
little extra money can you be saved the choice. The pipe-organ
and the tambourine don't really blend. This factor was high-
lighted right from the very start with the Bishops Report
through its failure to examine in any detail what were to be
the respective powers and limitations of Bishop and Presbytery
in the fine new set-up of Bishop-in-Presbytery. It is all a little
like saying: We have here a square peg, while yonder you have
a round hole; why should they continue in lonely isolation;
let's pop the square peg into the round hole. 'But', some hardy
sceptic maintains, 'it's well known that square pegs don't go
into round holes.' 'Oh, it's not easy; what with all the bigotry
and hatred we've inherited; what with the *Daily Express*
writing inflammatory articles; but given a little faith and
patience and Christian charity it's wonderful what can be
achieved.' To me this is poppycock, and the fact that it's
pious poppycock doesn't make it any the more palatable.

Life, so often as I have experienced it, is a matter of making
a choice and standing by the consequences. Either you believe
that authority within the Church vests in individuals set apart
and ordained within the Apostolic Succession for the sole purpose, within God's inscrutable design, of bearing that rule; or
else you believe in a conciliar form of Church government and
see the parish minister, answerable to his Presbytery, as carrying
the highest powers within the Church. You can say, as Anglicans seem to say, that without Bishops of their sort there can
be no Church, and in so saying find you have unChurched
those with whom you are conversing; or you can say, as we do,
that your system is 'conformable to the Word of God' and so
pass judgment upon none. What you cannot do is simultaneously to say both.

To some extent it may be that the difficulty stems from a
temperamental difference between our two peoples. The
Englishman is reputed to have a genius for compromise; the
corresponding quality in the Scot is a genius for controversy.
So long as he can find a formula that both of us can sign the
Englishman is happy in the knowledge that no-one is going to
be enough of a cad to enquire too narrowly just exactly what is
meant by some of the phrases in the document. Can you read

it in such a way that it is acceptable to you? Then put your
name to it and don't ask silly questions. We'll do just the same;
we shouldn't dream of raising a hornet's nest by asking needless questions. We in the north, on the contrary, would fall out
about why a comma stood where it did, and until the issue had
been clearly settled and the offending comma made into a
semi-colon not a scrap of signing would we undertake.

In the ill-fated proposals for the union of Anglicans and
Methodists—to quote a concrete instance—the service of reconciliation might possibly be construed as an occasion when I
would publicly recognise the validity of your orders, or it might
be regarded as an opportunity for me to make good a deficiency
in your orders (with, of course, the utmost discretion). While
you can read it in a way that is quite inoffensive you have a
shrewd suspicion that I am reading it in the other way which
is highly offensive. This kind of thing would never commend
itself to us in Scotland. I once heard the phrase used in an
ecumenical debate, 'this God-given ambiguity'. A little like
adding blasphemy to the sin of our accommodations.

No single thing has had a more powerful effect upon the
course of the ecumenical movement in Scotland than the
publication in April 1967 of the late Professor Ian Henderson's
book *Power without Glory*. Before it starts at all it nails its colours
firmly to the mast on the dedication-page—'This book is
dedicated to the good Christians in every denomination who
do not care greatly whether there is One Church or not.' It
appeared at a critical moment in the course of the negotiations
between the Church of Scotland and the Episcopal Church in
Scotland, and it set forth with the most shattering clarity what
the author believed to be the real issues at stake. It set the whole
affair in a wider national and historical context than most up
to then had understood.

I was proud to count Ian Henderson among my best friends.
For his ability as a thinker and a teacher I had the most profound respect, for his absolute honesty and the sheer courage
that went with it I had a great admiration, and for the gentleness and kindliness that were the real Ian Henderson I had the
fondest affection. When first I had come to Glasgow he had
been in hospital and I had thought it my duty to pay him a
visit—a Presbytery Clerk though he walks ungaitered will

normally be accepted among his people as *pastor pastorum*. Very soon the visit became a regular and ever-lengthening feature of my week and a close friendship developed between us.

Ian had been one of the original Committee of Fifty appointed after the fall of the Bishops Report. He had found himself consistently following an unpopular line at these get-togethers—controversy is definitely bad form in some circles—and he had found the easiest and pleasantest plan was just gradually to drift out until ultimately he was replaced by someone who had a greater enthusiasm for the way things were going. Later he came to feel a bit guilty about this. Had he, he wondered, sold out on his kirk and on his friends. At the same time he felt he was not well equipped to fight that kind of battle. What he did know about was writing, and he wondered whether he could not perhaps strike a blow for Presbyterian independence by writing a book.

Needless to say I encouraged him, although, frankly, I felt that while a book might well do a lot to get this guilt-feeling out of his own system it was not likely to affect, tremendously, the course of ecumenical events. We discussed the book from time to time, but it was when he gave me the text to read before sending it to his publishers that I recognised how appallingly wrong I had been. Here, I instantly recognised, was a work that would shake the entire country, here was a book whose sheer honesty would make it a force to be reckoned with, here was a summary of the ecclesiastical situation with its national undertones that none could possibly ignore, here was a work whose scholarship was as undeniable as its conclusion was inescapable.

The fact that *Power without Glory* was written in tones that were often bitter and sometimes extravagant would, I saw clearly enough, detract from its value as a balanced assessment of the situation; but I saw too that a balanced assessment, however valuable in portraying the past, was not likely to have much effect in shaping the future, whereas this brilliant broadsheet was certain to have a massive effect. I conveyed my views to Ian, advising that he take nothing out, tone nothing down. How right we were, and how tremendous was the impact.

What a tragic loss the Church sustained through the sudden death in April 1969, at the early age of fifty-eight, of this distinguished son. At the time of the publication of *Power without*

Glory he had been Moderator of our Presbytery of Glasgow, and how proud he had been of the fact and with what magnificent distinction he had carried through all his duties. I like to think he would have rejoiced in my own appointment to be Moderator of Assembly.

One day at last Assembly when I was standing-in as chairman I got a fair amount of bouquets—undeserved, I thought—for my handling of an awkward situation. We were dealing with the report of the Inter-Church Relations Committee, and in it was a proposal that Dr A. C. Craig, who had been on the Committee for very many years—he had had the distinction of steering the Bishops Report through a fairly hostile Assembly—should be continued on the Committee as an honorary life-member. As a counter-motion one member moved that this be not done—it was quite wrong, he thought, that anyone should be continued too long on any committee, this was particularly true in the case of the Inter-Church Relations Committee, and, in any case, life-membership was a nonsense. He spoke well and gained quite a bit of support and one or two people commented in fairly robust terms on the general theme of outstayed welcomes. The matter went to a vote and the counter-motion was carried by a considerable majority.

Archie Craig was sitting in the Assembly when the matter was raised and as the debate proceeded he looked a bit self-conscious and unhappy. Half-way through he had been about to slip out, but I had signalled to him to sit still. At this point, then, the question having been finally decided, I turned to him and I said, 'Dr Craig, none knows better than you do what a remarkable genius the Assembly has for distinguishing in any issue between the principle involved and the person involved . . .' Before I could continue there was a positive roar of agreement and approval, so that when it finally died down I had only to add, 'You can see clearly enough that if the Assembly don't want you condemned for life to the Inter-Church treadmill that is certainly not because they are unaware or unappreciative of all you have done in the sphere of Inter-Church relations as well as for the Church as a whole.'

I hope, by the same token, that I was able that June evening to enjoy the company of all the Bishops without conceding the principle.

CHAPTER 6

Piper in the Aisle

We were at a supper-party given in our honour in the home of
the British Consul General in Amsterdam, and although the
month was April strawberries were being served. I was seated
on the right of our hostess, Mrs Hughes, while on her left was
her own Anglican vicar who, by one of those queer coincidences
of which life seems to be so full, had attended the same Glasgow
school as I, my senior by a couple of years. Though this was
not something we had learned at Albert Road Academy, he
and I were agreed we should like some pepper for our strawberries. Our hostess obviously thought we were resurrecting
some schoolboy prank, and others sitting at our end of the
table were drawn into the discussion. It transpired that my
wife had caused some consternation at the other end of the
room by peppering her strawberries. We had thought the
custom to be an international one—it certainly does something
to bring out the flavour of the fruit to have just a sensation of
white pepper shaken over it. The event, though, reminded me
of another occasion when, as it were, we had thrown the whole
cruet at the unfortunate fruit. It happened on this wise.

One of the normally less onerous *ex officio* appointments of our
Moderator is that of Honorary Patron of the Magna Carta
Trust. There is no very obvious link between Runnymede and
the Royal Mile, and no very patent reason why the Moderator
should be involved. But, as always, there is a story behind it.
Some twenty years ago the American Bar Association erected
the Kennedy Memorial at the spot where King John is believed
to have signed the Great Charter that was to prove the basis
upon which, throughout the English realm, the freedom of the
individual was secured. That the king signed it with great
reluctance seems clear from the fact that it took five days'
confrontation with superior force to persuade him so to do;
that he would blithely have torn it up after the signing seems
clear from the fact that they made him sign four separate
copies which were sent to secure places in different corners of

the country. Signed it was, and reneged it could not be. On the earlier visit of the Bar Association when they made so much stir and commotion at Runnymede I was cynical enough, I'm afraid, to remark that the practice of law in the States had at length arrived at the stage signalised by Magna Carta—hence the interest. The real reason for their concern for the Charter was that one of the phrases from it had been incorporated almost word-for-word in the American constitution, and, whatever deviations may sometimes be countenanced in practice the American has a profound reverence and affection for his Constitution. 'To none will we sell, to no one will we delay or deny right or justice.' Considering that had been written in 1215 there was some justification for my cynicism in the recollection that as recently as 1879 it required a decision of the courts to establish that an American Indian was 'a person' within the meaning of the Habeas Corpus Act.

Merely to erect a memorial is not enough; it has got to be maintained; and for this purpose a Fund was established and contributions towards it are regularly made from the States. To enable the Fund to be rightly administered a group of Trustees—all of them, I think, *ex officio*—has been appointed under the Chairmanship of the Master of the Rolls and including such dignitaries as the Lord Mayor of London, the Chairman of the District Council of Egham and others. There are also many Patrons, including the Archbishop of Canterbury, the Roman Catholic Archbishop of Westminster, the Lord Chancellor, the Speaker—and the Moderator of the General Assembly.

Now as it happened a return visit to London was being made in July 1971 by the American Bar Association—about four hundred of them, I believe, along with camp-followers to the number of a further seven hundred. Not even the Metropolis can laugh off a visitation of these proportions. It was proposed that the event should be marked by adding a suitably inscribed stone slab to the Memorial at Runnymede. A representation of about two hundred assembled on a Sunday at lunch-time in a hall of the Royal Holloway College, part of the University of London, a masterpiece of Victorian grandeur and pomposity in red brick, on the A30 near Staines. Lunch was served here previous to our proceeding to the spot in a meadow by the

Thames between Windsor and Staines where, on 5th June 1215, King John, confronted with the united power of the Nobles and of the City of London, had been obliged to put his name to the Great Charter—in quadruplicate. We were thereafter to return to the College for afternoon tea on the lawn.

I cannot recall much about the luncheon menu until we came to the sweet course when the most luscious dishes of strawberries and cream were laid before us. At regular intervals along the table were shallow glass dishes equipped with spoons of about teaspoon size and containing what looked like caster sugar. Almost everyone in my line of vision added varying amounts of the sugar. But no-one seemed to enjoy the result! In all time coming the name Runnymede will instantly conjure for me a vision of salted strawberries—only later will Magna Carta come to mind. At least it gave us a sharp thirst for the afternoon tea. And, who knows, it maybe sent us forth to the meadow with the same unhappy taste in our mouths as King John had experienced so many years before.

Strawberries apart, it was a very pleasant day. The weather was lovely and the company most friendly. Naturally enough, I was, in my Moderatorial garb, an object of the most acute interest to our American friends who, almost without exception, decided that I was (a) real cute, (b) English, and (c) Anglican. I readily pleaded Guilty to the first count of the indictment. After lunch we were taken in buses the short trip to Runnymede where there was a brief ceremony in which Martin Sullivan, Dean of St Paul's, Lord Denning, Master of the Rolls, Lord Hailsham, the Lord Chancellor, and the President of the American Bar Association took part. At the subsequent tea on the College lawn we had quite a chat with the Lord Mayor of London and Lady Studd. Sir Percy commented on the fact that he and I had this in common: that we had only a year in which to make an impression, in which to put the stamp of our personality upon our job, and he felt it was all a bit inadequate. Many months later, after we had attended the Lord Mayor's Banquet in the Guildhall when the new Lord Mayor is welcomed and his predecessor thanked, I dropped a note to Sir Percy in which I reminded him of his comment about the shortness of the year and went on to say that I thought he had contrived to pack a vast deal into his term so as to make it a memorable one for the City. I only wish I had been able to do anything of comparable significance.

We had been staying at this time with my wife's sister at Hailsham in Sussex. The return journey from Staines on that pleasant Sunday evening, taking a deep wide sweep around the south of London and cutting across all the roads to the south coast, was enough to make us wonder why any car-owner in the South of England should venture forth deliberately and call it pleasure. How fortunate we in Scotland are—especially, perhaps, in Glasgow—to have so much coast-line and other beautiful and recreational country so convenient to us, and, comparatively speaking, such quiet roads to take us there. As, all these long years ago, the great men of the City twisted King John's arm, did they conceive they were establishing a freedom that would allow their descendants to possess each his own car and be at perfect liberty to join the bumper-to-bumper queue for a glimpse of the sea? The want of hindsight is a privilege of inestimable worth.

It was on the following Thursday that we were once again crawling along in a bumper-to-bumper procession. But this time it was in the late forenoon and we were driving through Streatham on our way to London where I was to take part in Westminster Abbey in the Memorial Service for Lord Reith of Stonehaven, first Director-General of the BBC, twice Lord High Commissioner to the General Assembly, who had died some weeks earlier. According, I believe, to Lord Reith's own direction the sermon was to be preached by the Moderator of the General Assembly. Eric Abbott, Dean of Westminster, that most gracious Christian gentleman, had been very kind in his invitation to me to take part. The Service was to be broadcast, but not televised—John Reith was ever a man who knew his own mind and his instructions were quite explicit. Some of his old friends were to be taking part—John Snagge had returned from retirement to do the commentary, and Sir Adrian Boult was to conduct the BBC Symphony Orchestra in the Prelude to the *Dream of Gerontius* and in part of Fauré's *Requiem*. The Revd Murray Leishman, Lord Reith's son-in-law, and Mr Charles Curran, the present Director-General, were reading the Lessons. The Archbishop of Canterbury was also present.

For myself, I had known John Reith by reputation over a considerable period although it was only comparatively recently I had come to meet him for the first time. He was a native of my own city and a son of a United Free Church Manse there, and in a variety of ways could have been said to be a perfect example of the high-principled, intellectual evangelical of the end of the last century. During his time at BBC his massive stature and his craggy features made him an easy target for the cartoonist, while his clear convictions and the stern determination with which he held to them made him a formidable foe no less than a trusty friend.

It was late in 1965 that I met him for the first time. I was at that juncture very deeply involved in a case at Glasgow University in which a number of students had been very severely punished, admittedly without trial, and—as I maintained—without guilt, a case that was shortly to attract the massive publicity which all along I had been trying to avoid. Lord Reith had just become Lord Rector of the University and had a seat on the University Court, which was the body to which we had appealed and which was at this precise point making very heavy weather of the case. As Lord Rector he would be official representative of the students and therefore, it seemed to me, he was entitled to be made familiar with their side of the story.

He proved a patient, interested, and most intelligent listener, and I had great hopes of what he might be able to do. He had, however, as it transpired, come into the struggle much too late, and that in two senses—first, that the matter was too far advanced for intervention by a newcomer to be either easy or effective, and, secondly, because he was becoming too old and unwell to be fit for the major pitched battle that alone would have achieved results. Indeed as time went on I came to be genuinely sorry for John Reith in his position as Lord Rector, for I think he found it a bitterly frustrating and unrewarding position. A few years earlier and how much he might have accomplished at Gilmorehill!

I had also met both Lord and Lady Reith quite a number of times during the two successive years when he had been the Queen's representative at the General Assembly. On each of these occasions he had made a quite remarkable opening speech, touching on things at the heart of the faith, and doing so in the most intensely personal way. In 1967 he had, I thought, sailed very close to the emotional wind, and there were times when the strain on himself must have been quite enormous—merely to be listening to him was strain enough for most folk. By the following year his health had deteriorated still further, and all through the Assembly he was dependent on an electrical pace-maker to assist his heart. The tax on his resources must have been colossal, but being John Reith he carried through every single duty to the full without pausing to count the personal cost. Once again I felt extremely sorry that this honour—and I know he regarded it as a great honour —should have come to him so late.

So I had very readily accepted the Dean of Westminster's invitation to preach at the Service, and had noted the stern injunction of the BBC that my part was to be confined to eight minutes flat (hoping that it wouldn't turn out to be too flat). And here we were on this pleasant July day proceeding through Streatham towards Westminster at a relentless eight miles an hour. Queenie and I were to be having lunch with her sister and brother-in-law in London after the Service, and then we were to be leaving immediately for the four-hundred-mile drive north to Glasgow. I was hoping that on that part of the journey we'd be able to average a better pace.

The Service proved in fact one of the most impressive events in which I have ever played a part. From all the reports that reached me (and there were certainly not a few) the radio version came over with profoundly moving effect—probably all the more effective for not being televised. In the long and varied history of Westminster Abbey it must have been a unique occasion, if not actually a traumatic experience. The Saltire Flag of Scotland, the St Andrew's Cross, was flying from the mast (full mast in accordance with Lord Reith's wish); we sang two Metrical Psalms to Scots tunes—the psau'ms o' Dauvit to the tunes o' Dauvit; the Moderator of the Scots Kirk wagged his heid in their poopit; and at the end a piper from the former Cameronians (John Reith's old regiment) marched with slow and measured step from the east end of the choir through to the nave playing that greatest of all laments, *The Flowers o' the Forest*.

The preparation of my own contribution I had not found an easy task. John Reith had been a highly controversial figure—as are all men who have ideas and the determination to see them realised. One wanted to do full justice to a truly great man, and at the same time one was determined to avoid anything that might sound like fulsome flattery. A true portrait, 'warts and all', seemed to be what was called for. But eight minutes flat isn't very long to paint in the features, let alone the warts. And in any case it was supposed to be a sermon and not just a character-study. No, not an easy assignment. So many people who heard the broadcast have asked me for a copy of the sermon that I am emboldened to reproduce it here at length.

For a moment this morning I would take you back across the centuries to the day when Solomon dedicated the temple he had built in Jerusalem. The elders of the people and the chiefs of the families were assembled, sacrifices had been offered 'past counting or reckoning', the Ark of the Covenant had been carried and laid in its place beneath the wings of the cherubim. It was then that Solomon turned to bless the people, and to tell them the tale of the temple and in particular how it had been in the heart of David his father to build such a house, but God had ordained it otherwise. 'Nevertheless,' God had said to David, 'thou didst well that it was in thine heart.'

Not without reason do the Jews adore and revere the memory of their Shepherd King, for it is to him that they owe their existence as a nation. He it was who knit the warring tribes together, who drove out their foes and established their borders, who gave them a capital city and a place among the nations and a pride of belonging.

More than that, it was David who in a day of idolatry held the Jews to their faith, who made them a peculiar people in the sight of God. For all his faults and inadequacies—all the more, it may be, for his personal weaknesses and failures—he was supremely a good and an upright man who stood firm as a rock for Jehovah.

Right it is—inevitable it is—that the name of David and the name of Israel should be inseparable names. So shall they ever remain.

Yet this man who had done so much to win a place among the immortals died, it would seem, with his greatest ambition unfulfilled, suffering from a consciousness of having failed. For it had been in the heart of David not only to establish a capital city wherein his people might dwell but to build a shrine wherein they might worship.

There are thus two assessments of the achievements of King David—the world knows him as the man who established a Kingdom; in the sight of God he is also the man who had it in his heart to build a Temple—and who did well that it was in his heart. Indeed of any man there are these two assessments—what he counted for on the world's evaluation of his work and what he was worth to God to whom the innermost secrets of the heart lie open.

In no case can this great truth be more clearly or more vividly seen than in the case of him to whose memory we are this day met to pay our proud tribute, John Reith, founder of the BBC, man of vision, who complained that he had never been given a big enough task to do.

In the eyes of the world he is most surely known—and will long be remembered—as the man who in the early days of broadcasting set the stamp of his particular and peculiar personality upon this new medium of communication, who made his unflinching demand for a kind of broadcasting, for a standard in broadcasting, for a purpose behind broadcasting, that has not only influenced the medium itself but through it has affected the lives of countless thousands in this land and throughout the whole world. So easily in these formative years radio could have become either the handmaiden of commerce or the instrument of government. It was Reith who out of nothing and in face of daunting difficulties created this unique public service we have come to take so much for granted. Like David, he founded a kingdom and he established it upon a sure foundation.

There were to this man distinctive qualities that contributed much to his success, that go far to explain his remarkable achievement.

There was about him always something of the Old Testament prophet—and that not merely in his appearance. He had all the prophet's conviction that his intuition was divine inspiration, that he spoke with the voice of authority, that he interpreted the will of the Almighty. With that there went—as there is bound to go—an undeviating commitment that refused to be turned aside. Friends and admirers called it single-minded devotion, unfriends and detractors called it an inability to conceive he could possibly be wrong. Call it what you will, it enabled him to get the right things done at a time when so many lesser men were convinced they knew better. T. B. Honeyman, who died the other day, tells that on assuming a difficult assignment he was warned by James Bridie, 'If you see a straight road, for God's sake pay no attention to advice.' How vivid a picture that conjures of John Reith.

As a prophet too Reith had that supreme ability to see the events that were happening around him in terms of moral values. Courses of conduct were not just expedient or inadvisable, they were right or they were wrong. Today there is a readiness to accept that events are amoral and that the extent to which we see them otherwise is just the extent to which we have affixed our human standards where they do not properly belong. This is no new philosophy. There have always been Ahabs and Jezebels and manufacturers of golden calves to preach just such a doctrine, and, thank God, there have always been Elijahs—and John Reiths—to refute it.

It was this deep sense of righteousness that inspired him when Lord High Commissioner at our Scottish Assembly to speak of 'the magnificent and majestic assurances of our faith,' to describe that faith as 'stupendous and exhilarating and almost incredible but true, and because true able to revolutionise the world,' and that led him to go on and say, 'We must believe our own faith, actually believe in it, in the sense of imagining it and realising it.'

For such a man 'compromise' was but a polite name for surrender, 'practising the art of the possible' but a way of describing the coward's failure, 'coming to terms with reality' but a euphemism for apostasy. 'No surrender' was his motto, and how true he was to it at no matter how great a cost.

This man, John Reith, was, too, a great Scotsman. Again, his very appearance had in it something of the rugged grandeur of his native land of green heath and shaggy wood.

For all its grey grimness it is a kindly land, and when the sun shines upon it it can be bonnie beyond words. At heart Reith was a kindly and a generous man with a real sense of humour—even if he was ever at pains to appear just rather than generous, even if he felt he had to make it clear that for him keeping faith mattered more than making fun.

Scotland is a land where to have climbed one mountain is merely to have gained a clearer view of the loftier peak ahead still unscaled, where to have gained a lovely vista is but to have espied a better vantage point still further ayont. Does this go some way to explain that inability of Reith's ever to be satisfied with what he had achieved, that stretching and straining and striving for the bigger and the grander and the more worthwhile thing that was still ayont, that made him to the end complain he had never been fully stretched.

Here he could have no continuing city, for he sought a city that hath foundations. And now he has won to that city. The spirit that could find no satisfaction in the things of time and space has

achieved its fulfilment in the eternity and the infinitude of God.
And to God we give the thanks and the praise.

> Thoughts hardly to be packed
> Into a narrow act,
> Fancies that broke through language and escaped;
> All I could never be,
> All, men ignored in me,
> This, I was worth to God, whose wheel the pitcher shaped.

'Nevertheless thou didst well that it was in thine heart.'

I hope it did something to bring John Reith alive, the John
Reith we had known and admired and, if you will, in the case
of some of the congregation, the John Reith with whom they
had fought and disagreed. For my own part I surely felt that
the Service as a whole was a most fitting tribute to a really
great Scot. And I am prepared to admit it owed more to the
piper than it did to me.

The notes of that magnificent tune he played, *The Flowers o'
the Forest*, were still seughing in my ears as we were driving
north. It was the second time we had heard it within a few
weeks, for just before setting off for the south I had preached
at the Annual Remembrance Service at the Scottish National
War Memorial at Edinburgh Castle. And again the solitary
piper had played that lament. The Last Post can somehow
reach down to the very roots of your soul but it's *The Flowers o'
the Forest* you find yourself continuing to sing.

There is, I am satisfied, nothing in the whole world quite to
be compared with the Scottish National Shrine—it is surely the
grandest thing the memory of war has ever inspired, the most
articulate expression ever shaped in stone of the sorrow and
sadness that are the price of war. Other memorials—the
Cenotaph in Whitehall, for example—are great silent tributes
to the dead, they are the spontaneous outburst of a community
that has been struck dumb by the tragedy and the pity of it all.
But that magnificent shrine rising up in the midst of the ancient
Castle of Edinburgh, with the rock that is Scotland cropping
up in its very heart, that is no silent memorial—it speaks. Yea,
it sings, it is a coronach in stone. I am sure H. V. Morton has
laid bare the secret of the matter when he says it runs back into
the difference between the character of the Anglo-Saxon and

that of the Celt, for the latter has always been able to express
its sorrow and to set its tears to music. The coronach, the
lament, the dirge is something that inevitably conjures up a
picture of a solitary piper and of the heart-wringing notes
lilting to us across the purple heather. The Cameronian piper
had been, perchance, just a trifle out of place marching down
the aisle of Westminster Abbey—he couldn't possibly have been
more at home than on the rock of Edinburgh Castle.

The lament itself, *The Flowers o' the Forest*, seems to catch up
all the bitter anguish of a world in travail. It is as though all
the pain that man has ever suffered, all the grief that has ever
torn the heart of woman, had suddenly wiped away its tears
and ceased its sobbing, for it had found a verse in which to
express itself and an air to which to sing it. The formless has
taken shape; mute silence has found a voice.

It comes from one of the saddest pages in the book of Scotland's story. In the spring of 1513 the Queen of France had sent
a ring to King James IV, most chivalrous perhaps of all the
Stuarts, begging that should Henry VIII attack France James
would take 'but three paces into English ground'. In the
summer of that same year Henry set sail for France, and James,
true to his promise, collected an army the like of which Scotland
can rarely have seen—Highlanders and Lowlanders, farmers
from Ayrshire and fishermen from the East Neuk of Fife, gentle
and simple, the cream of the nation's manhood. They
marched to the Borders and on 9th September the two armies
met where Till flows into Tweed. The Scots were in a
strong position on an eminence, but this they relinquished—
it is said on the chivalrous but ill-advised insistence of their
monarch. The battle was engaged, and a bloody battle it was
to prove.

Practically a whole generation of Scots was wiped out.
Houston of Houston, the laird of my old Renfrewshire parish,
fell with seven of his sons, and that story could be repeated
with varying details in every parish in the land. The English
were themselves so sore crippled they were incapable of following up their victory—in any case they scarce needed to. In
every corner of the land, alike from the window of the castle
and from the door of the hovel, women looked for husbands
and sons and lovers who were lying on Flodden Field. In every

heart there was sadness, in every eye there were tears, 'sighing and moaning on ilka green loaning, for the flowers o' the forest were a' we'de awa'.

In later years the Field of Flanders was to give us the poppy; it was the Field of Flodden that gave us *The Flowers o' the Forest*.

CHAPTER 7

Westering Sun

It was the final evening of our tour in the Presbytery of Loch-carron, whose bounds embrace the area of Wester Ross from Aultbea in the north to Glenelg in the south, and I had just dedicated a bright new Church Hall which the congregation at Kyle of Lochalsh had built for themselves. A Service had been held in the pleasant little Church, then the crowded congregation had filed across to the new hall where they stood around, packed very tight. All I had to do here was to unveil a little wall-plaque. In the course of the afternoon the Minister, Tom Kant, a Perth boy who had been ordained with us in Glasgow where he had served a long assistantship, had shown me how this was to be done. With the advantage of his six-foot-four he was able to carry out the necessary manœuvre from ground level, but for a more normally-sized mortal a small and somewhat precarious platform had been provided. Poised on this the difficulty was not that of pulling down the veil with decorum but of ensuring you yourself did not come down with it—void of decorum. Many and varied are the feats expected of a Moderator.

There was a time, for instance, when I was Moderator of the Presbytery of Paisley and I had been invited to open a new Church Hall. Here again we began with a service in the Church and then proceeded to the main door of the hall where my instructions were to knock loudly and say, 'Open unto me the gates of righteousness'. In front of the door was a cement platform approached by steps and surrounded by a railing—only the railing was not yet there. On the platform I stood alone, rehearsing my line while the congregation gathered all around. What no-one had told me was that, to conform with the fire regulations, the doors opened outwards. When I knocked and demanded that they be opened unto me my prayer was answered with embarrassing promptitude, leaving me no alternative but to leap off the platform down to ground level. The flash of camera bulbs on every side as I soared through space comforted me greatly. 'Moderator in Full Flight' must have been a popular caption.

All went well on this occasion, however, and having managed with some show of dignity to get back down from my little platform I was offering a word of congratulation to the good people of Plockton and Kyle on their achievement, and extending to them good wishes for the new activities in which they would be engaging. I had, I said, been involved in the dedication of bigger halls, of more expensive halls, of more elaborately equipped halls, but I had never, I confessed, been present in a hall where a more lovely picture was to be found framed in the window. For at that moment the September sun was setting over Skye, and against it the Coolins were silhouetted, and all appeared in such many-coloured autumn splendour, while in the foreground lay a cluster of islets in the sound, covered in seaweed and heather. A picture never to be forgotten. Little did I know that a few minutes later I was to be invited by the Session Clerk to accept a painting of the Five Sisters of Kintail 'as a little memento of the occasion'. It is a lovely picture and it hangs above the fireplace of our sitting-room at home where it acts, of course, as a continual reminder not just of Kyle but of our whole tour in these glorious surroundings. Yet for all its beauty I wonder whether it was not excelled by that picture framed in the hall window that autumn evening.

There had been to me something deeply touching about that picture of the westering sun, that view of a West Highland sunset, and I've never been able to get it quite out of my mind. For it seemed only too symbolic of what is happening in the area generally. An ageing, if not actually an aged, congregation (and Kyle, I am sure, because of the railway and the Skye ferry has more young people around and is livelier by far than most of the area), a want of industry of any kind, a complete lack of outlet for youth and its energies, an absorbing interest in theological controversies of a past day, a passionate love for a language with a great history and little if any future, and a tendency towards spirituous refreshments—sadly a West Highland sunset.

Not but what we had a most impressive tour and found plenty of evidence of interest and vitality. I had been especially keen to pay a call at a tiny little school at a spot called Kililan to the north of Dornie, at the head of Loch Long. The full name of my Renfrewshire parish was Houston and Killellan (pronounced 'allan') and it was the same Fillan whose name is perpetuated up here in this northern parish. He was the son of Kentigerna and an Irish nobleman, this Fillan of ours, and after the death of his father in battle he had come to Candida Casa at Whithorn in the south of Scotland to be with his uncle Comgan—whose name you find at Kirkcowan in Wigtownshire (pronounced as though the 'w' weren't there). As a result of the decisions of the Synod of Whitby in 644 the Romanising party in the British Church was gradually pushing its influence farther and farther outwards and imposing its reforms in what had been strongholds of the Celtic Church. By the early eighth century the movement had apparently reached Whithorn. Rather than accept the unwelcome new ways many of the older Celtic monks had moved quietly back, keeping beyond the range of the reformers' influence. Fillan and his uncle were among those who moved, and it was away up here to Wester Ross they had come, establishing finally a little cell in the glen north of Dornie. Kentigerna, Fillan's mother, followed at a later time and made a home for herself on the far shore of the loch.

A Strachan war memorial window in the west wall of the Kirk at Houston shows Fillan walking on one side of the loch, looking wistfully across the waters to the figures of his mother and his uncle on the farther shore. So, you see, it was quite by way of being a pilgrimage for me to come here in the steps of our own domestic saint, and to see in the brilliant colours of reality the picture I had so often admired in stained glass.

In due course they had turned their steps again to the south. I suppose news had reached them that the contemporary Herod was dead and that things would be easier again for the Celts. Fillan left his name in the valley of the Dochart between Tyndrum and Crianlarich (Strathfillan) and he left his mother on an island in Loch Lomond (Inchcailloch, the Island of the Old Woman). Then one day he crossed the Clyde just west of where the great span of the new Erskine Bridge takes today's traveller across, and he must have come up through the pleasant fields around Langbank to what is now Kilmacolm. Arrived at the kindly little hollow that is Killellan he deter-

mined, it would seem, that here he would pause awhile. And
stay here he did and that until his death in 749. A cell was
established, and here he taught and preached—a hollow stone
on a little knoll is claimed to be the spot from which he spoke
to the people. The well in a nearby field bears his name and
in the later days of the witches it gained great repute as a place
wherein children could be bathed to cure them of rickets. His
cell was called Cella Fillani, which in due course was corrupted
to Kilfillan, and ultimately to Killellan. At the time of the
Reformation it was a parish, and its local priest, Peter Maxwell,
was one of those who came into the new Church, went to the
University where he became a Master of Arts, and was thereafter restored to his former living. Killellan continued to be a
separate parish until 1760 when it was decreed it should unite
with the neighbouring parish of Houston, the union actually
taking place in 1771 when the death of the then minister of
Houston led to his neighbour from Killellan moving east and
becoming first minister of the united parish. Even with today's
transport it's a far cry from the uplands of Renfrewshire to the
shores of Loch Duich. It seems odd it should have that close
link from more than twelve hundred years ago.

Not all our time was spent visiting schools. We met, naturally
enough, the local congregations, usually at services which were
invariably followed by social get-togethers over a cup of tea.
We in the Church of Scotland look, at the moment, as if we
might depart from the Westminster Confession—I cannot see
us ever departing from the cup of tea. We found people keen
and enthusiastic, even if the inevitable absence of the younger
generation must make things both discouraging and difficult.
But what is there for young people to do once they have passed
school age? Nor is any useful purpose served in this connection
by establishing a pulp mill at Corpach or an aluminium plant
at Invergordon—that is merely to create new centres of population, not to cure depopulation. In some places depopulation
has got to such a pitch that only a handful of people are left in
a parish. It would be outrageous to close the Church, distances
being so great, and yet the numbers are such as scarcely to
justify the maintenance of a building, and most definitely not
such as to use the full-time services of a minister. Driving with
Aonghas Innes Macdonald through his parish of Gairloch I was

shattered to discover that though still in his parish we had already travelled farther from his manse than would have taken me from one end to the other of the Presbytery of Glasgow, the biggest presbytery in the world.

It is in these parts too that the unhappy divisions within the Presbyterian family make themselves most disastrously felt. In this corner of the country the Free Church of Scotland is very strong. These folk, the 'Wee Frees', represent the continuing line of that Free Church which 'came out' from the Church of Scotland at the Disruption of 1843 but which did not go into the Union of the Free and United Presbyterian Churches in 1900 (and was accordingly unaffected by the subsequent union of 1929). They are deeply fundamentalist in their theology, very strict in their moral code (as applied to others their unfriends would say), and inclined to regard the national Church as having betrayed its Presbyterian principles and taken on much of the character of the Babylon in which it dwells.

A further complication is the fact that in this area, too, the Free Presbyterian Church commands a great deal of support—indeed it had its origin in these parts. Some years before 1900 there were those in the Free Church who were unhappy with the way things were going in that denomination and who in consequence broke away and set up as an independent body. The reasons that had led to this were substantially the same reasons that obliged a number of Free Churchmen, particularly in the West Highlands, to oppose the Union of 1900 and in the end of the day to stay out of it. Anyone unacquainted with such matters might well think this was the ideal moment for these two dissentient bodies to come together. Anyone experienced in this field, on the other hand, would know that the fact that the two groups stood for the same things but had taken their stand at different times and in different circumstances was a very adequate reason why they should never come together at all.

So in almost every one of these small communities all three bodies are represented—the Church of Scotland, the Free Church, and the Free Presbyterian Church—and apart from an almost one-hundred-per-cent cross-the-line attendance at all funerals there is extremely little coming and going among them.

In the little village of Applecross, for example, all three denominations are present and, relatively to the size of the community, are flourishing. This means three Churches and Manses to be maintained, three stipends to be paid. Applecross is situated on the seaboard of a tortuous peninsula, and its population today is dwindling at an alarming rate. In spite of improvements carried out on the tortuous road—all fifteen miles of it—that links the village with Tornapress on the Lochcarron-to-Stromeferry Road it is still a somewhat daunting and even dangerous journey. A notice at the landward end of the road euphemistically explains that it is not recommended for L-drivers—surely bureaucracy has risen to a joke for once. There can be days—sometimes weeks—on end when the road is impassable because of snow. Not a human habitation is in sight along the entire journey. A new road is being built along the coast, but it is taking a lot of time and costing a lot of money, and I imagine is intended primarily as a tourist attraction. Normally the sea passage can be kept going, and a little boat from Kyle provides a connection for those who have —literally—the stomach for that mode of transport.

We paid a very pleasant visit to Applecross on the Sunday evening of our tour. Accompanied by the minister of Loch-carron, John Macleod, and his wife, with whom we were staying and who was interim moderator in the vacancy at Applecross, we motored over the pass and were entertained to tea at the home of the local Schoolmaster, who is also Session Clerk. The service was in the extreme West Highland tradition —we sang only metrical psalms, the singing was conducted by a precentor, the local postman, the pace of the singing was of the very slowest. There was a full congregation, including a number of visitors, some of whom we were assured were from the Free Church—a most unusual occurrence. We happened to notice what must also have been an unusual occurrence, that the visitors included the organist and his wife from the Church of Scotland congregation of St Andrew's in Liverpool. We were to meet again in September when I visited that congregation, and the event was made the occasion for a State visit by the Lord Mayor—with carriage and pair, outriders and all. Anglican and Roman Catholic Bishops and representative Free Churchmen were also present. That this should happen on

Merseyside was as nothing compared with the presence of a
few Free Church people at Applecross.

What things could be achieved in Applecross, not only for
the religious life of the community but for its entire wellbeing,
if only the three congregations—they are all Presbyterian—
could sink their differences and become one. And that pattern
could be repeated right throughout the West Highlands. It is
a great tragedy that the setting sun should always be casting
the shadow of at least three Church buildings.

'Bed and Breakfast'—you scarce pass a house on these quiet
roads but you see a board swinging from a pole at the garden
gate bearing the familiar words. To me it appeared quite clear
that the provision of 'B and B' had become the principal local
industry. Tourism certainly has increased enormously in recent
years and visitors from the south, from America, and sometimes
from the Continent crowd the narrow roads and misuse—so
often—the passing places throughout the months of summer
and autumn. Each cottage has its room ready, its nylon sheets
in situ, and its bacon and eggs in readiness for the morning,
along with the oatmeal for the porridge which will be eaten
with sugar when, as every schoolboy knows, it ought to be with
salt. If they themselves happen to be booked up they have
friends and relations—'cusseens' mostly—farther off the beaten
track to whom to direct the visitor so that none need go bedless
or baconless. The rates charged are such as compare more than
favourably with hotels'; for the visitor there is the added attraction of picking up a spot of local culture ('we actually lived in
the homes of the people'); and on the other side of the ledger
the charges represent a valuable source of income in an
economy where sources of income are in remarkably short
supply.

The 'Bed and Breakfast' notices are in most cases so arranged
that they can be easily removed on Saturday and Sunday
nights, for visitors are not then welcome. Usually, it is true,
guests will be accepted on Saturday provided it is clear they
are not to be leaving before Monday morning; but the influence
of Sabbatarianism is such that no amount of paying will induce
a hostess to accept guests who mean to travel or who have
travelled on the Lord's Day. Just why the worship of Sunday
with all the extreme literalism usually associated with the

Jewish Sabbath should have held such sway in these parts I do not know. It may well be that the lack of modern industries has relieved them of the pressures that have elsewhere led to an easing of the restrictions. A Sunday newspaper is anathema. The fact that it was put together during the week and printed on the Saturday is regarded as an irrelevance; and—again refusing to be logical—the fact that Monday's newspaper involved Sunday work doesn't militate against its sale.

The position is rather neatly epitomised in the story—apocryphal, no doubt—of the old lady who complained bitterly to her minister that one of his elders, a crofter, had been harvesting oats the previous Sunday. Recognising that it had been a bad season and that that blink on the Sunday afternoon had been one of the few opportunities to win the crop, the minister pleaded, 'But you know, Sarah, how the Gospel assures us that our Lord Himself plucked some ears of corn on the Sabbath day.' 'Ay, I ken,' she replied, 'an' I've never thoct ony the better o' Him for it.' The observance of the Sabbath is a standard by reference to which the activities even of the Saviour Himself have to be judged. You can't win in a situation like that. When at length the sun goes down over this so bonnie West Highland scene I feel sure it will be more considerate than to do so on the Lord's Day.

I had a happy reunion with John Macdonald during our visit. John was a fellow-student of mine, though he was quite a bit older, having been a school-teacher for some years before deciding to prepare for the ministry. A brilliant student he was. He is now retired and has built himself a fine modern bungalow at Alligin, in the Torridon district, looking out on one of the loveliest views imaginable. It stands on the site of a croft that has been in his family for many generations. So many memories we had to share that the afternoon was gone in a flash. One of my own vivid pictures was of a day around Easter-time in our final year at Trinity College. A group of final-year Divinity students from Edinburgh, Aberdeen and St Andrews as well as Glasgow was spending a week's holiday on the Isle of Iona as the guests of a Mr Russell, a paper-maker in Markinch. Our host had an idea that the spirit of that holy isle had something to offer to men who were about to dedicate themselves to a life of full-time service in the Kirk—hence his generous gift of the holiday. All this, it must be understood, was before Dr George MacLeod had conceived the idea of the Iona Community or had begun rebuilding the ancient abbey on the island.

It was a pleasant afternoon and about a dozen of us had engaged a little boat to take us across to the Island of Staffa to visit Fingal's Cave. The passage wasn't any too smooth and when we arrived at our destination our boatman intimated that he would sail past the mouth of the cave but that it was too rough for us to make a landing. John Macdonald immediately moved back to the stern and exchanged a few words in the Gaelic, whereupon the next thing we knew we were heading in towards the rocks and John was standing in the prow with the painter in his hand. With a sure-footed agility that must have come of long experience John leapt on to the slippery rock, guided the little craft in and steadied her until we had all, with varying degrees of indignity, made our way ashore. I realised then, as I have often done since, that to be able to cope in a parish you need a working knowledge of other things besides Hebrew and Greek and theology.

As befitted a visit to these parts, our trip was arranged on more leisurely lines than obtained in some other areas, allowing for the occasional purely personal visit and even making provision for us to enjoy most of a day at sea as guests of Major Macrae of Letterfearn in his yacht *Whaup*. The parish minister, who was also a Macrae (he has since retired), was there too. Sailing a yacht—indeed, seamanship of any kind—is to me a complete mystery and up to that moment I had been happily content to leave it so. But when our host went below deck to prepare lunch, leaving me in charge of the steering and the sails—and the two seemed in a mysterious way to be closely linked together—I got to the stage of regretting I hadn't given some thought and study to the matter in my more impressionable youth. Our skipper, however, was a man of great faith, as well as a proficient brewer of coffee, and in the providence of God, and due to the occasional intervention of the parish minister (who, I am confident, knew far more about the business than he was prepared to concede) we stayed afloat—luckily we had had a lot of sea to ourselves! We spent a most enjoyable day.

The effortless movement of the yacht seemed somehow to symbolise for us something of the spirit of these lovely parts and of their delightful people. It's hard, always, to tie them down to anything very definite (the lawyers' 'irrelevant and lacking in specification' usually applies to their answers to the most direct questions); they are harder still to stir up to any pitch of enthusiasm ('We do not want to get cento a paneec', as it was once explained to me); they are not readily overtaken by any sense of urgency. It's a popular story that tells of the professor of languages who had in great detail explained to a crofter the Spanish doctrine of mañana. 'Now Angus,' the professor went on, 'as you know, we in the Gaelic have the word "mara" which also means "tomorrow", and since we have the same kind of philosophy behind it I have a theory that there is a connection between the two. Would you not agree?' 'Oh no, professor, I could not at all agree with you about that. You see, as you were describing it to me I felt I could detect a certain note of *urgency* about mañana.' When at length the night descends upon these parts it will fall, I am convinced, in a quiet, effortless kind of way.

A most enlightening, as well as entertaining, incident from that time we had been at Iona as divinity students had been brought back to my mind. We were on our way home and were crossing the Island of Mull to connect with the steamer at Craignure for the sail to Oban—a forty-mile drive, most of it through a deer-forest—which could easily have fooled me since it hasn't a single tree. Quite a cavalcade of ancient taxi-cabs set off from Fionn Phort, myself up in front with the driver of the second vehicle. On discovering that I 'hadn't the Gaelic' he more or less ignored me, my best efforts at conversational openings producing mere monosyllabic replies. Near the end of our journey I got quite a fright as I saw something shooting past us along my side of the road. 'What was that?' I shouted. 'I theenk,' said our driver in the most unconcerned tones, 'that it would be a whee-el from the car in front.' Sure enough, the said car-in-front was now showing distinct signs of being in difficulty from shortage of wheels and the whole cavalcade came to a halt. The errant wheel was soon found. 'What will they do for nuts?' I asked our man. 'I theenk,' he said, 'we will all chust need to look for the ones that came off.' And suiting the action to the words, as one might say, he lit a cigarette, chose a reasonably comfortable portion of dyke and sat there while 'we' conducted the search. A somewhat ancient and rusty model of a jack had been unearthed and since no-one else seemed interested I had crawled beneath the disabled car and with the expenditure of much energy had got the jack jammed under the axle. When I surfaced and started cranking, however, nothing seemed to be happening, so that it was not wholly a surprise when my driver friend from the dyke commented in conversational tones, 'I theenk that chack is broken.' I had a certain temptation to say, 'I theenk I would like to punch you on the chaw,' but I remembered that a certain standard is expected of ministers-in-the-making. At long last three of the six nuts were found, a few strong men lifted the car, and since the thread was completely stripped off the nuts they were hammered into position and the journey continued at, it has to be said, a considerably reduced speed. Lest anyone should think we missed our boat because of the delay let me hasten to reassure him. Certainly we should have done, but we had three hours to wait, for the steamer had been 'delayed' by the weather. In these parts there is certainly nothing to inspire 'a note of urgency'.

What is to happen to the railway line to Kyle of Lochalsh? That is a question that is much asked but to which no final answer seems to be forthcoming. Yet upon that answer a great deal depends for this area in general, and for the village of Kyle in particular. This line, which runs from Inverness right across Scotland to the west coast, was for long the main link between the mainland and Skye and the Islands of the Outer Hebrides. The stretch of line along the south side of Loch Carron was, I believe, mile for mile, the most expensive railway line ever to be built in Britain, and the cost of maintenance of the long desolate stretch across by Achnasheen to Beauly must be extremely high in relation to the amount of traffic carried. But a life-line is not to be valued at the price of the rope. So long as the West Highland line from Fort William to Mallaig is continued, a sea passage to Skye is easy enough, while with improved road facilities to Ullapool, and a shorter sea crossing of the Minch, the need for the maintenance of the line to Kyle is being challenged. More than once there has been a definite threat to close it. Its disappearance could be yet another crippling blow to an area that has taken many hard knocks in recent years.

It is of vital importance, it seems to me, that as many connections as possible should be maintained between the district generally and the outside world. The tourist traffic and the bed-and-breakfast guest are not enough. Too easily these people will turn ever more in upon themselves, their own language, their own brand of religion, their own parochial interests—they will try to survive upon a tradition, try to make yesterday serve as a substitute for tomorrow. And that, as I see it, will be a sad day, a day to get the piper out and the coronachs sounding, for that will be a day when the shadows gather very thick. On that day, indeed, the westering sun will be setting to rise no more.

CHAPTER 8

Fair City and the Country Around

One of my professors used to comment on the fact that in the whole course of his extensive journeyings St Paul never conducted a ministry in the country. Always it was to the thronging seaports, to the towns on the caravan routes, to the places where the crowds congregated that the great apostle was attracted. This was to be explained, our teacher suggested, partly by the fact that these were the places where Paul could contact people who in turn might be counted on to carry the infection of the Gospel with them and spread it wherever they went; but partly also it was because people in busy cosmopolitan centres are accustomed to grappling with new ideas, they have minds that are open to accept the untried and the unusual, for them the effort to keep up-to-date has become a necessity of existence. In the country, on the other hand, you find always a deep-rooted conservatism; when change is adopted it is of necessity rather than of choice; the accustomed pattern represents the safe way; if a thing has always been done in a particular fashion it follows reasonably enough that that's the way in which it ought to be done, the way God meant it to be done. So Paul left the rural hinterland to those who would have more time to spend on it, more patience to await its awakening, while he himself got on with spreading the seed where some would quickly take root and whence some would be carried to faraway places.

That lecture had been much in my mind in those spring days of 1940 when I was being pressed to accept nomination for the vacancy in the parish of Houston and Killellan. I was at the time minister in the neighbouring parish of Linwood, where I had been for little more than four years, where things were going reasonably well, where there was a great deal of life and enthusiasm, and where I was both happy and content. I had become interim moderator at Houston on the death of the Revd George Muir after a sixteen years' ministry, and in that capacity had come to know many of the people well. At an early stage in the proceedings they had most generously invited me to consider becoming their minister and had been understanding when I declined.

Then through an odd concatenation of circumstances they had found themselves at the end of a vacancy cul-de-sac and so had approached me afresh with greater insistence. I was most hesitant. For one thing I had no desire to move from Linwood. For another thing I disapproved of an interim moderator accepting nomination in the vacant parish. Most serious of all, I wondered whether I should be able to make anything of it at Houston, for this, as I saw it, was the supreme example of what our professor had had in mind when he spoke of the difficulties of evangelising in the rural areas. If St Paul found the prospect daunting, who could blame me for hesitating? I had been born and brought up in the city; I had spent a long and happy assistantship in a positive whirl of activity in the busy parish of Springburn in the north of Glasgow; my charge at Linwood, while it was in the country three miles from Paisley, was essentially an industrial village. I had just no experience of the country and I asked myself very insistently whether I really wanted the opportunity to acquire any.

In the end, though, I had agreed to go; and if in the course of the next few years there were times when I wondered whether I had been wise, I could not say there was ever a time when I truly regretted my decision. Even St Paul might have enjoyed the country had he persuaded himself to 'settle down' there. Country people are not easy to get to know, but there's a great kindliness there when you do break through; they don't wear their hearts on their sleeves, but they do have hearts, and warm ones at that; they rather enjoy giving the impression of being simple, even stupid, but they have a profound wisdom all of their own; they are not easily stirred to any excess of enthusiasm, but neither are they readily carried away from their established loyalties. They have a wave-length of their own, and unless you can get on to that wave-band you have little hope of communicating—you should at least save yourself the disappointment of imagining they are going to fiddle about with their mental equipment for the sake of adjusting to your wave-length. They may be led, they will never be driven. It is highly unlikely that they will disagree violently and publicly with your proposal, it is just that when the time comes to do something about it they will not be there. And you must never make the mistake of imagining, because they have not openly commented upon something you have done, that they have been unaware of what was happening.

The last point is neatly illustrated in a story which has to do with an inspector of schools who arrived one morning at a country centre of learning, and, having looked around at the class, felt he would be hard pressed to know how to describe them in a twenty-questions game—as animal, or vegetable, or perhaps even mineral. He gave them a stirring harangue on the theme of wakening up, with a few remarks on other cognate topics. They took it with a grand indifference. 'Look,' he said, 'you're all asleep, sound asleep. Waken yourselves up. Pull yourselves together. Before asking any proper questions of you I want to make sure you're all alive. You, my lad,' pointing to a boy in the front row, 'you, give me a number.' After a period of thought commensurate with the intricacy of the question the youth slowly enunciated, 'Ninety-three.' The inspector wrote 39 on the board. They all gazed at his handiwork with admiration. 'There you are,' said the inspector, 'as I tell you, you're all asleep. Now give yourselves a good shake-up and I'll give you another chance. What about a girl this time. You, missie.' Missie was taken somewhat by surprise, but after a little hesitation ventured, 'Twenty-five.' This time 52 was written on the board to the complete satisfaction of the whole class. 'But this is terrible,' said the exasperated man, 'have you got no eyes in your heads, or are they still closed in sleep? You, boy, you give me a number.' To which he got the laconic reply, 'Sixty-six, an' mak' a bullocks o' that yin if ye can.'

I learned that lesson fairly quickly, and I have never fallen into the error of thinking because a matter was not commented on that it had not been observed.

One local habit into which I was a bit worried to find myself so quickly and so easily falling, was that of the double-negative, of never making a positive affirmation if you can contrive to express the same thing by contradicting a negation. Don't say 'It's good', say 'It's no' bad'. Don't say 'It's bad', say 'It's no' a' that guid'. Don't say 'It's a cold day', say 'I've been oot on a warmer day'; and if you want to be more emphatic and imply that it's really bitterly cold then you can affirm that you've been 'oot on mony a warmer day' or 'oot on a lot warmer a day'. I used to say we compared the adjective 'good' not, as most would, as good, better, best, but as micht be waur, micht be a lot waur, micht be an awfu' lot waur.

Talking one day to one of my members whose wife was making a remarkable, if not indeed a miraculous, recovery from an illness that had all but proved fatal I asked him—he was on his way home from the hospital—how he had found her today. 'Ah weel,' he conceded, 'I canna say she's went back ony.' A local shopkeeper was in the habit of expressing the hope when his customers reappeared after vacation that they were 'none the worse for their holidays'. Discussing the prospects of a young fellow who had just moved into what I thought was a remarkably poor farm I said I thought it wasn't perhaps a very great place. 'You'll no' be faur wrang,' said my farmer friend, 'I wouldna say it's the best ferm in the coonty.' We put new granite chips down on the walks around the Church. I thought it transformed the place out of all recognition and my conviction was confirmed when I overheard two elders discussing the new-look. 'Ye ken, John, thae chips havena done ony herm.' To which the other replied, 'No, Willie, they havena spoiled the look o' the place.' But the best example of all, perhaps, was the conversation I interrupted regarding a farmer's wife who had sustained quite serious injuries in a motor accident. 'It'll no' ha'e done her ony guid,' was the one observation. 'She'll no' be wan bit the better o' it,' was the rejoinder.

There must, I feel sure, be an explanation of this habit so widespread through the country areas of Scotland, but I've never discovered it. When considering any peculiar trait in the Scots character it is customary to attribute it, if possible, to John Knox or John Calvin, to the Kirk or to the Covenants, to the Hebrew Sabbath or the Metrical Psalms. I don't think that helps us very much here, for whatever the faults of the Kirk it was always very sure of its pronouncements, very convinced of the literal accuracy of every jot and tittle of its creed. For myself I am apt to conclude it is just a manifestation of that cannie nature that never advances farther than it can quickly retreat, that regards all exuberance with suspicion, that refuses to count chickens until they are hatched and hesitates to count them even then—it would much rather wait and see if they turn out to be good layers. And it's not so very far away from the position of the solicitor who may tell you that if the facts are not substantially different from how you have represented them he thinks it is not impossible that if the matter were taken to court and the other party did not produce some unexpected piece of evidence there was quite a possibility that you might not prove unsuccessful. (And you part with good money for that kind of advice.) In any case I found it a habit into which it was easy—I mean it was not difficult—to fall.

Country humour too is something which is quite distinctive and which, if you are to enjoy its full flavour you have got to develop a skill in detecting. It's very much an acquired taste. The ideal wag in the farmer's book is the man who can 'slip them in awfu' cautious'. Strangely, perhaps, the countryman doesn't take offence if the joke is turned back on himself; instead he inclines to have an affection for the person who can do this—'Oh, but he was able for me', is a mark of high regard. He will never indicate that a joke is intended and may not even expect its existence to be acknowledged unless by that slightest twitch of the eyebrow, the kind of thing which if you're not careful can at the cattle-market make you the unwitting and unwilling possessor of a calving heifer. Oh yes, this type of humour is there all the time. Over and above this, of course, there is the rumbustious laughter of the market-ring and the cattle-show, and there is the rough joke that goes its rounds in the country as it does elsewhere. Behind it all though, there is this quietly, unpretentiously humorous attitude that to me is of the very essence of living in the country. I'm not sure that St Paul would have understood it.

I remember talking one day to a young farmer about a man known to both of us who had appeared in our community just about a year before, a man of great wealth and position and importance as he had assured us. Now he had disappeared even more quietly and mysteriously than he had come, omitting even to leave a forwarding address. This was particularly unfortunate since so many local tradespeople had accounts to settle. 'They tell me, Mr Herron,' my young friend began. I cocked my ears, because from this opening gambit I well knew

I was about to hear a jewel of wisdom of his very own concocting. 'They tell me, Mr Herron, you should never steal anything in this world. You're far better to buy it and not pay for it.' With no greater solemnity, with no more profound air of seriousness did Euclid, I am certain, first state the proposition that the sum of the angles of a triangle amounts to a hundred and eighty degrees.

A minister friend tells of having moved to a new parish where in the first couple of months he was trying to get around the housebound. He was in a home where the lady, crippled with arthritis, was apologising for her inability to get to Church. 'Wi' a' this wet weather I've never been able yet to get doon to the Kirk to hear ye preach.' My friend, a modest soul, assured her that she hadn't missed much. 'No,' she said, 'that's what everybody tells me.' Another country minister recounts the tale of a widow whose daughter was about to sit her finals in medicine. Mother was explaining how difficult it was, how they didn't want you to pass nowadays, how anything was a good excuse for failing you, and so on. 'Oh,' said my friend, anxious to be sympathetic, 'I know how the standards are constantly going up. Why, even in divinity, since my day, the whole thing's much more difficult.' To which his hostess replied kindly, 'Maybe it's juist as weel you got through when ye did.' Or there was the case in my own experience. Years ago when the height of ministerial ambition was to be invited to do a service on what is now disparagingly referred to as 'steam' radio, I was visiting an old fellow who said to me, 'They havena gotten you on the wireless yet.' With fitting modesty I explained, 'No, they haven't got down to my level yet.' At once he sprang to my defence, 'I wouldna let you say that. Na, na, I wouldna let you say that. They had an awfu' puir man on last Sunday.'

Don't say these people didn't know what they were saying— fine they knew—only they had learned how to 'slip them in awfu' cautious'.

I am sure a thesis could be written on the subject of the humour of the Scottish countryman, and I'm sure it would prove much more entertaining reading than a lot of theses that have earned their authors honorary doctorates. It would be hard to write, though, for so much can depend on the way a thing is said, and how do you put that down on paper? And to anyone who doesn't know the Scots tongue it is quite impossible to transliterate, while translation can leave you unhappily without a joke. A pity, though, for the field is so very rich.

I was taken right back to my Houston days and reminded of many of the things I had there learned about country folk during the spells we spent in the Presbyteries of Perth and of Auchterarder, during the months of October and November. I had tried to arrange my visits to the country Presbyteries for times when the harvest would be likely to be over, for I was very conscious of the fact that whatever might be the attraction of seeing a Moderator it could not expect to compete with the claims of 'the hairst' on a good September evening.

Perth is justly proud of its ancient Kirk of St John the Baptist, whose minister, Willie Smellie, so closely associated with the famous 'Tell Scotland Campaign', had just intimated his retirement after thirty-five years' distinguished ministry in the parish and service to the life of the City.

It was in this Church in 1559 that John Knox preached with such violence and virulence—or so the story is commonly told— that the mob set to and destroyed the Church and everything lovely that was in it. What actually happened was probably somewhat different from that. Mary of Guise, Regent for her infant daughter, Mary Queen of Scots, had summoned the Scots preachers to meet her at Stirling. The City of Perth at this time had gone so completely over to the Reformed faith that when the Regent had demanded the suppression of heresy there the Provost had replied that while he could make their bodies obedient he could not answer for their consciences. Knox had at this stage just returned to Scotland after a period as minister at Geneva, and he hurried to Perth to join the preachers there. It had been agreed that 'the gentlemen of every county should accompany their preachers on the day appointed . . . without armour, as peaceable men desiring only to give confession with their preachers'. (Was this the precursor of today's peaceful picketing?) Erskine of Dun had gone to see the Queen Regent and he returned to tell of how once again she had broken faith with them, that having besought them to come no farther than Perth she had now outlawed them for non-appearance at Stirling. Knox's sermon that Sunday was concerned not only with idolatry and the errors of Rome but also with broken faith and deceit—not wholly irrelevant in the circumstances.

In any case, sermon was over, practically everyone had gone home, and all, no doubt, would have passed without incident. After sermon, however, a priest had spread a cloth on the altar in the Church and had begun to say mass when a boy cried out against it and the priest boxed his ears. It was all that was needed. The smallest spark can be dangerous when there is a lot of combustible material about. The mob rose up and literally tore the place apart. The monasteries of the Black and the Grey Friars were also visited and a deal of hooliganism and looting took place as well as the tearing down of the objects of idolatry—preferably those with a good second-hand value. Knox describes the perpetrators as 'the rascal multitude'. It's not hard, though, to understand how when normal restraints are lifted a hungry mob of underprivileged requires no theological impetus to set it to work.

Perth has a prison—two in fact, for there is a Senior Detention Centre on the outskirts of the city. An afternoon spent in the prison I found intensely interesting, partly because I was anxious to see at first hand the work they are doing there, and partly because the Governor used to be a minister of the kirk, having had a parish in Orkney and having been under our care in Glasgow for a spell while he was assistant to the Governor at Barlinnie Prison. I knew that most of the prisoners sent to Perth satisfied two requirements—they had been put away for fairly long spells, and their records were such as to create a real hope that their time behind bars might be used for remedial purposes. This, as I say, I was anxious to see in operation. I have seen something of our Barlinnie Prison in Glasgow, with its ancient buildings, its appalling overcrowding and its dismal hopelessness. All indescribably depressing. I was later to visit the open prison at Penninghame near Newton Stewart, to which carefully selected prisoners are sent to serve a part of their time, where there are no obvious bars, and where indeed the prisoner who was ill-advised enough to do so could escape without much trouble. I found it rather intriguing, incidentally, that one prisoner to whom I spoke in Perth told me he hoped to be seeing me in Penninghame the following month—an appointment which, in fact, he was careful to keep.

Prison always fills me with a feeling of waste—waste of good years of the prisoners' lives, waste of time and energy by the great army of men who have to look after them, and waste, too, of thought and care and attention by those in administrative posts who are dedicated to achieving a work of human reformation with machinery that is out-of-date, inadequate and designed with a totally different end in view. We urgently need to do some serious thinking about this business of the punishment of the offender, what it is meant to be and what it is supposed to achieve. Time was when it was accepted that the wrongdoer deserved to be punished, that is, to suffer, and that incarceration under the sternest and most brutal conditions provided all the treatment required. If inadequate the theory was simple. Then we got the idea that the evildoer was an individual maladjusted, or ill-educated, or inadequately equipped—or more likely all three at once—and that what he was requiring was remedial treatment. He was just a sick person needing to be healed. So we partially but not completely made the switch from a punitive to a reformative theory of punishment. We didn't, however, sufficiently sincerely believe in the change to equip ourselves properly for it. The result, as it appears to me, is that we have fallen between two stools—prison is no longer unpleasant enough to exert any very great deterrent influence; it is not nearly constructive enough in its approach to achieve any marked reformative effects.

I do not want to seem to be knocking the system just for the fun of it. Still less do I want to seem to be criticising the efforts of those who are trying to make the system work. If I am being critical it is of myself and my readers—ordinary law-abiding citizens who prefer to put an unpleasant business out of mind. We hear that the perpetrator of some dastardly deed 'has got ten years' and we think that's a jolly good show, it's high time these people were made to toe the line. We don't at that time wonder overmuch why the criminal acted as he did, we don't pause to ask what ten years in prison is supposed to be going to do to him or for him, we don't—at the end of the fifth year perhaps—remember him and wonder how he is getting along, we don't at any point ask ourselves what ten years of living in that utterly artificial society behind bars will do for a human personality. Nor do we ever ask what the people to whom we have remitted the responsibility of looking after him during this long section of his life are supposed to be doing about it. Had it been proposed that the Great Train Robbers should be hanged I imagine there would have been a terrific outcry. How many, I wonder, of those who would have shouted most loudly have paused to ask whether the slow, persistent disintegration of character that must result from thirty years spent in top-security wings of this prison and that is any kindlier or more humane a way of destroying a human personality than would have been sudden extinction.

Perth and Penninghame, let it be said, are far from being without their success stories. Many prisoners go out considerably better equipped to cope with life than they had been when they came in, and not a few of them make good. We must accept it that there are those who have dedicated themselves to a life of crime, who take it for granted this will mean wandering in and out of jail, and in whose case the only thing to be said in favour of a prison sentence is that it puts them out of circulation for a time. There are those too whose troubles do not arise from want of qualifications to cope with life, who will be trouble-makers in whatever society they find themselves. They are probably the biggest problem of all—not only do they resist reformation themselves, they exert a bad influence throughout the whole place. On the other hand the number of those who make one appearance in prison and one only is a very high number indeed. For this we have to be most thankful —and deeply grateful to men like the Governor at Perth and his staff, and to the representatives of the Home and Health Department at St Andrew's House, for their unremitting care in a field where there is so much to discourage, where disillusion must always be lurking round the corner, and where cynicism must be an most persistent temptation.

The prison is situated near the South Inch in Perth. It may be that on the North Inch they have found at least some part of a solution for delinquency—particularly of the juvenile variety—in the Bell Sports Stadium, a most impressive and unusual building erected there as the result of the generosity of one of the magnates of the distilling business. Facilities are available here for every form of sport, and there is a resident manager and his wife ready, able and willing to advise and organise. The stadium is in constant use and its facilities in perpetual demand. It is encouraging to see so many young people healthfully employed here who otherwise might possibly find mischievous outlets for their energy. It is an example that might well be studied by local authorities—of our cities in particular—for something of the kind, even if on a more modest scale, could greatly relieve the tedium of life in one of those concrete jungles called housing estates.

Among the many schools we visited was the High School in Auchterarder, with whose headmaster and his wife, Mr and Mrs John Clark we spent one or two very happy days. One of the younger classes was later invited to write what used to be called a 'composition' on the subject of 'The Moderator'. The results in some cases were quite remarkable—and revealing in a pride-shattering kind of way. I was interested to learn, for example, that the Moderator was 'nise but very oald'; that he wore 'funny kind of trowsers that cum down to his waste' (a trifle inadequate, perhaps); that he had 'a mashtash below his nose' (where better, after all, to have it); and that 'the mother woar a nis hat'. It took a small boy in the country school in Kirkcowan in Wigtownshire, though, to make the discovery that the Moderator is 'the boss o' the kirk'.

Most of our time in the Presbyteries of Perth and Auchterarder, however, was spent visiting farms, the agricultural school near Comrie, the cattle-market at Perth, and meetings of country folk in Churches and village halls throughout the county. Two events of this kind stand out vividly, though they were merely typical of many others.

The first was a dinner which Bill Shannon organised in the Laymen's Training Centre at St Ninian's, Crieff, for which he is responsible. The idea of such a centre had originated in that most fertile brain of D. P. Thomson, our free-lance evangelist for many years, and he had been able to convert a redundant Church building in Crieff and make it suitable for this purpose by the creation within it of meeting-rooms and dormitories. The work has expanded, and now under the energetic leadership of Bill Shannon the whole place has been redesigned, rebuilt and refurnished. All the year round conferences and training-classes—mainly but not exclusively for young people—are held, and a great outreach in evangelism is accomplished.

Bill had invited a number of representatives of various branches of the agricultural life of the community to a dinner in the Centre.

Things have changed a lot in farming too in recent days—as was illustrated in a story I told them. Earlier that very day I had been visiting a dairy farm in the parish and had been admiring the cows in the byre when one of the staff had pointed to a fine-looking heifer and had suggested I might like to milk her. 'Right,' I said, 'I'll milk her if you get me a luggie.' The luggie, I should explain was the special kind of pail with a handle sticking out like an ear (or lug), used for milking in the old days when that was done by hand. There wasn't such a thing on the premises! So far has mechanisation advanced on the farm.

The other had been a meeting of four congregations held in the hall of the little village of Balbeggie. They had decided to make it a concert kind of affair and I was to give an address. Each of the congregations concerned had undertaken to provide two items for the programme, and this they had done remarkably well. At one point when we had a fiddler playing a selection of Scots airs I shouldn't have been a bit surprised had someone suggested clearing the floor so that we could have a set of quadrilles—tell the truth I was tempted to propose it myself. It was that kind of meeting.

CHAPTER 9

Not as a Stranger

Eighty of us had assembled round a dinner-table—or rather series of dinner-tables—in Kirroughtree House Hotel just outside of Newton Stewart. It was the evening of the last day of our visit to the Presbytery of Wigtown and Stranraer, and a dinner had been arranged to be followed by a 'party'. Thus was a most fitting ending provided for what had been twelve wonderful days in a kindly and pleasant, if little known, corner of the country. Glasgow, Dumfries and Stranraer form the corners of a more or less equilateral triangle whose sides measure roughly eighty miles. Galloway—that ancient kingdom —stretches properly from the outskirts of the town of Dumfries through the counties of Kirkcudbright and Wigtown, and up into Carrick, the southern division of Ayrshire. Locally Kirkcudbright is known as The Stewarty and Wigtownshire as The Shire. The latter in its turn is divided into three—the Rhinns, the Machars and the Moors. There is a Presbytery of Kirkcudbright which accounts for the Stewarty while the Presbytery of Wigtown and Stranraer, the subject of our visit, starts as far east as Creetown on Solway-shore and stretches northwest as far as Ballantrae on the Ayrshire coast. Until 1963 there were separate Presbyteries of Wigtown and Stranraer.

As I say, about eighty sat down to dinner, ministers, elders and wives, and they represented every corner of the Presbytery area. The popularity of the evening presented difficulties with which, however, the management were willing and seemed able to cope. The social side of the evening—the 'party'—had been put under the care of John Andrews, Minister at Kirkmaiden, Scotland's most southerly parish. Now John is a very close friend of mine. As a student he had been a member of my parish of Houston when I went there, and his folk had continued with me through all my ministry. Of John's abilities as a 'party'-organiser I had no doubts—his father before him had earned a deservedly high reputation in this regard, and in the country we're great believers in heredity—'awfy' weel come' is a phrase that practically guarantees ability. In their typical cannie way Houston folk would have testified, 'You could dae an awfu' lot waur than get Finlay Andrews to run your concert for you.'

On the present occasion, as was to be expected, John did us proud. With him as compere, and his wife, Jean, at the piano, we had songs specially written for the occasion, wise-cracks by the score, some spontaneous, some smelling strongly of mid-night-oil, stories suited to the occasion and others that were just stories—a real nicht wi' Burns in the best south-country tradition. In many ways it seemed to me to characterise the spirit of the whole trip—so friendly and warm-hearted it was.

I remembered how, in that very hotel-room, close on a fortnight earlier, the Press had been waiting to interview me on my arrival, and when I had had a chance to study the programme of our tour one of the reporters enquired whether I had any comments. 'Only this,' I said, 'that it seems to me there are two things from which we're not likely to suffer— the one is leisure and the other is hunger.' Every moment of every day seemed to be accounted for and the number of lunches and dinners to be given by the County Council, by Provosts and Burgh Councils and by congregations suggested— on paper at least—a formidable gastronomic engagement. In the event it had proved busy enough in all conscience, but so enormously happy and rewarding; and if we had been well fed—well, here we were tackling the last dinner and showing no ill effects.

The minister of Wigtown, Raymond Vincent, had a wonder-ful song to sing in which the virtues of the Moderator were extolled in a way unlikely to contribute noticeably to the magnification of his ego. It was clever, it was well done, it was well sung. In spite of that I found my attention wandering a little, wandering back to a previous Sunday afternoon when I had preached in his fine old Church in what was once the county town (it contrives to retain a strong flavour of its erstwhile dignity), of the lovely view over the Bay towards Creetown, and of the monument to the two women who here died for their faith—an old body of sixty-five, Margaret Lachlison, and a young lassie of eighteen, Margaret Wilson. It was in the spring of 1685, during the Killing Times, and three

of them had been condemned to die by drowning, principally
because of their adherence to the teaching of James Renwick.
The third condemned was Agnes Wilson, Margaret's younger
sister who, among other things, was found guilty of having
participated in the Battle of Bothwell Brig (she had been seven
years old at the time). A trip to Edinburgh and the outlay of
what must have been for him a vast sum of money and the
girl's father, Gilbert Wilson (himself an ardent bishop's man)
had been able to win a reprieve for the thirteen-year-old girl—
what she could have known of treason to the king is ill to
conceive.

The bed of the little river Bladnoch is here cut deep in
Solway sand, filled over at high tide, at other times carrying
merely a trickle. In the bed of the river the two women were
tied to stakes, the older woman nearer to the incoming tide
so that the girl might see her last agonies and perchance recant.
It's said that near the end they dragged the lassie out of the
water to ask if now she would pray for the king. Yes, she said,
she would willingly pray for any who needed her prayers—'I
wish the salvation of all men and the damnation of none.' But
Major Winram produced a copy of the Oath of Abjuration
and, when she had repudiated this, back into the rising tide
they pushed her. Smillie adds a quaint postscript to the story.
Years after the event an old man might have been seen dragging
weary feet around the town of Wigtown, shunned by all,
carrying with him a great jar of water from which he sought
to slake an unquenchable thirst. He it was who had been
town-crier at the time of the drownings, and it was he who at
the last had pushed Margaret back into the tide, saying, 'Tak'
anither drink then, hinny.' It's hard today standing at that
bonnie spot to believe it could have witnessed a scene so
unutterably ugly.

Some years ago I had been attending a three-day conference
of the Liaison Committee of the Anglican-Presbyterian Discussion Group at what had once been a splendid private-house
at Riding Mill in Northumberland. We had got through our
business rather more expeditiously than expected and so had
finished just after lunch on the last day. I was on the point of
leaving for the drive to Glasgow when the Bishop of Clogher
in Ireland, who was attending as an observer, remarked to me

that had he known we would finish so soon he would have
arranged to catch the Stranraer ferry that evening instead of
going by Heysham the next day. I suggested to him that if he
cared to come with me I would make the detour by Stranraer
and see him aboard his ferry.

We were driving along Solway shore near to Carsluith, still
discussing some of the issues that had engaged the attention of
the conference, including, of course, the necessity for there to
be 'an episcopal element' in any reconstituted Church of the
future. 'Look,' I said, pointing across towards Wigtown where
Bladnoch flows into the Bay, 'over there you'll see a monument
to two women, one an old body and one a lass of eighteen,
who were tied to stakes and drowned by the incoming tide for
their resistance to the attempt to introduce "an episcopal
element" into the Kirk of Scotland. It would repay you to go
some time and look at that stone and others like it in every
other parish hereabouts and think what they have done for the
history of this people and how they have shaped the thinking
of this people.' Throughout this whole south-west corner, I told
him, he'd be hard pressed to find a grave-yard that didn't have
its martyr's stone; ay, and that he'd find many such a stone
ahint a dyke in some lonely far-off place, for not all of those
who died were accorded the dignity of consecrated ground.
Nor would they have asked for it, for they believed that
consecration came from within. 'Where is your kirk in Scotland
today?' someone asked a Covenanter in the dark days when all
seemed lost. 'Show me a man prayin' ahint a dyke,' was the
answer, 'and I'll show you the Kirk in Scotland today.' The
necessity for an 'episcopal element' forsooth!

My friend, I am sure, decided I was a typical instance of
Scottish bigotry. He could well be right. But then I'm just a
typical example of the material with which they've got to
work, those who would commend the 'bishop-idea'. In fact
what he did was to suggest that we were scared of a word and
that 'bishop' today didn't at all mean what it meant then, a
bishop now had no faintest resemblance to what our fathers
had so bitterly resisted. I have never seen the force of this
argument. In fact I have never seen the sense of it. If bishops
are so utterly different from what they used to be, then for the
sake of clarity let's find a new name for them. I don't like

drawing a distinction where there isn't a difference, but
neither do I like blurring a distinction by refusing to mark it
by a difference. In answer to that complaint, of course, we
hear about the element of continuity and the importance of its
being recognised. The 'historic', we are assured, matters no less
than the 'episcopal' in the conception of the historic episcopate.
Once again I take refuge in the doctrine that you can't have it
both ways—not even if you're a bishop. Either this is something
new, essentially new, in which case let's signalise the fact by
giving it a new name; or else it's the same old thing in a new
dress, in which case we don't want any truck with it any more
than did our fathers about whose graves the whaups are
crying.

Earlier on that same Sunday, before setting off for Wigtown,
I had preached at a District Morning Service in Monigaff, the
little village across the Water of Cree from the town of Newton
Stewart, whose minister, Ronald Farquhar, is Clerk of Presbytery and looked after us with patient care throughout our stay
in the Presbytery. Then, later still that same day, we went on
south to Whithorn, the spot so closely associated with the name
of St Ninian and the beginning of the Christian faith in what
we now call Scotland. Years ago as a student I had preached
here occasionally and had fallen under its charm. I felt no
sense of grievance that no-one claimed vividly to remember
my earlier visits! But you do sometimes get a surprise in that
regard. Not so very long ago I took a service in Penicuik and
talking with a group of people afterwards I remarked, 'You
know, I preached here as a probationer in 1935.' 'Yes,' said a
lady, 'I mind that fine. And I'll tell you what you preached
about.' It must have been quite outstandingly bad to be so
memorable.

As I say, Whithorn had cast a spell upon me in those days.
Apart altogether from its historical associations there were its
natural features, its great rolling fields, at that time of grass
and oats and turnips, its enormous herds of neat, fine-boned
Ayrshire cattle, its Clydesdale horses so delicately set on their
white-spatted feet, their farm-closes each with its dairy and its
cheese-loft and flanked by its vast stackyard. Things had
changed a bit now, the oats had given place to barley, the
turnips had as good as disappeared, there was grass that had

been cut for silage and some hay in bales, the Ayrshire cows had
lost their horns and here and there a herd of Friesians was to
be seen, the Clydesdales had vanished, the cheese-lofts had
gone and the stackyards had made way for silage pits and
milking-parlours—but otherwise life seemed to go on much as
usual. It had been a busy Sunday that, as I recollected it, with
its three separate services and the people to meet between
times.

It had been as nothing, though, compared with the following
Sunday. For that day we had driven twenty-five miles to the
Parish Kirk of Inch, near to Stranraer, for Morning Service,
and thereafter had lunched with the Earl and Countess of
Stair in their home at Castle Kennedy, which is close by. We
had time, unfortunately, for only the briefest walk through the
famous gardens of the house before we had to set off for the
twenty-mile run down the length of the Rhinns to the village
of Drummore, in the parish associated with the name of St
Medan. There in the village kirk I preached at another Service
and followed it with the usual tea-party at which, in this case,
we met many old friends. For I claim the closest links with
Kirkmaiden.

It was here in the village of Drummore that my father had
been born just ninety-eight years before. He lived and worked
in different parts of the parish until at the age of eighteen he
left it for good having resolved, it would seem, to come to
Glasgow and make his fortune. The former part of this programme he carried through with expedition and complete
success. He found a job with the then Glasgow and South
Western Railway Company ('the Soo-west' to its friends) and
there he remained until his retirement forty-seven years later,
having seen the change-over to LMS in 1923 and just missing
nationalisation and 'British Rail'. Work on the railway was
steady—no small commendation in those uncertain days—but
it was certainly not the kind of employment at which fortunes
were made. Still, I suppose, after the degree of poverty that
was all too common in the country districts it must all have
seemed remarkably opulent. My grandfather had died while
father and his older brother were still children, and so their
mother had opened a little shop in part of her house at the
Southern School just three miles from the lighthouse at the

Mull of Galloway—thus establishing Scotland's most southerly trading concern. At the age of ten father became a 'half-timer'—that is to say, he and his brother between them put in a full day's attendance at school and a full day's work at a nearby farm. At the age of twelve he left school altogether and began to 'work a pair o' horse'—to do the full work of a ploughman. Life was real, life was earnest for the widow and the fatherless in these good old days. Some of father's more hair-raising tales of the places he had to go and the things he had to do made me at least wonder what children had been made of that they were able to come through unscathed. Whether they were all that unscathed is, I suppose, a good question; it was certainly a case of survival of the fittest.

We could have spent a long time in the hall at Drummore that afternoon, talking to old friends, reviving memories of yesterday. Before we left our good friend John M'Guffog presented us, in name of the congregation, with a picture of the former parish kirk that was built in 1638—Kirk Covenant they sometimes call it. It's little used now, for the former Free Church in the village is so much more convenient; but it stands up there on the hill-top at the crossing of the main roads of the parish, and it speaks of days lang syne.

We had no time to waste, though, for we were to pay a call on a meeting of the St Giles' Society, a voluntary organisation for disabled people of all ages, that was that afternoon visiting the farm of Auchleach, near Ardwell. If you didn't know about such things you might well imagine that visiting disabled people of any sort would prove a depressing experience, but on the contrary the 'patients' are invariably able to give a fillip to their more fortunate neighbours. That certainly applies to the St Giles' Society. While there I met a man who claimed that at Neil Ramsay's farm of Dunbae near Stranraer when I was 'a hafflin' his father had taught me to plough. This was not true. What his father had done was to try to teach me to plough—a vastly different thing. But he had taught me how to harness a work-horse, and about the same time I had put in quite a bit of practice at hand-milking cows, so that I can claim two skills not universally shared by young farmers today.

From Auchleach we hurried on to Stranraer where I preached at a service in the Old Parish Kirk in which I had taken an occasional Evening Service in days gone by for my friend Russell Walker, now retired. When at length we set off for the twenty-five mile drive back to our hotel we felt we had not had an idle Sunday.

As we sat at the 'party' that final night enjoying the homely programme I could not but think how wondrously 'couthie' country folk can be. I remembered how a few days earlier we had been at a get-together of, I think, voluntary social workers held in the church hall at Newton Stewart, and I happened to ask someone whether there was still in the district a lady I had never met but whose father, Willie M'Creadie, had been a reader in *The Glasgow Herald* when I was a copyholder there back in my student days. I had had a great regard and affection for the man—who was old enough to be my father and sometimes spoke to me as if he were—and I felt I should like to say Hullo to the lady. Oh yes, my informant said, he knew fine who I was talking about but she wasn't here tonight. That was all. About fifteen minutes later the lady was produced. Someone, it seems, had been despatched straight from the hall to her house to tell her she'd better get her hat on and come on down the street for the Moderator was wanting to see her.

On another night we got back to our hotel fairly late to find a stranger there awaiting us. 'You were speirin' for me the day, I hear,' he said. There had been a luncheon given by Newton Stewart Town Council that day, and in the course of chatting with the Provost at the table I had spoken of a holiday we had spent in Glen Trool with Jimmie Little, the herd at Glenhead, and his wife. They had had a small boy, John, a most delightful child of about ten, and his father was already wondering whether he would 'stick to the hill'. He was the only child in the Glen at the time and rather than transport him to school each day the County wanted to 'board' him in town. This, Jimmie thought, would spoil him for the hill. I asked if he was still around and was told he was driving a lorry for Solway Precast Concrete. Nothing more was said, but a message, apparently, was got to John that he'd better get away and see the Moderator, who was asking for him. It was gey late before we got to bed that night. It's like that in the country.

That holiday when we had first met John Little had been the first year of our marriage and I had proudly taken my wife to Glen Trool where I myself had spent many happy days. We had fixed up for a fortnight at Glenhead, about a couple of miles beyond the head of the loch. It had rained every day and all day throughout the fortnight—or at least it had felt like that—and Queenie had never quite come round to sharing my enthusiasm for Glen Trool as a holiday resort.

As a teenager I had gone frequently for short holidays into the Glen of Trool, when it was little known and little visited. I had stayed with the shepherds, introduced, as it happened, in the first place by Willie M'Creadie of the *Herald* reading-room to Willie Graham, who was then at the Buchan and whose father at Auchengashel was so well known as a breeder of Belted Galloways. More than once I had stayed at Culsharg, a lonely cottage on the Buchan Burn, about a mile and a half from the nearest road and now, I believe, used as a storage hut for the forestry. A pleasant place it was in those days, lying with its back to Benyellary and facing a pleasant meadow down by the burn. Its hirsel included one side of the Merrick and part of the shore of Loch Enoch, with its glittering silver sand which, it was said, men used to shake on to a greased handle to make a whetstone for their scythes. The ominous-sounding and grim-looking Murder Hole in the corner of Loch Nelderkin was on the out-hill of Buchan, and the kindly-named but treacherous Silver Flow of Buchan was just off Culsharg land towards the Back Hill o' the Bush. S. R. Crockett, while writing some of his books, had stayed for a time with the Macmillans at Glenhead (two descendants of the family, retired missionaries, have returned to live in the Glen), and it is said he had given a copy of *The Raiders* to his host with a request for an expression of opinion. The book review which came to him verbally some days later was, 'Ony coof [silly person] can write a book, but it tak's a man to herd the Merrick.' I was proud to think I had at least helped to herd a bit of the Merrick.

Crockett, I feel, fared better than did another Galloway writer, John Mactaggart, who at the age of twenty-five under conditions of great secrecy produced an amazing volume of local lore under the title *Scottish Gallovidian Encyclopedia*. He had expected neither comfort nor encouragement at home in his dedication to this writing task—hence the secrecy and hence

the fact that the first his father knew of the project was to see
the book in a local shop-window. 'John,' he said to his errant
offspring, 'we at hame have aye kent ye were a fool; the 'hale
warld'll ken noo.'

An intensely interesting race are the shepherds—'the hirds'—
utterly apart and different from the arable farmers, following a
lonely path through life, followed at a respectful distance by
their dogs. And whatever you think of the herds you've got to
admire the dogs. But don't, please, imagine they're going to
admire you in return—they're simply going to ignore you. Tall
spare men, the herds, quiet and silent they stride so effortless-
seeming over their hills and by their burns and lochs, thinking
much but rarely giving expression to the results of their medita-
tion. Indeed their capacity for silence is quite phenomenal. I
remember one cottage where, at the time when I went about
these parts, it was said that the herd and his wife had had a tiff
about some debatable subject twenty-nine years before, and
that since then they had not exchanged a single word—each
was waiting for the other to admit error by making the first
advance. No normal human being could do it.

Then there is the tale of the Galloway shepherd who had
been separated from his wife by death after forty years of
conjugal bliss. A friend offering sympathy was saying how much
in his lonely cottage he must be missing the partner of a lifetime. 'Ay,' conceded the herd, 'ye canna live wi' a body for a'
thae years an' no' miss her when she's awa. But d'ye ken what
I'm gonna tell ye—I never really liked the woman.'

I knew that Rab Johnston, my host at Culsharg, had been
for a time on a farm on the banks of the Cree not far from
Newton Stewart, a pleasant place with, as I saw it, much to
commend it compared with the isolation and hardship of his
present post. I asked him one day what had led him to make
the change. 'Och,' he said, 'I couldna be doin' wi' the stir and
commotion, ye never could get awa' frae the soond o' a ploo.'
And to think that for most of us the sound of a plough symbolises
peace, quiet and seclusion.

As these recollections were piling in one upon another my
attention, I fear, was more and more straying from the party.
I was recalled by a remark from my neighbour at the table,
Paul Monteath of Stranraer St Andrew's, Moderator of the

NOT AS A STRANGER 107

Presbytery and the evening's chairman. He had been a
minister at Thornliebank when I had gone to Glasgow, and I
had introduced him to his present charge—that is to say, I had
followed the ancient custom of preaching at his first service,
'preaching him in' as it is called. He was talking of the day he
had taken us round the new industrial area of Stranraer, showing us some of the light industries that have been brought in to
diversify what was once exclusively an agricultural economy.
My wife, naturally, found especial pleasure in seeing the manufacture of the most attractive children's clothing and the
designing and manufacture of the neatest little shoes; but for
me the highlight of this part of our tour was a visit to the
Creamery where we were able to see cheese manufactured on
the grand scale.

In spite of all the automation and mechanisation the process
is still essentially the same as it has always been and as I so
clearly remember it in a day when every farm in Wigtownshire
had its dairy and daily manufactured its quota of cheddars.
That had been a day, surely, before men were conscious of
'the working week', for the average dairyman began his day
by going out around 4.30 to bring in the kye—aided by a
storm lantern most of the year. Milking began at 5.30 and went
on till 7, after which there were calves to feed. A half-hour stop
for breakfast and then the byre and the pig-houses had to be
'mucked'. Meanwhile the cooking of the milk began in the
great vats, the 'crud' had to be cut and stirred, and finally the
whey run. I loved the non-scientific way they gauged when the
whey should be run—a momentous decision that determined
whether the cheese would be right as it should or would be
sweet or acid. A handful of crud was squeezed dry, then pressed
against an old blacksmith's file that had been heated in the
boiler fire. When pulled away it should leave a fine growth or
'breard' an inch long. Then a hurried lunch and the crud had
to be milled and the chisets filled. By the time yesterday's
cheese had been larded, and the day before's bandaged, and the
day before that's turned, and the pigs fed, it would be at least
3.30, and the time till the kye had to 'fetched' again at 4.30
was free time. After the evening milking the vats could not be
left till the milk had cooled to at most eighty degrees, and before
refrigerators this could be 9 or even 10 o'clock. And it went on

for seven days a week. Little wonder there's not a farm in the
county still making its own cheese.

At Creetown we had been interested to visit the works of
Solway Precast Concrete, the largest single employer of labour
in Galloway, and to learn that the new London Bridge is faced
entirely with slabs that have been cast here north of the
Solway. Interesting, too, we found it to learn that the granite
chips that strengthen the finish of all Britain's new motorways
come from the quarry at Carsluith.

We had reached a welcome break in the proceedings at the
party and I was taking the chance of a few words with the
minister of Portpatrick, Samuel M'Naught, recalling our visit
to his parish on the Irish Channel. Often I had been to Portpatrick in the past—on sunny days and on stormy days—but
never before had I had the opportunity of going aboard the
life-boat, or of seeing inside the coast-guard station, or of
talking to the staff of the wireless station. Few of us know how
much work goes on behind the scenes to secure the safety—and
contribute to the comfort—of those that go down to the sea in
ships. As we were shown over the life-boat with all its gadgets
and its safety devices—in spite of which, we in Scotland have
known to our sorrow, they can capsize—I was reminded of
some of father's stories of the life-boat that used to be stationed
at Port Logan, in Kirkmaiden parish. She was just an open
boat, and the source of her power was the strength of the men
at the oars, the local fishermen who volunteered for this
dangerous service. Interestingly enough the money to provide
her had been largely gathered in Edinburgh at the instigation
of R. M. Ballantyne, that remarkable teller of tales of whalers
and fur traders, and she had been called *The Edinburgh and
R. M. Ballantyne.* In the circumstances it was imperative that
full advantage be taken of tides and currents and it was necessary therefore that she be launched from the spot most advantageous for getting to a wreck. Besides which, of course, she
had on occasion to go to a rescue on Luce Bay, right on the
other side of the peninsula. For these journeys by land the
power was provided by four or five pairs of horses supplied
by the local farms, and my father was at a time responsible
for one of the pairs. To our modern automated ears it sounds
incredibly slow and pathetically inefficient and it must have

made tremendous demands on human strength and physical endurance. Yet they had a fine record of rescues to their credit, and the old boat was scrapped as recently as 1926. It is the pattern of the boat that changes, the spirit that makes men volunteer for such service remains the same.

In and around the 'twenties when I used to be much about the district, sheep-farming had been at its lowest ebb. The hirsels I had known were of the poorest quality and were capable of supporting only pure-bred blackface stock on which the return was slight. As a further complication the terrain was so treacherous that the stock had to be reared on the ground— they were bound to the ground as they called it—or 'bun tae the grun' as it sounded. There just wasn't a living in sheep, yet it was difficult to get out. Then forestry came along, govern- ment-sponsored, and thousands upon thousands of acres have been given over to coniferous forests. This has, of course, altered the whole face of the countryside, some say for the better, while others maintain it has taken away its distinctive character and its beauty. It has surely driven out the shepherd completely from some areas and instead of the lonely farmstead you find little forestry villages scattered in pleasant corners. A new look for the countryside, a new pattern of living for its people.

Kirroughtree House Hotel on the outskirts of Newton Stewart where the party was being held and where we had been accommodated throughout our stay had, interestingly enough, been at one time the home of a family of my own name, a name not uncommon in Wigtownshire. Only they had spelled it with one 'r' while I have always affected two— *Herron*. I never fail to be amused at the way some people lay great stress upon the detail of the spelling of their family name and how they base the most momentous conclusions thereon. I have a theory that the spelling of proper names has arisen in most cases from the whim or prejudice or ignorance of some session or parish registrar of yester-year. I vividly remember a day when my father was holding forth with much conviction about the sanctity of that second 'r' in our name—someone had had the temerity to challenge it. To prove his point he dug out his birth certificate and was dumbfounded to find that the person who had written that out had known nothing about

the second 'r'. It was all a bit embarrassing. Yet the headstone
in the local kirkyard where his parents lie certainly supports
the two-r theory. And I at least can claim two 'r's in my birth
certificate—I've just been checking it to mak' siccar!

It was in 1855 that compulsory registration of births,
marriages and deaths was introduced in Scotland and local
registrars appointed. In many cases the person chosen for this
new part-time post must have been of limited educational
accomplishment. Before that, baptismal and other registers
were at the mercy of persons of very varying ability. And the
people instructing the entries must often have been much more
familiar with how their own names sounded than with how
they ought to look on paper. I am sure that the final 'e' in
Browne, for example, must have originated as a flourish in an
Italian-type script, and that the 'p' in Thompson may well
have been the old-fashioned 's' in Thom's son.

The too-well-educated registrar was also a danger, for he
could think he was putting a thing right when in fact he was
making it wrong. I remember a *Herald* sub-editor who 'corrected' the Rhinns of Galloway to the Whins of Galloway. If it
doesn't conform to anything in your knowledge change it, it
must be wrong, is a simple and satisfying enough working
principle. An obvious example is the local parish of Stoneykirk.
This is locally pronounced Steeniekirk which is correct, for
the ancient kirk was dedicated to St Stephen, abbreviated in
these parts to Steenie. A field covered with stones, however,
would also be described as steenie, and there seems little doubt
that someone somewhere along the line thought he was cor-
recting an ignorant mispronunciation by making it Stoneykirk.
Likewise there is the neighbouring parish of Kirkmaiden which
is dedicated to St Medan (from Medan's Kirk to John o'
Groats, as Burns puts it). But someone obviously concluded
from the sound that it had something to do with a young lady
and corrected the spelling accordingly.

So, for all I know, the Herons of Kirroughtree may have
been relations of my own—though I should think it extremely
unlikely. I have never been one who wanted to dig overmuch
into my family history, having a shrewd suspicion that people
who go around turning up stones that have lain quietly for
years are liable to find queer nasty-looking beasts scurrying

away from the unwelcome daylight. Not that I've any reason
to expect that my family tree would prove any less respectable
than the average, it's just that I prefer to leave well alone. In
any case I haven't the skill in covering up which is attributed
to an American (they love this kind of delving) who was
preparing a family tree with laudatory notes on the various
branches and twigs, but who was a bit put out to discover that
one ancestor had had the unfortunate distinction of dying by
judicial electrocution at Sing-Sing. He was equal to the occasion, though, and the note read, '. . . who was appointed
to the chair of applied electricity at a well-known American
institution and remained at his post to the end'. I was much
amused at an American who said to me the other day, 'Sure
the *Queen Elizabeth* is a big ship, but she couldn't carry half the
passengers that were on the *Mayflower*.'

So, you see, it was not as strangers that we had come to grey
Galloway, a land I had always loved and with which we had
so many ties. As a boy I used to read much of S. R. Crockett
and got myself much steeped in local lore. Crockett lies in the
kirkyard at Balmaghie—the Kirk abune the Water o' Dee, as
it has been called—and near to him lie yet another two of the
martyrs of the Covenant.

The closing 'party' that night was for me as much a sentimental as a social occasion. As we sang the final *Auld Lang Syne*
the tear was not far from my eye. And not far from my mind
were the poignant lines from Robert Louis Stevenson's poem,
written in distant Vailima and dedicated to Crockett:

> Be it granted me to behold you again in dying,
>   Hills of home! And to hear again the call;
> Hear about the graves of the martyrs the peewees crying,
>   And hear no more at all.

CHAPTER 10

Amazing Grace

'What has been your most difficult assignment?' It's a question
no-one has asked me. A pity, for I should have little difficulty
in giving an answer. That day in February, I should say, when
at Windsor in the Garrison Church of the First Battalion of the
Scots Guards I preached at the Memorial Service for the five
boys who were killed during the unit's four months' tour of
duty in Northern Ireland. Keith Crozer, the chaplain of the
battalion, I had known when he was minister of a Perthshire
country parish, and I felt very honoured when he conveyed to
me an invitation to take part in the Service; but as the date
approached I found myself more and more worried about
what to say. The occasion seemed so emphatically to demand
some kind of clarion call for an end to the madness that is
Northern Ireland today. But the more I thought of it the more
I wondered. What had I to contribute towards solving these
problems? What status had the Church entitling it to make
any pronouncement except in the most general terms—the
kind of thing already said and repeated *ad nauseam*. Even more
important perhaps, what comfort would such a declaration be
to those families who were being brought from as far afield as
Caithness and Islay in the hour of their sorrow? In the end I
preached a short and extremely simple sermon on the subject
of the life to come. This, I felt, was the one thing I alone had
the right to do, the one message which was the unique possession of the Church, the one word which if I spoke it not
would remain unsaid. And this I must add—I have rarely if
ever addressed my words to a more attentive audience. In a
letter afterwards the chaplain wrote, 'I can honestly say I have
never heard a reaction to a service like there was to this one.'

It was a memorable service. Holy Trinity Church in Windsor,
which is the Garrison Church for the Battalion, is a large
building, and it was filled for the occasion almost to capacity—
with over seven hundred Guardsmen, with the relatives and
friends of the boys who had died, with ex-officers of the regi-

ment and of others which had served in Ulster, and with
interested members of the public. The praise was led by the
Band of the Junior Guardsman's Company, the lesson was read
by their commanding officer, Colonel Richard Mayfield, and
the Anglican and Roman Catholic chaplains assisted Keith
Crozer in the conduct of the Service. What a tragic situation!
Five lads, varying in age from eighteen to twenty-three,
giving their lives in a quarrel in which they had neither interest
nor concern; one shot in the back on patrol on a Sunday
afternoon, one killed with a bomb while preparing lunch for
his mates, one killed in an explosion on the 'peace-line'; one
leaving a family, one recently married, one with a baby he
had seen but once. What an appalling waste. What a senseless
business generally is this war that isn't a war that is being
fought in the streets of Northern Ireland.

Yes, I had been sore tempted to say something about the
cause of this pitiful waste of young lives. Not that I had a
solution of what, humanly speaking, seems an insoluble problem, but I could have roundly criticised those responsible
because they had not come up with a solution; I could have
bitterly condemned the spirit of intolerance, the dedication to
memories of events that would be well forgotten, the religious
zeal that assumes such grotesque sectarian shapes—I could well
have attacked all of these things. But I'm glad I resisted the
temptation. I don't think it would in the least have helped
anybody, whereas I hope what I did say may have helped to
lighten somebody's heavy burden of sorrow.

There is a movement in the Kirk today that wants to see
us more deeply involved in politics. Some say quite straight-
forwardly that they refer to party politics. Others draw a
distinction between politics and party politics, though how the
distinction is to be maintained in practice I cannot conceive.
The Church and Nation Committee Report at the past Assembly
was much concerned to press this need for political involvement.
For myself I regard this kind of development with some misgiving—I'm probably in a minority but that merely intensifies
my conviction that I may well be right. As I once assured the
Assembly, I am one of those who recognise there are two sides
to every question—my side and the wrong side.

As I see it, it's when men have no longer a gospel to preach that they take refuge in preaching politics. When they've no longer good news to proclaim they feel constrained to offer good advice. When they're no longer very sure that Jesus saves they feel the responsibility for mounting a rescue operation of their own. I recognise, of course, that the Church and Nation position can easily be defended. Of what use is it to preach about brotherly love and a fair-do for the under-dog, to preach about a better order of human society and making this world into the kingdom of heaven, to preach about a caring fellowship and the claims of the hungry and the under-privileged and the third world, unless you're going to take some steps to ensure that these things are achieved and realised. And since they are achieved only at the level of political activity there is clearly a need for us to be involved in political activity. Otherwise we're just making platitudinous noises. It can all sound most convincing.

But I still think that when a politician comes to the Kirk it should be to get his faith fortified, not to get his party political convictions clarified. There are plenty of agencies offering the latter service; it is the Kirk and the Kirk alone that dares to offer the former.

It seems a little strange, does it not, that our Lord should have been content to preach about brotherly love and to manifest it as far as Calvary and that He should not have undertaken any kind of political involvement or even made any specific attack on the social evils of His time. Slavery, for example— where does Jesus make any direct reference to it? Or the place of woman in the society of His day—where does He in terms condemn it? One might go farther and remember that one of the temptations He rejected at the outset of His ministry was that of entering the sphere of practical politics by providing free bread for the masses.

I'm not unmindful of the fact that one of the highlights of the Assembly is generally the day of the Church and Nation Committee Report, a day which can be counted on to bring the gathering alive. Undoubtedly it's always an intensely interesting and entertaining day's debating. How it ranks in the matter of edification is another question. For long this report was taken on the Monday of the second week, and as the Garden Party at Holyroodhouse was held at 3 o'clock that afternoon the anxiety of commissioners to enjoy the social event set a definite limit to the oratory and hurried on the discussion. But recently Church and Nation has moved to Tuesday and the Garden Party to Saturday so there is no longer that clash of interests to give it momentum. (You know about the country elder who explained to a friend that there was some word of their minister leaving and the Session 'thought they wad like to gi'e him a wee bit momentum'.) The report usually covers a vast number of topics—national, international, social, economic, industrial—even religious. Nor is it content to deal with its various themes in general terms, it makes detailed pronouncements on specific points. This couldn't fail to produce a lively debate. And there is, no doubt, a considerable value in having these matters aired in an open forum north of the Border, particularly in the absence of any kind of Scottish home-rule. I wonder, though, as I have already hinted, whether the exercise has any other value.

To me it always appears that what we have in such a debate is a company of Scottish Churchmen discussing matters of national interest, not the Church of Scotland reaching decisions on political issues. I feel too that we are able to discuss these important matters with a zest and enthusiasm that are all the greater because we do not have the responsibility of reaching the ultimate operative decision in regard to them. There are, I think, two points here that should be borne in mind. First, that solving other people's problems is a stupid and futile business. A minister said to me the other day, 'We have a sixteen-year-old son who's proving a bit of a problem for us at the moment—not but what every maiden lady in the congregation knows the answer to it.' Secondly, that the well-intentioned amateur is one of the most dangerous of human beings. 'I was only trying to help', can be a most exasperating explanation from somebody whose interference has created havoc. From the point of view of the Church of Scotland a great part of the agenda of the Church and Nation Committee seems to me to represent 'other people's problems'. In the highly specialist domains represented by most of these problems commissioners at the Assembly are usually cast for the role of well-intentioned amateurs. And the real pity of it is that so many people see this part of the Assembly business as the one occasion when the Kirk genuinely goes into action in the world. It's hard to convince people today that the Gospel is good news—not good advice, not even good works.

Long years ago I heard a story which I have since unsuccessfully tried to verify. It has to do with Samuel Rutherfurd, the author of *Lex Rex* which, three months after the Restoration, was, by order of the Committee of the Estates, burned at Edinburgh and St Andrews—little wonder considering it stated, among other things, 'Power is a birthright of the people borrowed from them; they may let it out for their good, and resume it when a man is drunk with it.' At the time of the story Rutherfurd was minister at Anwoth near Gatehouse-of-Fleet, before he had gained such fame as Professor at St Andrews. In that day the Kirk was very deeply involved in politics and every pulpit was a platform for the denunciation of the powers-that-be—'preaching up the times' they called it. Someone challenged Rutherfurd that he was not doing his share. 'What about That One,' he asked, 'does he preach up the times?' Every Sunday without fail, he was assured. 'And what about That Other One, what does he do?' His denunciation of the powers of wickedness in high places was drawing crowds from far and near. 'So all the distinguished men of the Kirk are preaching up the times?' Every single one of them. 'In that case,' said Rutherfurd, 'it won't matter if one insignificant little man preaches up the unsearchable riches of Christ.'

The service in the Garrison Church at Windsor had not been my first introduction to the situation in Northern Ireland. Along with Edward Marr, my Senior Chaplain, John Mowat, Clerk to the Presbytery of Aberdeen, and my friend Highet Allan, Session Clerk of Mearns on the outskirts of Glasgow, and accompanied by our respective wives, we had attended the General Assembly of the Presbyterian Church in Ireland, which was held in Belfast just a week after our own Assembly had risen. We have a system whereby the Presbyterian Churches of Scotland, Ireland, England and Wales send 'corresponding members' to one another's Assemblies. These are full members with all the rights in the matter of speaking and voting that belong to normal commissioners, though I don't imagine these rights are often exercised beyond the formal address which one of the party is always invited to give. It is in every case very much of a social occasion, wives accompany their husbands and there are a variety of lunches, tea-parties—even breakfasts—to be attended. Ireland being Ireland no opportunity for a light-hearted talk is ever allowed to pass, so the tea-parties can be very cheery affairs. It's amazing that for all they have suffered and for all the agony they are enduring the Irish people have never lost their sense of humour. Maybe it's a very good thing. It's a great pity, though, that so easily they seem to lose their sense of proportion, and a great pity too that they seem never to have acquired an ability to forget. Walking along a street you will see painted in huge letters on a wall, 'Remember 1690'. I should have liked to get a paint-gun and put on the opposite wall, 'Think about 1990'. It's said that an Irishman one day forced his donkey to ford a stream that was in spate. The unhappy beast narrowly escaped drowning. A week later, the waters having completely abated, they came to the identical spot and the donkey refused to put a foot into the trickle of water. Not all Paddy's coaxing, not all his swearing, not all his beating could budge it an inch. 'You stupit beast,' he said, 'your memory's better nor your judgment.' A wise word, is it not, and worthy to be pondered.

During our stay in Belfast we were the guests of the Lord Chief Justice, Lord M'Dermott, and his charming and active wife. Two of her brothers have been Moderators in the American Church. Their younger son is a minister in Dublin. For it has to be understood that the Presbyterian Church in Ireland has charges throughout the whole country, most of them, naturally, in the 'six counties' but catering for Presbyterians throughout Ireland as a whole. This fact had led to some trouble when we were there. The opening evening of the Assembly is quite a national event, attended by representatives of government and other leading personalities. As well as the Governor and the Prime Minister from Stormont a representative of the government of the Republic is always invited. In today's atmosphere this in itself is enough to create a 'situation', and I understand the police spent a good part of the forenoon of the opening day searching the premises for odd-shaped parcels. Everything, fortunately, went off without incident. The fact that the National Anthem is almost a 'test' of loyalty in Ulster no doubt accounted for the Republican representative and his wife standing throughout the singing with lips firmly sealed. At the same time one can see how even a little thing like that could verge on provocation. Professor James Haire was retiring as Moderator, being succeeded by Dr F. Rupert Gibson, whose tragic and untimely death at Christmas-time was so sad a blow for his Church. At his Funeral Service, at which, unfortunately I was unable to be present, representatives of all denominations in war-torn Ulster were able to sit together for the first, and unhappily the only, time.

James Haire I knew very well. He had been a close friend of Ian Henderson, and we had met on a number of ecumenical committees. The first occasion of our meeting, though, went much farther back to a day when J. Stuart Cameron, whose assistant I had been for three years in Springburn, had been called by the congregation of Malone in Belfast and we had been over for the induction. Jimmie, who was still very much of a lad at the time, had been deputed by his father to take some of us out in the car on a free forenoon. I have always remembered how he told me that day as we drove around that before you can even begin to understand an Irishman you have got to realise that he can feel so intensely about a principle as to lead him to do things utterly foreign to his normal nature. He illustrated the point with the story of the two countrymen who decided that the system of land-tenure was so iniquitously unjust as to demand the death of its local representative, the factor. It was known that he passed a certain point at precisely 5 o'clock every Friday evening so the pair, duly armed with loaded blunderbusses, prepared an ambush. The hour for his passing had come and gone with no sign of him. By 6 o'clock they were getting really anxious. Said Michael, 'I do hope, Pathrick, that nothin' has happened to the daicent man.'

We had very much enjoyed our stay in Belfast and our participation in their Assembly. They are a wonderful people, the Presbyterian population of Ireland, and their Church in these difficult days is standing firm for reason and moderation without yielding on essential principle. It would be interesting to be able to assess how far the comparative non-participation in violence on the Protestant side is due to the existence of a solid bloc of faithful Church people. At least one had to admire enormously the courage and patience and faith—and good

humour—with which their ministers are carrying on in face of
difficulties that would daunt most of us. At the time when we
were in Belfast there was something of a lull in the hostilities
and you could move around the centre of the city without being
too conscious that anything unusual was afoot. You hadn't to
go far, though, to see the ravages, and everywhere you sensed
an indefinable atmosphere of unrest.

To see how other people conduct their business is always an
interesting, and sometimes an instructive, experience, and there
were one or two features of the Irish Assembly that appealed
to me. A question, for example, when asked by a member from
his place on the floor, was repeated by the Assembly Clerk at
the microphone. While in some ways this was cumbrous and
awkward it had the advantage of securing that the question
was a simple, direct one designed to elicit information and not
a speech ending with a question-mark designed to influence the
voting. The thing I liked best, though, was a system whereby
they have a man at a little table in the wings doing nothing,
apparently, but supervising the time of speeches. So soon as a
chap comes to the rostrum this man takes a reading. According
to whether the speaker is proposing an original motion, speaking to an amendment, contributing to the discussion, or what
have you, he has a specific number of minutes allotted to him.
One minute before his time is up the recorder presses a button
which causes a little bulb on the rostrum to light up. Ten
seconds before time-up another button is pressed and this time
a buzzer sounds. All that is needed to make the device perfect
is that ten seconds after count-down a third button should be
pressed and cause a trap-door to open, when the offending
speaker could finish his oratorical masterpiece in the basement.

I had a further contact, albeit at second hand, with the
happenings in Ulster when at the beginning of December I set
off, accompanied by Dr Tom Nicol, Assistant Chaplain
General, now minister at Crathie, on a flight to Dusseldorf
en route for visiting our Scots units in the British Army of
Occupation of the Rhine. This trip had, understandably, been
organised long in advance and by the time December came
round many of the troops were no longer in Germany, having
been drafted to Northern Ireland to face the bombs there. It
could be, of course, that this made my visit all the more

worthwhile, for the women-folk might be expected to require all
the morale-boosting they could possibly get. There they were with
their children in a strange land, far separated from their own
friends and with their husbands facing danger far away. That
the powers-that-be were very conscious of all that was involved
had been brought to my notice a few days earlier when during
my stay in London I had had a brief meeting with Lord Balneil,
Minister of Defence. We had spoken of my forthcoming visit to
Germany and he had told me how important it was in his view
that the lines of communication between Ulster and the Rhine
should be kept open and easy. He had gone so far as to suggest
that if I thought, once I got there, that anything could be done
to help in this regard I should not hesitate to get in touch with
him.

In one respect at least I found that the lines of communication were functioning better even than anyone in authority
seemed to know, or might have approved. The Queen's Own
Highlanders (the Seaforths and the Camerons were united in
1961) were officially stationed in the Garrison at Osnabruck,
though the boys and their chaplain, Matthew Robertson, were
in fact on duty in Belfast. The chaplain had contrived to
return in his own car so as to be on parade for my visit—I
noted that no-one was indiscreet enough to ask him how it had
been done. I was most glad to meet him, and later his wife,
who it transpired was a grand-daughter of the schoolmaster in
my first parish of Linwood—do I overhear someone saying it's
a small world? It's said that an old body learned that her
soldier son was in a hospital one of whose nurses was the
daughter of a near neighbour remarked, 'It's a wee world.
Just to think o' oor Willie's broken leg being in the haunds o'
a kenned face.'

It was a great joy for me on the Sunday to conduct a Service
in Matthew's little Church in the barracks. It's a converted
stable—suitable enough, surely, at the Advent season—and
they had made the rings for the halters, still set in the wall, a
feature of the decor. After Service we were drinking coffee in
an adjoining canteen when one woman after another came up
with a little brown-paper parcel, 'Padre, could you give that
to Angus?' 'I heard that you had the car, padre, and I wondered
if it would be a bother for you to take this for Archie?' And so

on. Surrounded by his haul all he needed was a red cloak, a white beard and a reindeer or two. I was expressing the hope he wouldn't have too much bother explaining it all at the customs-post, when a lassie came over and said, 'Och, padre, if I had juist thoct I could ha'e rowed mysel' up in broon paper and you micht ha'e ta'en me.' Not all that much wrong with the morale, I thought.

Another day we were at Herford visiting the Royal Scots Dragoon Guards, or at least those of them who were left from the Ulster draft. A couple of jeeps pulled up in the barrack-square and a number of young soldiers piled out. These, it was explained to me by Major Buckley, who was my guide at the time, were under eighteen and too young for Northern Ireland. They were undergoing instead a course of training as vehicle-drivers. They were all Scots boys and maybe I would care to have a word with one or two of them. So it was represented to the boys, in suitable square-bashing language, that they might care to line up, which they did with a great deal of shuffling and spacing-out and military precision generally. There would be, I imagine, sixteen of them and they ended up in a neat square all standing uneasily 'at ease'. I moved over to the first boy who stared straight through me without an eyelid so much as flickering as I advanced. By way of an easy opening gambit I asked, in the friendliest tones I could muster, 'And where do you come from?' He clicked his heels together, saluted, and spat out at me, 'Perth, sir.' The words hit me with all the malignant precision of machine-gun bullets. Involuntarily I ducked to the side and found myself looking at the boy next in the line. Before I had time to utter a word he went through the same performance as his neighbour and spat out, 'Falkirk, sir.' I had, all unwittingly, set off a chain reaction, and helplessly I had to stand there and get sixteen places of origin literally fired at me. They looked so defiantly apprehensive that I might be thinking of putting them on a charge for having come from such places that I hastily suggested to the major that maybe we should not any longer keep them from their lunch.

It was in that same barrack-square at Herford that an hour or so earlier they had laid on a very fine concert in my honour. The Royal Scots Dragoon Guards represent a fairly recent

amalgam of the Royal Scots Greys and the Third Carabiniers—
they are a very highly specialised and heavily armoured spear-
head today. The Greys had had a pipe band and the Carabiniers a brass band. The united band of pipes and brass had
marched and counter-marched across the square playing for
my enjoyment, and they had concluded their programme with
a number with which not long before they topped the pops—
Amazing Grace. I thought it a surprising achievement for such a
piece. A very splendid and deeply moving rendering it had
been. Months later in a house in the States our host said he had
a very special treat in store for us and proceeded to play a
record of it. He did not know he was taking me back to that
cold grey December day in a German barrack-square.

For me the unforgettable episode in our visit to Germany
was the evening when we went from Hohne to the site of
Belsen Camp, that epitome of the horror that was Nazi Germany. The whole area has been cleared and everywhere silver
birches are growing. Apart from an obelisk in one corner of
the area the ground contains no memorial except that on every
side there are mounds, each one of them with its simple stone
saying, 'Here lie 4500, April 1944', or 'Here lie 6000, May
1944', or whatever the pitiful facts may be. Now Belsen was
not an extermination camp with gas chambers and cremation
ovens; it was just a simple camp where people were imprisoned
and died from disease, hunger, neglect; died by the hundred
daily with no-one so much as to drag their bodies outside the
huts let alone to bury them. The British Director of Medical
Services, one of the first to enter the camp after liberation,
wrote, 'No description or photograph could really bring home
the horrors that were there outside the huts; and the pitiful
scenes inside were much worse.' The whole miserable disease-
infested place was burned to the ground immediately it had
been cleared—let it not cumber God's fair earth a moment
longer. There is a legend that to this day no bird ever sings in
Belsen. I had heard that story and had treated it as a nice
piece of poetic fancy. Now I'm prepared to accept it as a
solemn prosaic statement of sober fact—the bird that wanted
to sing in Belsen would be remarkably insensitive to atmosphere. A terrifying and a memorable experience to walk in the
grey dusk among these silent silver birches. Not all the hospi-

tality that was lavished upon us by the Fourth Tank Regiment, which we were visiting in their quarters at Hohne, could obliterate that picture from my mind.

It had been on the Saturday morning of our stay at Osnabruck that we had driven to Bielefeld to be entertained by representatives of the German Evangelical Church. In the afternoon we were introduced to Bethel, 'Village of Mercy'. Bethel is a suburb of Bielefeld; it has a population of around eleven thousand; seven thousand of them are patients, mostly epileptics of the worst kind I have ever seen, but they include also many mental defectives; the other four thousand represent the nursing staff. What goes on in the houses of that suburb in the way of dedicated caring defies description as completely as did the brutality of Belsen. At lunch in Bielefeld we had spoken with a German pastor who had spent three years in Auschwitz because he defied Hitler using the Bethel patients as guinea-pigs in his chemical experiments. It cannot be denied that Bethel is no less an expression of the German character than was Belsen—the nurses, for all their self-sacrificial caring, had the same tendency to heel-clicking, and could as easily have been taught goose-stepping, as the monsters of the concentration-camp. Each is a perfect exemplification of one or other of the extremes to which a certain type of character can aspire.

Isaiah, I have often thought, had the right idea when he envisaged the great day of the Lord as a time when men would beat their swords into plough-shares and their spears into pruning-hooks—the steel that makes a sword a deadly instrument of war will make a plough-share fit to turn a goodly fur. What counts is not the material that's used, but the use for which the material is shaped. There is nothing necessarily corrupt in a nation capable of producing Bethel—even if it has driven the birds to silence in Belsen.

On leaving Hohne we continued westward to Hanover to visit the vast military hospital there—in the maternity unit alone they are responsible for a thousand military personnel deliveries a year. At lunch I had a long chat with the Medical Officer, Brian Peake, who told me that as a student he had been at the relief of Belsen. Half of the hospital of which he is now in charge had been commandeered for the use of those whose lives might still be saved. Not only had they commandeered the hospital beds, he told me, they had gone about the country commandeering chickens, eggs, food, and anything they thought could be of service in restoring the victims. All of those with whom they dealt claimed ignorance of what went on inside the barbed-wire fences. It was perfectly possible, he agreed, that this might have been so. And even if they had their suspicions they were not, I am sure, encouraged to pursue their enquiries too persistently. There are things we are better not to know. Had you or I been in their shoes, who knows, we too might have thought the wise course was not to know too much.

Strange creatures we are, all of us, strangely and wonderfully made, capable of the ugliest misdeeds, but capable also of acts of heroic self-sacrifice; nicely balanced on a ledge, Belsen on one side, Bethel on the other. 'There, but for the grace of God . . .'

They were grey, depressing winter days that we spent in Germany, but for all that I have many happy memories of my tour—memories of dinner with the Commander-in-Chief, a Scot, Sir Peter Hunt, in his house at Rheindalen; memories of visits to RAF personnel, to the camp at Bruggen and to the hospital at Wegberg, and not least of being hoisted into the cockpit of the latest supersonic fighter (the enemy would have been well off his mark by the time I was got into position); memories of a wonderful mess dinner with the Dragoons at Herford; memories of the gracious hospitality of Brigadier David Young and his wife at Talavera House at Osnabruck; memories of the shine the batman there impressed on my shoes; memories of meeting a group of subalterns in the Herford mess that included a boy from Houston whom I had baptised, a son of Major Macrae who had taken us sailing at Letterfearn, a boy from my nearby parish of Howwood—happy memories all of them.

But somehow the thing that stands out grim and vivid, like a gibbet on a hill, is that walk through the silent silver birches where no bird sings. It still comes whiles to haunt me and I feel unutterably depressed—and then suddenly I hear the seugh of the pipes playing *Amazing Grace* and I feel my hope restored and my courage renewed. Grace sufficient for all our needs.

CHAPTER II

'Man's Inhumanity to Man'

We arrived in Gibraltar just in time to be involved in the Burns Supper. We flew in, in fact, in the early afternoon, having travelled to London on the overnight train. As the plane was preparing to land, my wife, seeing a very grand Daimler and a very distinguished-looking reception-party lined up on the tarmac, remarked that there must surely be someone of great importance on the plane. Having by this time identified our minister on Gibraltar, John Lawrie, and his wife among the company I said, 'Yes, my dear, it's you and me.' And so in fact it was. We were to be the guests, during our stay on The Rock, of the Governor and his wife at their official residence, The Convent. Sir Varyl Begg is a descendant of a former Moderator of the United Free Church of Scotland and justly proud of the fact, and though he had had to be in London at the time of our arrival he had made arrangements for us to be very officially and properly received.

While I was not in my official 'uniform'—it's not really designed for British Railway sleepers—we were both reasonably presentable. Unlike one of my predecessors of whom it is told that he was visiting one of our stations abroad involving a flight of some fifteen hours. Convinced that comfort mattered more than dignity he travelled in an old suit of disreputable tweeds. After 'reclining' hour after dreary hour in a plane seat he thought that a shave and a wash were called for but decided it would be better to wait till he got to his hotel where he could have a bath and change in comfort. There had, however, been a break in the communication-line, and he did not know that his host had arranged a full-scale parade of everybody who was anybody on the local scene, a piper in full regalia, the Press, photographers, the red carpet, the lot. The poor, grubby, un-shaven Moderator suddenly found himself the centre of all this, with the local television cameras working nineteen to the dozen. With this in mind I had been at pains to warn John Lawrie that we should be arriving as ordinary citizens.

The reception on the tarmac over, we were driven to The
Convent where we met Lady Begg and Sir Varyl's mother, and
had a chance to relax for an hour—something that didn't
happen very often in the course of the five hectic days we spent
on The Rock. The Governor's residence did in fact begin life
as a convent and part of the building is used as a Garrison
Church by the Church of England padre. There is also, of
course, an Anglican Cathedral, the Dean here being chaplain
to the naval forces. That part of The Convent which is used
as the residence is a commodious and gracious place, and there
is a beautiful level garden, a thing doubly precious where land
is so scarce and level ground almost unknown.

Scarcely had we had time to admire the garden ere we were
whisked away to the Lawrie's Manse at Scudhill for tea. Before
going to Gibraltar in 1964 John had been for twenty-seven years
minister in Glasgow at Blackfriars Church in Dennistoun, and
the service he had rendered there had been as distinguished as
it was faithful. I was much impressed when meeting people in
Glasgow and telling them we were going to Gibraltar to find
that their reaction in so many cases was to ask to be remembered
to John; and on our return they didn't enquire how we had
enjoyed The Rock, they asked how we had found its minister.
A reputation like that cometh not but by hard work and
devoted caring. Latterly John had been a martyr to bronchitis
during our Glasgow winters—hence his move, which from this
point of view had proved a complete success. So we were
happy to be with them in their Manse. I wonder just how many
Scots folk—particularly Glasgow ones—have been entertained
in that Manse. 'Given to hospitality' is one of the virtues of
which St Paul has a word to say. It's not maybe one of the
more spectacular virtues, but it's one that achieves much, and
I'm sure that in the kind of situation represented by our Kirks
on the continent, the Manse matters as much as the Kirk.

Then in the evening we set off for the Burns Supper. I've
attended a few Burns Suppers in my time, but the Gibraltar
one was unique. I've never been at one where less attention
was paid to Rabbie's verses or where more to-do was made
about the haggis. I began to think there might be more than
a mere joke in the story told by my friend Ben Johnston of
Inverkeithing that on one occasion he was under contract to

fly out to propose the Immortal Memory at a Burns Supper organised by RAF personnel on Gibraltar. The English wife of one of the officers in Fife meeting him on the street one day said, 'Oh, Mr Johnston, I'm so pleased to hear you're flying out to Gibraltar to propose the health of the haggis.' That could easily enough have been taken to be the object of the exercise the night we were there.

Furth of Scotland the vaguest notions obtain about this haggis that figures so prominently at every well-conducted Burns Supper. That it is something distinctively Scottish is universally agreed; that it appears along with the lion rampant and the thistle on the armorial bearings of the Archbishop of St Giles' would be unlikely to be denied; that it is meant to be eaten is readily conceded, but whether with a fish-knife or a claymore is not so certain. We Scots, on the other hand, recognise the haggis on sight and may even have explored the mystery of its interior. But haggis is not a twentieth-century Scottish dish. At what other season is it regularly eaten? I imagine few stomachs of today can successfully cope with more than a meagre helping. Even its culinary bed-fellows, the mashed neep and the champit tattie, are waning in popularity in a calorie-conscious community. It may still be true that 'auld Scotia wants nae skinkin' ware that jaups in luggies', but I doubt if it's true to add, 'if ye wish her gratefu' prayer gi'e her a haggis'.

What is there about this cult of the Burns Supper? There's a silly story about the proverbial Welshman, Irishman, Englishman and Scotsman, to the effect that a pair of each had been entombed for some days in an air-raid shelter. When at length the rescuers won through they found in one corner the two Welshmen singing Cwm Rhondda *con spirito*, in another the two Irishmen divesting themselves of their jackets to settle a nice point about Irish Home Rule, in a third the two Englishmen looking at one another with stony hostility for they hadn't been introduced, and in the last corner the two Scots animatedly arranging a Burns Supper for they thought it must be getting near the 25th of January. A silly story, but it has a point; for, to the Scot abroad at least, the Burns Supper seems to have established itself as a national festival. It's a strange thing that a people who for long would have nothing to do with the

Christian Year should be so devoted to a date; a people who threw a stool at the head of a Bishop for trying to introduce a liturgy should so love all the highly formalised performance of carrying in the haggis, addressing it, trenching its gushing entrails bright, reciting 'Tam o' Shanter', toasting the Lassies —and all the rest; strange that a people not notable for wearing their hearts on their sleeves should enjoy such a welter of sentimental slobbering. Anything less typically Scottish than the standard Burns Supper it would be hard to conceive; yet it has established itself as the occasion when Scots are Scots the world o'er.

I've been at Burns Suppers at which I didn't think Rabbie would have been very happy; I've been at some where I think he might have passed the time thinking up some scathing lines to immortalise the occasion; and I've been at some at which I'm sure he would really have been in his element. That night at Gibraltar I don't think he might have seen any very serious reason why they should have put his name at the head of the programme, but if my picture of the poet is anything like accurate he would thoroughly have enjoyed the fellowship and the warm friendship and the general spirit of good cheer that pervaded the whole evening. I don't know what proportion of Scots was present—I imagine it was pretty small—and I'm sure that for all the languages that are to be heard on The Rock— and it is a kind of Babel—none sounded stranger than the Ayrshire Scots of the 'Address to the Haggis', that great chieftain o' the puddin' race—an exercise which, I'm sure, some thought was being performed in Gaelic.

As I say, Rabbie, I feel certain, would have enjoyed himself that night at Gibraltar, for he was a man of broad sympathies and deep understanding, and the honest abandon and the spontaneous enjoyment of good fellowship he would have found much more acceptable than some of the unutterably dreary speeches that have been made in his honour.

I was much amused, incidentally, at another Burns Supper which we were to attend on our return from Gibraltar as guests of Sir James Miller, that amazing man who has been both Lord Provost of Edinburgh and Lord Mayor of London (the order is chronological and without prejudice to any other question). It was the Liveries Supper and the speaker was

Alastair Dunnett, editor of *The Scotsman*. In the course of his speech he complained of the Englishman's love of singing 'Auld Lang *Zyne*', suggesting that if he feels he must change S's into Z's he might begin with one of his own songs—for instance, Zing a Zong of Zixpence. My own complaint has always been about the substitution of Old for Auld and Long for Lang— why not anglicise it properly and make it Old Long Since?

Isn't it strange how many people there are who though they can understand and appreciate a joke are quite incapable of reproducing it? They normally explain it by saying they can never remember a joke, no matter how recently they have heard it. I am sure myself it is not really a deficiency of memory at all but a failure to understand what it is about the joke that makes it tick. It was at that same Liveries Supper that Sir James told the story of the two men who had left a party in a somewhat exalted condition, and meeting some time later one had asked the other how he had got on after they parted. 'I had a real bit of trouble,' he said, 'I was lifted by the police and spent the night in a cell.' Replied his friend, 'My but you were lucky; I got home.' The very next day I heard someone who had been there retell the story. He missed out the catch-line 'My but you were lucky' and seemed surprised, if not actually offended, when nobody laughed. He hadn't forgotten the line; he just hadn't seen its importance.

There was no occasion in the course of our Gibraltar evening to refer to 'A man's a man for a' that', but the line about man's inhumanity to man making countless thousands mourn was much in my mind in the course of the time we spent on The Rock. The island is quite unashamedly an instrument of war. There's no other reason for its existence. There's no other explanation why Britain should hold on to it so desperately in face of constant and increasing Spanish pressure. To the outsider it may seem obvious that what is so clearly a bit of Spain, geographically speaking, should be restored to Spain. Yet it's not in fact so easy to write off centuries of history, and the Gibraltarians are the ones most bitterly opposed to any suggestion of a return to their ancestral allegiance. The present situation on The Rock is nigh intolerable. The border is permanently closed on the Spanish side. This has resulted in a loss of employment for thousands of Spaniards who used to

cross from La Linea daily to work—for the labour requirements of The Rock far exceed any labour force that could
possibly be housed on it. The result is that workers are now
brought over from Morocco. As a further aggravation Spanish
air-space is now closed to planes to and from Gibraltar. This
makes landing on an inadequate air-strip still more hazardous
and leads also to a cat-and-mouse business of watching for and
complaining about accidental and trivial infringements. There
is a small colony of Scots on the Spanish mainland for whose
spiritual wellbeing John Lawrie is responsible. He used to drive
over from time to time, which took an hour or so. While the
border was still open the deliberate delays were such as could
cause the journey to stretch to over twelve hours, so that his
easiest way was to fly from Gibraltar to Africa and then fly
back from Africa to Spain. And now, of course, that is the only
possible way. Man's inhumanity to man can, at the lowest
estimate, cause a great deal of inconvenience.

The only place suitable for aircraft to land on Gibraltar is
the isthmus, and across this an air-strip was constructed parallel
with the Spanish border. In the nature of things it had a
maximum length of half a mile. To extend it there had to be
built what is literally a pier running out to sea, and this now
continues the strip for half a mile, giving a mile-long runway
altogether. Thus there is a constant and very real danger of
disaster. The incoming plane dare not touch down too soon or
it will reach the sea before the air-strip begins; it dare not
delay too long in touching down or it may run into the sea at
the other end. The problem is accentuated by the fact that the
Spanish air-space restrictions make it impossible to have a
straight run at it. To meet the needs of the emergency that
could so easily arise there is a most elaborate inshore rescue
unit on constant stand-by. To add to the difficulties, while the
east end is easily accessible by sea from the harbour, to get to
the west end involves sailing right round the peninsula and
even at the forty knots of which the rescue vessel is capable
this takes time. The unit is equipped with a huge rubber
dinghy with outboard motor and this can be launched immediately on the west side. But here too there is a problem—
an offshore reef causes huge waves that can lift the propeller
out of the water long enough for the craft to lose more way

that she has gained. So they begin by firing out to sea a fair-sized anchor with rope attached, and by hanging on to this they are able to progress, or at least literally to hold on to what progress they have made until the propeller is once again under water.

In the grounds of The Convent has been gathered a considerable collection of articles of historical interest, including a number of great, solid cast-iron shot five inches in diameter which, the legend explains, were fired into the fortress during the Great Siege—they were fired in red hot and the soldiers called them 'hot potatoes'. Metal was not too easily come-by on the island, so the defenders preserved these hot potatoes (once they had sufficiently cooled, presumably), fixed them in pairs with short lengths of chain and then returned them to the enemy. When you read about such exploits you wonder about the claim sometimes made that on humanitarian grounds we should stick to 'traditional weapons'. Things like hot potatoes and cannister and chained-shot and a cavalry charge were not designed with any kindlier intent than the hydrogen bomb, nor, I am sure, were their effects any less terrible from the recipient's point of view.

These things were much in my mind one day when we were shown over the modern battle cruiser *Antrim*. Rear-Admiral Hugo Hollins, who is now Flag Officer, Gibraltar, had been captain of the *Antrim* and we heard about her when he and his wife entertained us one day to lunch at The Mount. Captain David Lomar, the present captain, met us and showed us around. Instead of a bridge on top she's got a control room in the heart of the vessel—an affair of computers and radar-screens which, so far at least as I could follow the explanations so patiently given to me, not only tell you where to steer the ship but also tell you what targets to hit and when best to do so. The actual shots that are fired cost, I was told, £60,000 each, and they regretted their inability to put on an exhibition show for my benefit and hoped I would understand. For these missiles again, so far as I could follow it all, it's practically a case of affixing a label with the name and address of the proposed recipient and then putting them into space. Even if the addressee has 'gone away' in the interval the shot will pursue him with a pertinacity sadly lacking in our normal postal service. At least that's how it all sounded, although I'm sure it's not really so simple even with all the scientific aids of which the ship seemed in all conscience to have plenty. She was built on the Clyde, at Fairfields', at a cost of over £23,000,000. Hotter-than-hot potatoes!

For two hundred years the Royal Engineers have been represented on Gibraltar, and some part of the result of their activities has been the constant burrowing into the heart of the rock so that today there are many times as many miles of roadway inside the rock as there are on its surface. It began with the digging of the galleries high up on the rock in the attempt to get guns up to an advantageous position for attacking the attackers—returning the hot potatoes, with chains on. Before they had gone far with their blasting it was impossible to work because of the sulphur fumes. So they cut what were meant to be mere ventilating shafts but what came to be additional gun emplacements. An interesting series of galleries has resulted. But now they are digging nearer sea-level, and they have constructed a complete network of roadways (including an 'M1'), of magazines, of rooms and chambers. It would be possible, we were assured, to conduct a whole war from inside The Rock. Of what value that would be once the airstrip had been destroyed and the harbour bombed seemed an interesting question, but I did not ask it. Some things must be left top secret.

We visited all three Services under the guidance of the three Anglican chaplains, and we saw a great deal of the work they are doing to preserve the peace of the world, by being prepared for war. Last Assembly was much engaged—as have been many Assemblies in the past—with what has come to be called 'the doctrine of the just war'. I am sure I do not have anything new to contribute to that discussion. Let me just put on record how deeply I was impressed by the devotion and dedication of our men on the field and by the profound sense of responsibility with which they approach their terrifying task. It is not an enviable task. But as things are in our present-day world it seems to me to be a necessary task. And it is for us, the ordinary people of the world, rather than for them our conscripted specialists in war, to take the steps that shall ensure the coming of that day 'that man tae man, the warld o'er, shall brithers be for a' that'.

I felt that John Lawrie was doing his bit in a quite significant sense in this direction. For I think that, of all the services I conducted during the whole of my year, the service I took in St Andrew's Church in Gibraltar on the Friday evening of our visit was probably the most international and inter-denominational. The Roman Catholic Church was represented by no less than the Bishop of the diocese, as well as the local chaplain and a considerable number of laymen in positions of importance locally; there was a goodly number of Anglicans, and the Presbyterians and Free Churchmen were of all shapes and sizes. Racially I would hesitate to begin to produce a list. The Church was filled. A great tribute, I felt, to our Scots Kirk and a great personal triumph to our man on the spot. The Governor had assured me that John was the most highly respected man in Gibraltar, and after that Friday I could well believe it.

We left Gibraltar the following evening on a tight schedule. I was to be taking a service in Glasgow the next day at 11 o'clock in the Church of Roy Tuton, my junior chaplain, and it was to be televised and put out on the ITA network. The plane journey was pleasant and we arrived at Heathrow in good time (the previous night the airport had been fogbound and the plane had not left Gibraltar). A military car took us to Euston where we caught our sleeper, and that hammered on through the night, keeping good time all the way. We arrived in Glasgow, crossed the Clyde—all spot on time—and then sat for an interminable time waiting to move into the platform a few yards away. We got in, though, on time and all was well. While we were waiting it occurred to me to wonder whether there might be anything like the gun-and-anchor device used in the inshore rescue operation that we could fire on to the platform to get off the train and on with the broadcast. Maybe it was as well we managed without it!

CHAPTER 12

Native of No Mean City

It was during the war that one morning I read in the newspaper that the Government had appointed a committee of agricultural experts to look into some question of food production. I was visiting one of the farms in my parish and the subject happened to be mentioned. 'Tell me, Alex,' I asked, 'what exactly is an agricultural expert?' This I did more for mischief than for information, for Alex was a particularly shrewd citizen and his observations on many topics were well worthy to be recorded. 'Well,' said he with a solemnity befitting the gravity of the subject, 'tae let ye understaun', an agricultural expert's juist an ordinary fermer faur enough awa' frae hame.' Does not the Scripture assure us that a prophet is not without honour save in his own country. It's unlikely he'll ever be accepted as an expert amang his ain folk.

This doctrine I was quite prepared to apply to the circumstances of my own case. I had never been beset by any serious doubts about my ability to carry off the position of Moderator in Orkney or London or Paris, in which I was no more than a name and to which I came draped in the trappings of office. In districts where I was unknown I could reasonably hope that the breeches and the lace would both lend me dignity and help to conceal my deficiencies. But in Glasgow, my native city, in and around which my whole ministry had been performed—here the proposition was a vastly different one. Here were people who had been at school with me, who had worked beside me, who knew the members of my congregation, who had had ample opportunity of observing that the feet were of clay, and not very well fired clay at that. Here was an audience unlikely to be deceived by mere outward appearances. In a word, here I was not 'faur enough awa' frae hame' to pass as an expert—agricultural or ecclesiastical. Here, as the cynic might put it, I was among friends. Like the chairman in the story who in opening the proceedings said, 'I'm not going to call you Ladies and Gentlemen—I ken you all too weel for that.'

That was why I was so proud and happy that Glasgow should have been so obviously pleased at my nomination for Moderator and should have done so much to mark the occasion. Both the City and the Church—at Presbytery and at local congregational level—went out of their way to do me honour, and my brethren in the Presbytery were extraordinarily generous both in enabling me to have leave of absence for my period of office and generally in their understanding and help throughout. Of the vast pile of letters that had come to me at the time of my nomination none had been kindlier than those bearing a Glasgow postmark. For all the criticism that is hurled at it, for all the bad publicity it gets on the mass media, anyone who knows Glasgow at all knows well that it is no mean city—there is no more generous, open-hearted place in all the earth.

I could echo the words of the famous Glasgow comedian of yesterday who sang, 'I belang tae Glesca'. From personal experience I could not go on to reaffirm his further claim that on a Saturday nicht after suitable refreshment he came to feel that 'Glesca belangs tae me'—but at least I could understand and sympathise with the sentiment and with the conditions which gave birth to it. As happened to a minister who relinquished his seat on a crowded bus to an inebriated soldier, burdened with packs and bayonet and gas mask, who was being criticised on all hands for his failure to keep his feet in the passageway. 'Thenk ye, Minister,' said the inebriated warrior, 'ye're the only man on this bus who understands what it's like to be fu'.'

I was born in Glasgow, and although I can claim no personal credit for that fact I have always been very proud of it. Ours is a city that gets more than its adequate share of adverse publicity. Indeed, as the name of Whitstable is associated with native oysters, of Sheffield with cutlery, of Aberdeen with grey granite, so the name of Glasgow is for many associated with violence and thuggery. The stranger could be forgiven for imagining the average Glaswegian going around brandishing a bicycle-chain in one hand and carrying a razor in the other. In spite of all that the media have done to create and perpetuate this image, however, I have been surprised to discover how different is the picture of our city in the minds of many people.

For they think of it as first and foremost an intensely friendly place. This certainly is the impression I have gathered in countries as far away as Denmark and Holland. And equally certainly it represents what has been my own experience. No mean city but a greatly generous one.

It was in Glasgow that I received all of my education, the early part of it in two of the city's public schools where, I should say, the standard of teaching was extremely high. And then for seven years I attended Glasgow University—returning for another four sessions some twenty years later. It was during my first year at Gilmorehill that I fell under the spell of A. A. Bowman, Professor of Moral Philosophy, who I imagine did more than any agency the Kirk has ever been able to establish to direct men towards the ministry. Not that he did so in any deliberate fashion. It was just that his idealism—based on Kantian principles—conveyed itself so forcibly, just that his respect for human personality stamped itself so indelibly, just that his own faith manifested itself so winsomely, that none could escape being influenced. Outside the circle of my own home no single person has affected my own life so profoundly. And I am sure there are countless others who would bear the same testimony. Someone once said to me 'It's tragic that A. A. Bowman should have gone and not a single memorial to him in Gilmorehill.' 'Rubbish', I replied, 'Scotland's full of living memorials to Archie Bowman.'

Not but what there were others whose teaching meant much to me in those formative years—particularly perhaps those in the Theological Faculty, men one had the privilege of coming to know intimately and well. One feature which in my view was of great significance in this regard was that these men, whatever their academic qualifications, had all had the experience of serving for varying periods within the parish ministry. Today in so many cases young men of academic promise are moving straight from College into minor lectureships and so through an unbroken chain of academic posts into chairs. This is, of course, very much in line with the present-day tendency towards specialisation. Sometimes I wonder whether the cynic may not have been right in describing the specialist as someone who knows more and more about less and less until ultimately he reaches the stage of knowing everything about nothing. It is frightening, but true within my own experience, to say that I have never come across anyone more admirably cast for the role of Innocent Abroad than almost any one of the members of a Senatus Academicus when confronted with an everyday wordly problem of any complexity. And the respect so rightly accorded to such men within their own specialist sphere seems to blind them to their utter inadequacy outside of it. A blundering fool can be bad, a blundering professor can be much worse. A year or two in a parish is a discipline from which the most learned can profit much. It could be, of course, that the parish would not benefit to the same extent!

No list of institutions in which I gained my education would be complete which omitted the reading-room of *The Glasgow Herald*. In a day when the State recognised no obligation to assist with education beyond the level of school-leaving, the *Herald* performed an invaluable service for many Glasgow students by employing them on a part-time basis as copy-holders. The hours were from 5.30 in the evening till 1.30 next morning and the week ran from Sunday to Friday. Throughout the winter two students 'shared a desk'—that is to say they supplied a week between them, dividing the three nights each on any basis that was mutually agreeable. During the summer all the part-time men went on to a full-time basis, thereby providing the additional man-power to allow for holidays for the whole staff. From our point of view the one major snag in this otherwise excellent arrangement was that the holidays ran from the beginning of May to the end of September and so included the period of the degree examinations in each of these months. But no system is perfect. Going to bed at 3 and getting up at 7 is a habit to which you can accustom yourself. Though I must confess that when it was all over I found it even easier—not to say pleasanter—to accustom myself to a more normal routine.

It was just after the General Strike of 1926 that I started on the *Herald* staff. Vividly I remember that ill-fated venture of the trade unions to support their comrades in the coal-mines, and even more clearly I remember the spell of short-time working that followed in its wake and that got round to affecting even steady jobs like father's on the railway. My getting started in the reading-room and my consequent ability to bring in a pay-packet must have meant a great deal to mother who had managed so miraculously and without complaint over what I can now see constituted a period of the most acute difficulty. I can recall them still, those days of 1926 when the strike broke. Father, a devoted trade-unionist all his days, so deeply committed to the strike and all it stood for; and mother, capitalist and conservative (not that she had ever had any capital to conserve) who saw in the strike a threat to everything for which she had struggled and sacrificed so hard. In the early days father, idle by his own choice, saying, 'This is it; we can't desert our fellow-workers'; in the later days when he was idle by the company's choice, mother saying, 'What did I tell you?' They were not happy days in what up to that time had always been a happy home, and I was glad beyond words of the excitement and thrill of 'a job' to lift me out of the domestic depression, and even in a modest way to help to lift the depression. For by the standards of those days the rate-for-the-job was good—nothing less, in fact, than 14/6 a night.

To some extent, I suppose, I owed my job to that same General Strike. The *Herald* had been a 'union-shop', but the firm maintained that by walking out without notice, as they had done, the printers were in breach of their contract. The want of newspapers in those days when radio was still in its infancy created a situation so desperate it's difficult even to picture it today. In an attempt to cope with this the so-called *Emergency Press* was set up, and staffed by all sorts of people of limited experience and of no experience at all. As an exercise in typography it left much to be desired, as a means of disseminating news to a news-hungry populace it was an enormous success. Then one day in the columns of this *Emergency Press* there appeared an advertisement stating that Messrs Outram proposed to engage staff on a non-union basis, preference being given to former employees. No little stir was caused by this announcement, but in the event the majority of the printers went back on the new terms. There were some who did not, and in the general confusion and reorganisation I was able to secure one of the coveted posts as a copy-holder. And there I stayed for close on seven years. Except for a little break. After I had been on the job for nearly a year it was discovered that I had begun at the age of sixteen whereas the Factory Acts had ordained that no-one should be so employed on night work under the age of eighteen. The discovery having been made I wasn't allowed even to finish the week. But they did start me again on my eighteenth birthday.

It was a discipline in which one learned many useful lessons—or at least enjoyed the opportunity of so doing. Incidentally, how useful that distinction has often proved in the writing of testimonials—an exercise on which I think my brothers of today don't have to spend so much time as we did at the start of my ministry. There is on record the story of the lazy man whose testimonial read, 'Any firm that can persuade this man to work for them will be more fortunate than most.' One of my Houston farmers was approached by a former ploughman who said he was on the trail of a job and wondered whether he would give him a 'character'. 'I could gi'e ye that,' said his appreciative former employer, 'but I think ye micht manage better withoot it.'

As I was saying, it was a most useful discipline. One very valuable lesson for a young man destined to enjoy the considerable protection which the ministry affords was the experience of working with other people and of doing so at a very low point on the status list. At the bottom of it in fact, for with the possible exception of the office cat the copy-holder was the lowest form of life known in the printing business. All type after being 'set' is 'proofed' and the proofs are 'read'. This represents a joint effort in which two participate—first the reader, a tradesman printer who holds the proof and marks the corrections upon it, and secondly the copy-holder, a person of limited ability (or, it was frequently alleged, of none) who holds the 'copy'—that is, the manuscript from which the printer had worked in setting up the type. It was the copy-holder's duty to read aloud from the manuscript, and in those days a great deal of it was literally manuscript, and some of it quite illegible at that. If any howlers did slip through to the paper it could usually be shown that the fault lay squarely with the copy-holder.

A useful discipline, too, that of learning to be particular about detail, to be fastidious about spelling (particularly about the spelling of proper names), to be careful about the correct form of designations, to be consistent in style. All of this side of the business should properly have been attended to at editorial level. But in the rush to get copy out, much of it was neglected and so it came to us. After all, we were at that point 'where the buck stops', so we had to do the checking. *Who's Who*, *Debrett's Peerage*, *Post Office* and *County Directories*, *Whitaker's Almanack*, *Pears' Encyclopaedia*—these were our library—along with *Webster's Dictionary*—and they were much consulted. It is from these days that there dates my horror of wrongly-spelt names—for to me these have always seemed a mild form of insult to the person addressed. Before discovering who the person is I acquire a deep dislike and a profound distrust of the correspondent who has marked the envelope 'Rev Adam Hearne'. Even awarding me degrees I don't possess annoys, though it should doubtless flatter, me.

With a view to achieving consistency in matters where there is room for diversity in practice we had a house-style which provided, for example, that words like sheep-stealer, cattle-dealer, pig-breeder be hyphenated, while certain other terms including crossbred, greyfaced, shorthorn were treated as one word. This led on one occasion to our achieving an unhappy distinction when we reported a meeting in Perth of the 'Blackfaced Sheep-breeders of Scotland'. Punch produced a most effective little picture of a group of Zulus supported on Harry Lauder walking-sticks and accompanied by tartan collie-dogs. A useful discipline here too, if you will—of learning always to bear in mind the object for which the rule was devised rather than slavishly to follow it.

One's general knowledge, too, was considerably widened in consequence of a spell at a reader's desk, and—what can be equally important—one learned where to go in search of the answer when one didn't know it off-hand. There are many departments of human activity where, I'm sure, it's a pity to clutter up the mind with a mass of detail—sufficient to have a neat mental classification of what the authorities are and where they are to be found. For quite a few years in the reading-room I had as my reader one, Jimmie Mackintosh, who in the matter of general knowledge and common sense had one of the best stocked and best equipped minds it has ever been my good fortune to encounter. Of formal education he had enjoyed little, having left school at fourteen, having been all sorts of things from a message-boy to a 'super' in the theatre, before becoming a signaller in the Royal Artillery in the First World War. When in a discursive mood he had stories to tell of all sorts of adventures, from dashing across the stage in the old Theatre Royal as a Scottish soldier and then a few moments later pursuing himself in an English uniform hastily donned behind the scenes, to breaking-in South American mules at Redford Barracks in snow and ice—and as he told them it made great listening. Much of the spare time through the day with which constant night-shift provided him he spent walking the streets and haunting the docks, and, being equipped with a keen eye and a retentive memory, he knew Glasgow as few people do, and his acquaintance with commercial geography was phenomenal. And he had a vast fund of common sense, that most uncommon of all the senses. For there must be a dozen people with perfect vision or hearing or touch for each one fully fitted with the sense called 'common'. It was an education to be with this man who himself had been so little educated.

Probably the most valuable experience I had in these seven years was that of getting to know something from the inside about how newspapers function both editorially and typographically. I am happy to record that throughout my ministry my relations with the Press have ever been of the most cordial; reporters I have found a kindly bunch who in all my experience have consistently matched courtesy with courtesy and met confidence with confidence. Not infrequently I have fed them background information to help them in their understanding of a situation, with a proviso that it must not be used. I have never yet been let down—I could have been in real trouble if I had. They can be annoying, mighty annoying; they can be a perfect nuisance; but they have a job to do which is of supreme importance to the nation, for, as I see it, without a free Press democracy could not survive, and we have a duty to co-operate with them even when, as often happens, the matter is one we would be happy to see battened down under hatches. News has been defined as what somebody somewhere doesn't want to see published. It's hardly an exhaustive definition, but it's true as far as it goes.

When visiting London during my year I was very proud to be given a luncheon in the Fleet Street office of *The Daily*

Express by Sir Max Aitken, and also to be given a luncheon at the BBC by Mr Charles Curran, the Director-General. For I devoutly believe in the importance of good relations between Church and Press and between Church and Radio.

Of all the many irritating features of Press relations easily the worst from the point of view of a person like the Moderator is the anxiety of the newspapers to secure statements straight off the cuff and then to treat them as official pronouncements—to confuse ex-cuff with ex-cathedra, as one might say. It's highly unsatisfactory. It happens like this. A high-powered Commission is set up by the Government under the chairmanship of Lord Kilbrandon to examine the working of Scottish marriage-law and to make recommendations. The Commission sits for months studying the subject in all its complexity, considering written submissions, hearing evidence, consulting registrars and others, and so on. A full, detailed and painstaking report is prepared, running to, we'll say, 120 pages of closely printed and closely reasoned material. One afternoon my phone rings and a voice explains, 'This is your old friend Bertie Blogg of the Daily Distress. Sorry to disturb you and all that, but . . .' and he goes on to wonder whether you know that the Kilbrandon Report on Marriage-law is now out on a release for tomorrow morning. The main provisions are . . . and he mumbles into the phone a few blurred and scarcely-comprehensible phrases, ending with the inevitable, 'Would you care to make a comment?' You may well explain that you're deeply interested in the subject and if he'll let you have sight of the Report you'll let him have your comments in writing in a couple of days. Wearily he explains that he's trying to produce a newspaper, not to write a history-book, and could he have your comment now. Being a good-natured chap you decide to oblige and so make some half-baked observations. If they're sufficiently ill-considered you'll likely be reported fairly fully; if they're positively irresponsible you'll be quoted in black type, your photo will appear, and you'll find yourself described as a 'Kirk Leader'. If you can contrive to 'rap' the proposals this will give especial satisfaction and may even secure your photo appearing on the front page. The only comfort I'm ever able to glean in such a situation is to reflect that the glory of a seven-day wonder is that by the eighth day it's forgotten altogether.

I'm sure too it was these years in the *Herald* that helped to equip me for the Convenership of our Church's Committee on Publications. The work on which we were here engaged I found intensely interesting and challenging, and I like to think that during the nine years of my Convenership the Committee made some progress. Not that anybody should be a Convener all that long—five years at that time, now four, is the maximum which the Standing Orders allow. But just when I was reaching the end of my five-year stint we carried through a massive programme of reorganisation in consequence of which the Committee on Publications became the Department of Publicity and Publication, and I agreed to stay on for a couple of years longer to supervise the transition; then for another; then for yet another. Our activities were many and varied. We produced a monthly magazine, *Life and Work*, with a circulation in the region of two hundred thousand; we ran bookshops in all four cities; we conducted a small publishing house, the Saint Andrew Press; part of the time we were responsible for a newspaper, *The British Weekly*; and latterly we ran a Press, Publicity and Information Office that turned out to be an instrument of the utmost value. For all the success that attended our efforts—and it was considerable—I can claim little personal credit beyond a degree of quite remarkable good luck in choosing the right people for the various appointments.

There is no question today whether the Church can afford to be in publicity—the simple fact is that today the Church cannot afford not to be in publicity. It could with complete accuracy be said that the Church has always been a press agency, its business being to spread news—the Good News. At a time when the public is so much dependent upon the media for providing them with ready-made judgments or at least with pre-packed evidence on which to form their own judgments, it is essential that the Kirk should be in closest touch with these media and should be acutely self-conscious in the matter of the image of herself which she is projecting. An office like our PPIO, well-staffed with professional people who are good Churchmen, and well-equipped to do its job in an efficient up-to-date fashion, is, it seems to me, an absolute necessity for any Church that is to make its mark in the space-age world.

It was particularly pleasant to reap something of the harvest of my own sowing in this field. Little had I thought when I persuaded Bruce Cannon to take on the appointment of Press Officer, and made other arrangements with the aid of Denis Duncan for the equipping of the new office, that I would later as Moderator so much benefit from what that office would be able to do for me.

While I am abundantly satisfied with our efforts at establishing contact with the Press I have never felt that as a Church we were taking the fullest advantage of the opportunities for evangelism which television offers to us. I do not myself know the answer, but I feel there must be an answer. I do know that we have a fair amount of television time put at our disposal both on BBC and on Independent channels, and I know that there is a vast body of goodwill and readiness to help on the technical side in the production of suitable material. And while many interesting, instructive and helpful programmes are getting across I still feel that we're missing out disastrously on the full exploitation of the medium's potential We're providing pleasure for the bona fide Churchman, a nostalgic feast for the lapsed Churchman, an invaluable service for the house-bound, and interest for the unconcerned. But I cannot believe we're presenting the challenge of the Gospel with sufficient force to the uncommitted. If it's worth the money for the manufacturer of a detergent to spend thousands of pounds for a few seconds of time in which to convince people that his product can make their underwear whiter than white, then surely in all the minutes that are so freely given to us as a Kirk we should be able to do something really significant in commending the cleansing properties of the Gospel.

All of which is very far removed from the reading-room of *The Glasgow Herald*, and yet I think the two are closely enough linked in my own life-story; and I am eternally grateful for these years, for the people with whom they brought me in contact, and for all the insights they provided.

CHAPTER 13

Biggest Presbytery in the World

It was towards the end of March, a couple of months before I was due to take up office as Moderator of Assembly, that the Presbytery of Glasgow organised a lunch in my honour to be held in the City Chambers. To mark the occasion of my 'elevation' they presented me with my robes of office and a cheque. The affair was an exceedingly happy one, but for me the true pleasure lay in the thought that my brethren of the Presbytery should have felt they wanted to do this for me.

It was, I suppose, no more than a coincidence, but I saw it as a most fortuitous one, that the Moderator of Presbytery at the time should have been Jack Stewart, Minister at Colston Milton, one of our northern Church Extension charges; for Jack had been a youth in Springburn Hill Church when I began my ministry as Assistant there—little more than a youth myself. They were hard bitter days those of 'the hungry 'thirties'. I went to Springburn in 1933 when the depression was at its most depressing. The principal industry was the building of locomotives—there were no fewer than four separate works in the district—but there were other industries too, mostly connected with the railways. Then there were two locomotive running-sheds, Eastfield and St Rollox, employing, normally, considerable numbers of men. When I went to Springburn Hill there were over three thousand names on the Communion Roll, and of the fifteen hundred or so families which this represented I am sure that more than half must have been dependent in some way and to some extent upon the railway. They were the days of the 'pay-off'—they hadn't got round to calling it 'redundancy' then; the days of the hated means-test and the only slightly less detested 'dole'; days when a man was terrified to grow old, for no firm would engage a worker over the age of forty, and after six months unemployment a man's name was taken off the books and he had to be re-engaged. There was at that time a very special significance in the text, 'Now the man was above forty years old on whom this miracle was performed.'

Ministers today understandably complain about the difficulty of visiting where work claims the attention of the whole household throughout the day, and 'the telly' throughout the evening. There was no such difficulty in those days. It was only too easy to see the whole family at home of an afternoon. I doubt if there were a dozen families in the whole congregation where there was full employment; I am certain that in a couple of hundred cases there was full unemployment. I think of a father, three big strapping sons and two clever lassies, all trying to fill in idle hours week after week in the hope that a job would turn up for at least one of them. Yet life went on somehow, and, generally speaking, spirits remained high. There was marrying and giving in marriage, bairns were born; though, only too tragically often, we had to bury as well as to baptise them. The mothers had often come to child-birth ill-prepared and ill-fed, there was not the wherewithal to care for the children so that illness when it came took its toll. My abiding picture of Springburn Road is of an undertaker's car with four men sitting in unaccustomed navy-blue suits, the two in the back seat having a little white box across their knees. When people talk to me about 'the good old days' I'm afraid it is that picture that springs to my mind. Just how people kept going as they did, just how they were able to believe that things were bound to get better soon, was more than I could understand. In the winter you'd hear them say, 'Surely things'll tak' a turn efter Ne'erday'; and in the spring it was, 'If the Fair was by there's bound to be an improvement'. There were those too who didn't worry overmuch, witness the following conversation which I overheard between two girls in a paper-shop. Said the one, 'Did ye ken that Maggie Smith's gettin' mairit next Friday?' Replied the other, 'Naw. Wha's she gettin' mairit on to?' (A girl in Springburn always got mairit 'on to' someone.) 'It's yon big chap, Willie. Ach ye're bound to ken him. She's been gaun wi' him steady for a while.' 'Oh ay, him. But I didna ken he was workin'.' And then the punch-line, 'Naw, nether he is, but he's a rare dancer.' It's all a matter of getting your priorities right.

It's an odd thing in a way that we Scots have applied the hated title 'bishop' to one of the kindliest relationships that the

Kirk knows—that between an Assistant and the Minister he serves. I had been tremendously fortunate in having as my bishop Rev J. Stuart Cameron, at that time at the very zenith of his powers as a preacher, a pastor, an administrator and a presbyter. With the unfailing help of his wife, Stuart Cameron was able to run Springburn Hill congregation with extreme efficiency and to create within it a spirit of the warmest friendship. It was a haven of light in a day of deep darkness.

When I see some of today's shoddily-dressed, hair-encrusted students I think of what we were like in those days. Our bishop was a stickler for the proprieties and it must have been quite a sight even then—it would be regarded as a vast joke today—to see the pair of us complete in frock coats and silk hats walking down the hill together after a Sunday Service. And yet I venture to think that beneath these two 'lum hats' there was to be found a quite unrivalled knowledge of the men and the women and the children who formed the membership of that vast congregation, of their problems and their difficulties and their sorrows. Not even a good knowledge of the congregation, though, can save you from the odd stupid mistake. I remember Mrs Cameron asking me one day whether, since I lived on the south side of the city, I would visit a Mrs Walker who had just been admitted to the Samaritan Hospital. By one of those queer freaks of mental aberration that I suppose can afflict any one of us I presented myself next day at the Victoria Infirmary and enquired at Information as to the whereabouts of Mrs Walker. They hadn't any trace of her. But they insisted on making further enquiries. They were still busily engaged on these when I realised I had come to the wrong place, but I hadn't the heart to tell them. I assured them, though, that I must have been misinformed and not to bother; but to no avail, they persevered with their further research. I felt sure they were going to admit a Mrs Walker specifically for my benefit, so keen were they to oblige. Hurrying away at length I hastened to the Samaritan to resume my search. I was really surprised when they too denied all knowledge of any Mrs Walker. Later in the day I sought out Mrs Cameron and told her my sad tale. 'O dear me,' she exclaimed, 'did I say Mrs Walker—I will call that woman Walker—her name's Fraser.' When Shakespeare wrote his famous line about a rose by any other name he was, clearly, not thinking about the business of keeping hospital records.

From all of which it must be easy to understand what pleasure it gave me to have Jack Stewart presiding and his wife participating at the ceremony in the City Chambers. For I had been ordained in the Church at Springburn Hill, and that on the evening of Whitsunday, a day supremely suitable, surely, for invoking the presence of the Holy Spirit. It was the first time there had been an ordination in that Church, for all their ministers had come already ordained and all their assistants had left as licentiates. Stuart Cameron was desperately enthusiastic about the event and for weeks beforehand he 'plugged' it on every possible occasion. He had printed, I remember, twelve hundred copies of the Order of Service, and as these were handed out at the door supplies ran out while still the congregation poured in. Amazing to me that Jack was able to produce one of these very Orders of Service on that day thirty-seven years later.

Jack himself has had a quite remarkable career. A prisoner of war throughout most of the period of hostilities he returned to studies after his release, qualified for the ministry, and went to start a new cause in a part of that very parish where he had been reared, a part where during his boyhood corn had grown and cows had pastured. He is still there, having built up one of the healthiest congregations in our city, and that by dint of sheer hard work, unswerving devotion and personal magnetism —in all of which Maisie has played her full share. I believe there is much room today for a type of ministry new and different from the traditional; but when people tell me that the older type of preaching and visiting ministry has had its chips and is now meaningless I point to Jack's parish to refute their contention. Given the proper circumstances I am sure that kind of ministry has still much to offer to the Kirk.

Here we were, then, sitting side by side at the top table—the one Moderator, the other Clerk of what is usually claimed to be the biggest Presbytery in the world. I do not myself know what is the truth of this claim and, not being an American, I am not unduly concerned one way or the other. Certainly it is the biggest Presbytery in the Church of Scotland, and certainly it is as big as any Presbytery ought to be. Some would say it is too big. No-one should find it surprising that the biggest city in Scotland has the biggest presbytery, and unless Glasgow gets smaller—as it is doing—I cannot myself see the Presbytery being appreciably reduced. The number of charges has been steadily dwindling due to readjustments of one kind and another following upon the great movement of population that has occurred in recent years. A comparison between the time when I was in Springburn and today shows in round figures that in these thirty-five years twenty new charges have been created on the perimeter of the city and that a hundred and twenty have disappeared from the centre. At present the ministerial strength of the Presbytery is almost exactly three hundred and there has to be precisely the same number of elders, giving us a total strength of six hundred. It's big enough to constitute a kind of mini-Assembly, and for many purposes it is on these lines that it has to be organised.

It was in 1952, while I was still in the early stages of my studies in law, that I was appointed Clerk to the Presbytery of Paisley. This, naturally, was a part-time job, but Paisley with sixty charges was big enough to ensure that the work was both interesting and instructive. And though Paisley is the largest town in Scotland (the four places that exceed it in population-figures are all cities) it is sufficiently small for people to know one another and for there to be a very keen consciousness of belonging. To be a Paisley buddie is a real distinction. This spirit added greatly to the enjoyment of my position and may go some way to explain why, on my nomination as Moderator, I was invited back to the Presbytery of Paisley to be presented with the Inverness cape which is one of the most useful items of the Moderatorial attire.

I suppose it was inevitable when the Presbytery of Glasgow advertised for a successor to Dr John Sinclair, who was retiring after fourteen years as Clerk, that my attention should have been directed to the notice and that a number of people should have suggested that I ought to apply. Had all these hints come from Paisley people I might have been a trifle worried, but not a few friends in Glasgow, as well as others whom I scarcely knew, put in their word in support of my being interested. I was far from sure what to do. I was extremely happy in Houston, happy in the Presbytery clerkship there, and happy with my legal interests in Paisley which had latterly built up to quite a connection. Besides, a naturally lazy and unadventurous nature inclined me to leave well alone—or to work away with the devil I knew, according to the way you care to put it. On the other hand I had got to that stage in life—the half-century mark—when I had either to move or to decide I was staying put for the remainder of my time in the ministry. Nor could one ignore that there was much to attract in the Glasgow possibility. Not having myself seen the advertisement I did not know there was a closing date for applications. There were those who said to me, 'Just slap in an application and if they get around to making you an offer you can decide whether or not you want to go.' This I found utterly unconvincing. My attitude was that if I applied it was because I both wanted to go and meant to be successful. Hence my hesitation. In the end I wrote an application and had it typed, and for some days left it lying in a drawer in my desk; then I signed it, put a stamp on the envelope and carried it around in my pocket for a few more days; then I made my decision and popped the letter into a pillar-box. All unaware, I had posted it in time to arrive on the closing day for the receipt of applications. I was duly appointed and have been forever grateful that I didn't carry the letter in my pocket for yet another day.

In any Presbytery at any time the duties of the Clerk are full of interest and rich in reward. Nowhere is this more true than in Glasgow where they are so enormously varied, and at no time has it been more true than in this day of massive change. On a strict interpretation the duty of the Clerk is to arrange the business for meetings, to keep a record of the decisions reached, and to carry through the necessary correspondence and executive action arising out of the business transacted. All this has its importance, but there is little here that could not be done—probably much better done—by a properly qualified layman. The Clerk, however, has also a duty to be an adviser to ministers and members on all matters of law and procedure, as well as on more ordinary things. This is where the human element enters in so largely and where in consequence the interest mounts. I find people's attitude to Church law quite intriguing. There are those who see in its provisions a simple but effective weapon with which to fell their opponent (given,

of course, the right to interpret the law in their own way);
there are those who go in constant fear and dread of the law as
something that will surely one day trip them up; there are
those who see it as a chain to fetter others but as an irrelevance
to be set aside, as red tape to be cut, when it gets in their own
way. There are those who want to be constantly quoting it and
those who want to be constantly repudiating it. For myself I
have always urged ministers—they are the worst offenders—
to keep the relevant Act in the background as something to
which they can appeal should all else fail. Convince people that
the course proposed is the right and proper one and add, if
you like, that it enjoys the further advantage of being the only
course they can legally follow. In face of my strong advice to
the contrary a man once insisted to his Kirk Session that out
of a certain sum of money that was available they were bound
to make first of all 'an appropriate supplement' to his stipend.
The possibility which, to his great amusement, I had outlined
to him in advance materialised—they voted him a shilling!

It might be said in passing that there can at times be a
considerable element of embarassment in this aspect of the
work of the Clerk. How often have I had the experience of an
elder coming to see me to discuss 'something that happened at
the Session last night', and while he was sitting there to receive
a phone call from the minister wanting advice 'on a row that
blew up at yesterday's Session meeting'. On occasion it is
difficult to believe that each is describing the same event. When
you're designing your office it's of first importance to ensure
that there is a way out that doesn't lead past the waiting-room.
In ordinary legal practice the difficulty is met by sending the
second client to another solicitor, but I have no other Presbytery
Clerk to whom I can direct the other party. In any case my
job is not to set the scene for litigation but to try to get the
parties together for reconciliation.

The third element in the work of a Clerk is that of being a
minister to the ministers, of being pastor pastorum. This, of
course, is no part of the official duties, and no minister is bound
to accept the Clerk in this capacity. It is this in fact which constitutes the real strength of the Clerk's position. It's because a
man's not bound to come to me, because he's perfectly at
liberty to tell me what to do with my advice that I'm often able

to help him. In some ways this is the most thankless, even if it
is the most rewarding, aspect of one's work. For in the case
where a minister comes to you when he's in some serious
trouble, and you are able to get the tangle straightened out
and the man set on the rails again, then nobody in the Presbytery knows anything about it. And, believe me, this kind
of exercise is never easy but always exhausting both physically
and spiritually. It's only your failures for which you get any
credit, for they are the cases that have to be duly reported to
the Presbytery with a view to action at an official level. But if
there is little credit there is enormous satisfaction in dealing
with human problems in all their most intensely and intimately
human aspects. Thanks to the teaching of Professor Bowman
I've always been able to see this kind of situation as the problem
of a man involved in a difficulty, never as a 'case' involving a
man. And I like to think that under God I've been able on
occasion to help a brother in need.

They had been eleven wonderful years these we had spent in
the Presbytery of Glasgow and I felt they had reached a high
peak at the moment when, after suitable speeches by the
Moderator and the Lord Provost, Maisie Stewart 'robed' me
in the full splendour of my Moderatorial gown—with all its
tassells. It was with a full heart that I thanked the fathers and
brethren for this further expression of their goodness and goodwill towards me. I went on to say that many people had asked
me during the past weeks just what I hoped to do as Moderator,
and that while my immediate reaction had always been to say
'to keep out of trouble' I realised there was more to it than that.
Because, for all the disclaimers we care to issue, the Moderator
has come to be looked upon as a kind of leader in the Kirk.
I went on—

I am convinced that people in the Kirk today are anxiously
looking for the emergence of leadership, are intently listening for
the voice of prophecy. They see the Kirk in dire straits and, for all
the lip-service they insist on paying to democratic techniques, they
don't for a moment imagine that salvation is going to come from
more meetings of more committees, even if they are called commissions, or that a solution will emerge through the mere counting
of heads, even if the votes—or the heads themselves for that matter—
are fed into a computer.

So much criticism is being levelled these days at our committee system. Generally it's criticism on the fringe—about the size of committees, or about how often membership changes, or about how the budget is prepared. But deep down behind all this superficial fault-finding there lies a terrible impatience with a system whose results have been so dismally inadequate. People want to hear the Kirk speak out loud and clear a message for the day and its problems, without apology and without equivocation; instead they hear a heated debate on the precise position of a comma in the first amendment to the second counter-motion on the third section of the deliverance. They want to see the Kirk going places; instead they see a group of Churchmen gathered round a committee-room table studying travel brochures. A cumbrous, expensive and laborious committee system has produced little more than a condition of loquacious inertia.

After some comments upon the relation of the Moderator to all this, and after a reference to the Duke of Plazatoro who, you may remember, led his regiment from behind because he found it less exciting, I went on to say—

I doubt if anybody would want to have—I most certainly would not want to be—a Plazatoro Moderator, leading the Kirk from behind the pages of the blue-book of Assembly Reports or from behind a well-thumbed copy of Cox's *Practice and Procedure*. Less exciting—yes. Safer—yes. But if we can't stand excitement we should never have come into the service of the crucified Christ, if all we want is to be safe we should most surely never have entered its ministry.

It is my earnest hope and prayer that in this year it may be given me on occasion to say a word that will help the Kirk in facing the problems presented by this age of such wonderful opportunity if also of such daunting difficulty. At least I promise you this—that if I feel such a word has been given me to speak it will not be fear of the excitement that will keep me silent. I hope that in seeking to discharge the peculiar duties of this peculiar office in my own still more peculiar fashion I may not unduly embarass either the Presbytery of Glasgow or the Kirk as a whole. But I should be less than honest did I not hasten to add that I will feel a great opportunity has been missed if I don't contrive to give you all at least some gey anxious moments.

All of this was fully reported in the Press next day—all fairly enough except that *The Scotsman* chose to present the whole thing as an attack on a moribund committee system, and, as *The Scotsman* is the Edinburgh paper and is read by the Committee Secretaries and by the Establishment in general, I saw myself getting off to a very bad start and felt real glad to know I would have the Presbytery of Glasgow to return to for shelter when it was all over.

CHAPTER 14

Church in a Changing City

It was by courtesy of the Lord Provost that the City Chambers were put at our disposal for the presentation of robes. For this I was extremely grateful not only because of the splendid setting which the rooms provided, but also because of the way in which it emphasised the link between the Church and the City—a point further underlined by the presence of the Lord and Lady Provost. Later on in the course of my year the Lord Provost, Sir Donald Liddle, himself an elder of the Kirk, gave a Civic Reception in our honour, and this again was held in these same rooms. A very pleasant evening it turned out to be.

The City Chambers in Glasgow (or the Municipal Buildings as we called them in my young days) represent one of the finest examples I know of Victoriana at its most confident and resplendent. Begun in 1883 as the outcome of two competitions in design, the outward appearance of the building is one of rather grand and somewhat pompous and self-conscious solidity, but it is inside that you meet what might be described as grandeur on the grand scale—marble staircases, mahogany wainscoting, stained-glass windows, and ceilings that must have provided a headache (and a backache) for both plasterer and painter. It is, I am sure, a reflection of the Victorian Glasgow that produced it, of the wealth it had accumulated, of the position it had established for itself, but, even more, of the feeling of utter confidence and security it had been able to maintain even in face of the occasional set-back. In a way it might almost be seen as a gesture of defiance at the failure of the City of Glasgow Bank a few years earlier, with all that that had meant. The men who commissioned, designed and built the City Chambers were not irked by care or fretted by doubt— today was surely theirs, and, they thought, tomorrow also. In may ways it's a lovely place, even if a little frightening in its self-confidence. It has been described as 'the grand civic gesture par excellence'. Were it to be destroyed—by fire, for example—it could never be replaced. It's not just that we don't have that kind of money today; we no longer know that degree of assurance.

The City Chambers provided, as I say, a most beautiful setting for our function. But my principal concern was that in a way it symbolised the link that I believe still exists—even if of a more tenuous kind than at one time—between Church and City. After all, the motto of our city is not just, as some would be happy to see it, 'Let Glasgow flourish' but is 'Let Glasgow flourish by the preaching of the Word and the glorifying of Thy Name'. I doubt if there ever has been a time when it was more important than it is today to maintain the closest bond between those responsible for the government of our city and those whose duty it is to direct the affairs of the Church within that City. For Glasgow today is a changing city, changing at a rate and to an extent greater far, I am sure, than was the case during the Industrial Revolution which created the present city. A Church which claims to serve the people of that city, if it is to keep pace with these changes, must itself be constantly and drastically altering the pattern of its agencies, the method of its organisation, the mode of its presentation of the Gospel. As I once remarked in the Assembly, we cannot hope to solve the problems of the Space Age with the ecclesiastical machinery of the Industrial Revolution.

It was in the middle of the nineteenth century that Glasgow grew to such an amazing extent. The great new industries that were being established in the city were attracting people by the thousand, and their housing needs were being met by the erection, by private enterprise, of great streets of tenement-type houses, solidly built and well-designed and well-equipped according to the standards of the time. Having been built as an investment they were let to the tenants. A few years ago I had occasion to look into the history of a congregation whose Church was being torn down to make way for the Inner Ring Road, and I was interested to discover that it was just over a hundred years since a group of people had made an approach to the Free Church Presbytery for permission to put up this building 'on the western fringe of the city . . . to serve the new community that is growing up in that part'. I was reminded that my own father used to tell of how when he came to Glasgow just before the turn of the century he had lodged in that very part and from his window could see the corn being harvested and the cattle grazing. And today the Inner (sic) Ring Road passes through it.

The solidity and stability of these buildings has in the long term been one of their great disadvantages. Because long after they have ceased to provide an acceptable degree of amenity they have continued to stand firm. So when the great wave of rehousing occurred between the wars it was to fresh fields and pastures new that the planners turned, the city boundaries were extended in every direction and vast 'housing schemes' sprawled over what had been the green fringe of the city. There seemed to be a kind of naïve conviction that every man is still at heart something of the original Adam, and that given a home with a piece of ground attached to it a multitude of miniature Gardens of Eden will emerge and the pubs and the slums disappear. Hence the emergence of the 'four-in-a-block cottage-type' of design that set the pattern for so much of the housing that grew up between the wars. Unhappily the money that should have bought spades and mattocks and hoes went instead in most cases into bus fares back to the old familiar haunts. And neglected gardens are even more depressing than tar-macadam. So the garden idea was abandoned and the later sprawl took a different form; but there was still sadly lacking any kind of character that could have given rise to a sense of community or any kind of amenity that might have made the people want to spend their time in the area. Hence the concrete jungle.

Clearly all of this colossal movement of population presented the Kirk with an enormous problem, though in the early stages it was basically a simple problem of finance—if any financial problem can be called simple. The city was more than adequately supplied with kirk buildings but these were all in the older areas, and if any significant attempt was to be made to help people as they faced the new start in life that was offered to them on moving into a new home equipped with all mod cons then the Church had to be on the spot and not a mile and a half down the road. Thus the great Dr John White and his National Church Extension project, with its motto of 'the Church in the Midst'. In the years between the wars, and in the years after the last war after the building restrictions had been

lifted, Church Extension has done a quite amazing job in the
erection of Churches and Halls in the new housing areas—and
not least within the Presbytery of Glasgow. I can think of
forty Churches in the Presbytery that belong to this era and
that owe their existence to Church Extension. Given the money
there was little question of how it ought to be used.

The rehousing situation is totally different today. Two
factors have been responsible for the dramatic change that has
taken place. First that there were no more pastures new.
Apart from any question of whether it was desirable to go on
sprawling in this kind of fashion, the simple fact was that there
was no more virgin land on which to spill out. Secondly there
was the relentless deterioration in the quality of the older
properties within the city. Thanks to a short-sighted policy of
rent control a situation had arisen where property-owners had
no money to spend on their buildings beyond the most urgent
repairs, and over the years this has told a tale, even on the solid
Glasgow tenement. As well as being sub-standard many buildings were becoming unsafe. So attention had to be turned to
the extraordinarily challenging but also extremely complicated
business of redesigning and rebuilding almost the whole of that
city which the Industrial Revolution had thrown up.

Obviously so basic and fundamental a scheme of replanning
provided an unprecedented opportunity for looking at the road
pattern. A system designed for tramcars and horse-drawn
vehicles leaves much to be desired in a day of buses and
private-cars. So in simple terms we begin by laying down an
inner ring road with motorways and express-ways branching
off in every direction to provide safe, fast lines of communication with the whole of the country around. The city thus
carved up with roadways—segmented like some enormous
grape-fruit—can then be planned in Comprehensive Development Areas to provide for residential, commercial and industrial
needs. It's easy, of course—and tempting—to represent this as
a case of planning a system of roads and then fitting a city into
the blanks that have been left; it's tempting to suggest that
when it's finished you'll be able to reach the centre from the
southern perimeter in five minutes flat, that you won't be
allowed to stop there because of the parking restrictions, but
that a further five minutes flat will take you out to the northern

perimeter; it's tempting to taunt that you've made such elaborate arrangements for motor-cars to get to Glasgow that there'll be no Glasgow left for them to get to. Such criticisms are, I think, unfair. It would be a pity, naturally, for Glasgow to be blotted out for the sake of building a fast road to it; but it would be a pity too in this day of the motor-car to have a city to which and in which you can't drive safely and quickly.

Frankly, the thing that worries me most about our wonderful network of roads is a lurking suspicion that one day—and perhaps in the not-too-distant future at that—transport will take a new form and our grand new motorways will be as worthless tomorrow as our abandoned railway-lines are today. Planning must of necessity work on the assumption that progress will continue up a ramp. In fact it sometimes goes up a step. Had our forefathers been wise in their generation they would have done a survey—in depth, I doubt not—of the increase in the number of horse-drawn carriages coming into the city daily and we should have had the city-centre cluttered with stables and hay-lofts. And we today would have been confronted with an even more intractable problem. An equally dramatic change in the pattern of transport is not beyond the bounds of possibility, and that even before the last interchange spaghetti is completed.

The situation today, then, is that we have in Glasgow a rebuilding programme of quite unprecedented magnitude. It is not just that changes are occurring, it is that the stable things against which we should normally have been inclined to see the changes occurring are themselves disintegrating and dissolving before our incredulous eyes. In my closing speech at the Assembly I told a story which has subsequently gained wide currency. 'I moved recently into a new office at the west end of Bath Street in the new Renfield Church Centre. A friend was coming to see me the other day and I had explained to him exactly how to get there. He is a Glasgow man born and bred and would have claimed to know every inch of the city, but he has been in a country parish for the past ten years. He got to where he thought Charing Cross ought to have been and was looking around the wilderness of desolation trying to identify some landmark when he espied what was obviously a citizen in 'bunnet and muffler' admiring the activities of the earth-moving equipment. Touching him on the shoulder my friend said, "Tell me, if I go along here will I find Elmbank Street?" "Ay," replied the citizen, "if ye hurry".'

As I see it, one of the most promising features of this fast-changing city is the emergence, for the first time since the city was built, of something like a parish system. The new roads are to be available only to vehicular traffic and therefore create barriers comparable to the old railway lines. In this way the city finds itself divided up into segments. With schools and shopping centres and community facilities all conspiring to draw people into the heart of the Development Area, there seems a real opportunity for the creation of a community consciousness and pride-of-belonging such as has been found in the past to a limited extent in only a few places—Dennistoun, Springburn, Tollcross spring readily to mind. It is in this kind of situation that the Kirk has its duty and its peculiar opportunity—if it has the courage to accept a new pattern suited to the needs of today.

It was at this very juncture in the history of the Kirk that I came to be Presbytery Clerk in Glasgow and found myself of necessity grappling with the multifarious questions raised by this changing situation. Immediately I realised that we had to act quickly and decisively if we were to dictate the shape of our future, and not be dragged along at the heels of a housing programme. Immediately too I recognised the folly of the position that had at first been adopted, of saying that the Church must not be interfered with in any of the changes. As if we could carry on as though nothing were happening in the midst of a revolution! It was clear to me also that the only point at which one can intervene effectively to determine the emerging pattern is at the drawing-board stage. Once the bull-dozers have moved in it is far too late to do anything— except get out the dust-covers. Unhappily congregations incline—perhaps naturally enough—to want to wait and see how things are going to work out before they commit themselves to decisions that will deeply affect their own future. It's amazing how people who claim to stand for a faith prefer an insurance. The message that we can't afford to wait is increasingly getting across today, but in the early days it was indeed hard to convince people that they must try to envisage

what things were going to be like in ten or fifteen years' time
and to take steps now to equip themselves for that future.

As it happened, the area which was on the Planning Department's drawing-board at the time when I drew in my chair to
the Clerk's desk was the district of Anderston, which was to be
radically affected by the building of a new high-level bridge
over the Clyde as part of the west flank of the Inner Ring Road.
A very interesting district it was. Anderston was at one time a
village of weavers lying midway between Partick and Glasgow.
Further east was to be found another clachan, Brownsfield, in
the green fields north of the river before one reached Glasgow.
At the time when it came to be enveloped in the city Anderston
was one of the most heavily populated districts. At one time or
another it has contained no fewer than fourteen congregations
of what is now the re-united Church of Scotland, but when my
attention was directed to the area the congregations were down
to three in number. Once the work of rebuilding was completed the total population of the area was to be as low as six
thousand—scarcely enough by modern standards to justify a
single congregation. Obviously then our objective must be the
achievement of one new well-equipped Church to replace the
three out-of-date structures that were there. When a local authority compulsorily acquires property it pays compensation
at the rate of the current market value of property of that kind,
a figure hotly and laboriously contested between the seller's
agent on the one side and the District Valuer on the other.
When, however, the subjects are such that there is no normal
market for them, and where there is a bona fide intention to
continue in spite of the disturbance, compensation is to be at
the rate of the reasonable cost of equivalent reinstatement. So
I approached the Corporation with a proposal whereby they
would meet the cost of a new Church and Halls in Anderston
and we in return would give them not just the one Church that
lay in the way of the bridge approaches, but all three of them.
I put my proposition first to the planners because, as I saw it,
they were the people most likely to be attracted by the thought
of three cleared sites and least likely to be frightened-off by the
price. Then I moved to the Town Clerk's department, and
finally to the District Valuer. In the end we got the agreement
of them all.

So far so good. Instead, however, of that being the end it was just the beginning of my troubles. What I had now to do was to sell the idea to the three congregations—for with us there is still a great measure of autonomy residing with the congregation. Meeting after meeting was held with office-bearers, first in their separate groups and then jointly. How clearly I remember trying to portray—with maps and sketches and word-pictures—this ring road that would go 'under Sauchiehall Street, then over the blue trains in front of the Mitchell Library, then under St Vincent Street, then start to rise to cross the river at a great height'. As the whole area affected was then solid with buildings and as most of my audience had all their lives known it this way it was, admittedly, far from easy for them to envisage all this.

It was a great day for me, no less than for Archie Russell, the minister who had worked so hard all the way through, when in 1968 the then Moderator of Assembly, James Longmuir, came through to Glasgow and in a televised service dedicated the new and well-designed building that is now the Church of the Parish of Anderston. For not only had I established a Church; I had established a principle and a pattern. When we discuss a comparable situation with office-bearers today the phrase inevitably emerges, 'along the lines of the Anderston project'.

One thing that has greatly pleased me has been that since the new Church of Anderston has become a going concern many sceptics and critics in the Corporation have come round to seeing that the Church has something quite unique to offer in the way of community service. In the last few years Local Authorities have been made increasingly aware of their obligations in regard to social work, and, like the proverbial new broom, they have taken great pride in sweeping very clean, being a little contemptuous of all the cleansing devices that had been in the field for a long time beforehand. Now the sharp edges are wearing off the bristles of the new broom and Local Authorities are coming to recognise the difficulties in this department of work, and at the same time are inclining to recognise that the Church has something to contribute, something that no other institution can possibly supply. There were not wanting in Corporation circles those who saw in the bill for a new Church in Anderston (£220,000) a piece of highway robbery perpetrated by an unprincipled Presbytery under the guidance of a smart lawyer for Clerk. More and more those critics are being heard now to say that it has been the best spent quarter of a million in the whole project—for they have a piece of quite vital community work that cost them nothing more than the capital outlay of buildings. This clearly is a view I very much want to encourage. For I devoutly believe that in creating these new Comprehensive Development Areas the local authority and the Church have a common problem and a common responsibility and that they will succeed or fail together. The future therefore has to be visualised as presenting the same challenge and opportunity to both of us together—that of creating new communities in which people will want to live, not just schemes to which they will be directed and from which they will yearn to return. Existing legislation, if it can be liberally construed, provides the mechanism for a joint exercise in planning that could lead to the creation not only of new houses for people to live in but of a new and better way of life for people to enjoy.

There are in the city a considerable number of Comprehensive Development Areas—twenty-nine in all—and each of them has differences from the others and presents its own peculiar problems and difficulties. In such a situation to evolve even the most general kind of pattern must be a gradual process. It has to be borne in mind, though, that it's not a problem lying wholly within the field of Corporation planning —the Kirk itself within its own structure has many long-accepted patterns at which we must take a long, hard look, asking about their suitability and acceptability in the changing situation of today. At the moment, for example, there are in Glasgow 162 charges and I imagine that fifty is as many as we are entitled to expect to maintain on any long-term view of the future. At the same time I am sure that 162 ministers is not at all too many. After all, a sixth of the population of Scotland is in Glasgow, and even at present strength we have only about a twelfth of the ministerial manpower. If something along this line—reducing the number of charges and maintaining the ministerial strength—is to be achieved there must be drastic changes in our traditional pattern and the Church-on-the-corner with its one-man ministry cannot survive. And while most of our people are prepared—even keen sometimes—to talk about change, few of them are willing to welcome its implications when they come home to roost in their own parish.

One very interesting experiment of recent times culminated in the creation of the Renfield Church Centre, in which our Presbytery Offices are now situated. For close on a century Renfield Street Church had stood at one of Glasgow's busiest crossings, the corner of Renfield and Sauchiehall Streets. In days gone by it had been a preaching station outside which the queues had formed of a Sunday evening, but the demand for that kind of thing is no more. The hall accommodation was utterly inadequate, the condition of the fabric deteriorating, the congregation dwindling, financial difficulties increasing. Various approaches had been made from commercial concerns, culminating in an offer of close on £700,000 for the building for redevelopment. The congregational constitution was such that a sale could be concluded by the trustees only if seventy-five per cent of the members attending a congregational meeting voted in favour. Although it was forcefully pointed out that, at this capital value, for every man attending on a given Sunday it was costing close on £10 to provide a spot on which to place his posterior, it took two attempts before the required majority was secured. The congregation then united with another whose buildings were threatened by the Inner Ring Road; a disused but very lovely Church in Bath Street was purchased, as was also a block of offices next door to it. The Church was completely cleaned up, refurnished and redecorated, and the offices were demolished and on the site was erected a great complex of halls, meeting rooms, gymnasium, lounge and public dining-room. The whole venture cost the kind of money which in normal circumstances the Kirk would not have at its disposal. It's early days yet to pass any kind of final judgment on how the experiment is going to work, and how far the very heavy outlays are going to be justified, but at the moment the signs are exceedingly hopeful. And it's good that we've been able at the very least to make the experiment.

One problem which ought not to be our particular affair at all but which is coming to create for us a great deal of trouble, and to occupy an inordinate amount of attention, arises from the fact that not uncommonly our Churches represent buildings of historical or architectural interest—one is the only example of a Church designed by an architect of international repute ('people come from all over Europe to see it'); another has a steeple which provides a punctuation-mark in an otherwise horizontal building-line ('take down the steeple and the whole character of a most attractive street is lost'); another has unique fenestration ('the greatest living authority refers to it specifically in his book'); another represents the only example in Britain of this particular treatment of the west front ('some would say this was a cause for gratitude'); and so on. What is to happen when such a building no longer houses a viable congregation? Had it been a grocer's shop of peculiar design and all the customers had left the district I don't imagine any question would arise; but somehow with the Kirk it's felt that the same rules should not apply.

When two congregations unite there is invariably controversy as to which set of buildings is to be used, and it's most unfortunate when outsiders exert pressure in favour of one of them for reasons which have nothing to do with their adequacy or suitability to serve the needs of the united congregation. Let it be that it has been at length decided that a building in this category is superfluous to our requirements. What then? Of recent years there has been introduced legislation which provides for buildings being 'listed' thereby putting restrictions upon their demolition, alteration or change of use. The owner is given no opportunity to make representations on the matter— he can only say Goodbye to his asset as it is rendered unrealisable.

This issue of the fate of the superfluous building provided us a few years ago with quite a *cause célèbre*. The case was that of the Park Church on Woodlands Hill. The position here is that on this hill there is a group of magnificent Victorian terraces— quite unique in Britain, I understand. In the heart of the area soon after 1843 the Free Church built its College, distinguishing it with a great square campanile. Beside it they built the College Church (now the library of the college) and this carried two much smaller square Lombard towers. Some years later a Parish Church was erected just opposite the College to

the design of William Rochead. The nave was of a fairly plain
and uninteresting Gothic design, but at the east end was a
beautifully decorated square Gothic tower, and—more by
accident than by design, I'm sure—the four square towers
dominated the crown of the hill and together formed a most
pleasing skyline.

The Victorian residences—I hesitate to call them 'houses'—
the Victorian residences have over the past thirty years been
steadily and relentlessly converted into offices. While the façade
of the terrace-front has been scrupulously preserved, the
interiors (often surpassingly lovely) have in many cases been
completely gutted, while at the rear emergency-stairs, toilets,
strong-rooms have been affixed in the most outrageous fashion.
The result inevitably has been that the area as a whole has
ceased to be residential and the Park Church in the centre of
it all was faced with a fast-dwindling congregation, all that
remained of it being drawn from outwith the district. The time
came when the Presbytery could no longer allow them to have
a minister. What to do with the building? The site was a
prestige one in the very centre of an area of high-quality offices.
Clearly enough we recognised that for such a site we could not
expect to get planning permission in principle in any straightforward way. So we engaged Derek Stephenson, an architect of
distinction, and he came up with a plan for an eleven-storey
office-tower of attractive design and superior finish. For this
specific project we applied for planning permission, believing
that given that permission we could sell the plan—and the
site—to a developer for a considerable sum. We had a model
constructed and did a number of mock-up photographs showing
the end result. The publication of these hit the headlines and
produced the most amazing outburst I have experienced in
years. The Presbytery were characterised as Philistines, Shy-
locks, Rachmans, money-grubbers, and many other unpleasant
things besides. Needless to say, the Clerk was seen to be the
worst of the lot—a positive Goliath, chief of the Philistines.
Everyone, it should be said, seemed to agree that the office-
tower represented a most attractive plan, but, they said, not on
the Park Church site.

As time went on it became apparent that in face of such
clamant opposition the Corporation Planning Committee

would not grant the necessary permission, so we turned our minds to producing something that would commend itself. Consultation was had with the planning officials and together we explored three other possible ideas. Eventually it was indicated that sympathetic consideration might be given to an office-block of four storeys on the site of the nave, the tower being retained and completely restored. A full-scale project was prepared along these lines and a fresh application lodged. Again there was opposition. It was now discovered that the nave no less than the tower was of great architectural merit. All kinds of suggestions were mooted for a use for the building as it stood, ranging from a museum of armour to a shopping-precinct under cover. It would be true to say that the degree of thoroughness and dogged perseverance shown by the police when beating the woods for the murder weapon was equalled by the preservationists in their search for an acceptable use for the building—but all with a quite conspicuous lack of success. The same lack of success was later to attend an appeal issued by the Corporation for an indication of contributions that would be forthcoming for the purchase and preservation of the premises. People were prepared to give advice; they drew the line at giving money.

Although they had no use for the Church, the Corporation—as they were bound to do in terms of the statute—now offered to buy it at the price it might have been expected to fetch had we been free to develop. This figure we calculated at £80,000 and the highest the Estates Department was prepared to go was £25,000. The margin was too wide. I think we might have settled for £50,000—at least it's a lot of money to gamble with, especially when it's not your own money. Along that line, then, we made no progress. Why, you may ask, were we so anxious to realise the full price, why not allow the citizens to continue to enjoy the skyline in exchange for a nominal figure of compensation? Quite simply because a Church which is trying to serve the needs of a changing city cannot afford to throw away its assets—there are few enough of them in all conscience. Normally our buildings are more of an embarrassment than an asset, expensive even to demolish. But here was a site the value of which could erect two modest Church Extension projects where they were desperately needed on the perimeter of the

city. Had that building on Woodlands Hill belonged to an
otherwise penniless old man would it have been argued that he
could survive on social security while his asset, which could
easily have brought him £4000 a year, remained frozen so that
the citizens might take pleasure in the sight of the icicle? That,
as I saw it, was very much the kind of position in which the
Church was being placed.

The final outcome (it took some years to achieve) was that
planning permission was given for the modified scheme and a
developer was found prepared to pay £126,000 for the site
alone. This enabled us to build a Church at Giffnock, to make
a grant of £30,000 towards additional halls for an East Kilbride
congregation, and to put in hand the building of a Church at
Priesthill. But for this profitable sale none of these projects
would have got off the ground.

At the time of writing a Glasgow congregation with no great
financial resources is whipping up £5000 to repair part of its
steeple. Admitted that the steeple is a particularly lovely one,
agreed that it represents a punctuation mark in an otherwise
horizontal line, conceded that it has either to be repaired or
demolished and that the latter too would prove a costly
proposition; still, from the point of view of the congregation,
it's a mighty expensive comma, there are so many better uses
to which they could put £5000. I stand firmly by what I once
wrote in the course of a heated newspaper controversy on the
subject, 'Ours is a Ministry of the Word, not a Ministry of
Works; our interest is in men, not in monuments; our concern
is to build up live congregations, not to shore up dead buildings.'

Conservation (like 'environment') is very much in the air
today, and let us be grateful that an interest is being taken to
preserve for the generations to come some at least of the great
works of the generations that are gone. But there must be a
limit to how much can be preserved, and standards of significance must be established. A city should have a museum; it
should not be a museum. We in the Church are perhaps unfortunate in that so large a proportion of our buildings are
either of historical or of architectural interest. With the result
that—or so it feels—we get more than our fair share of the
retentionists' attention. For having erected and maintained
through a couple of centuries a building that has been a thing

of beauty for all to admire (free of charge) it's a poor reward when you no longer require the building but desperately need the price of the site to be told that you must keep the building there in all time coming and do without the value of the site. Had your forbear had the good sense to put up an ugly thing that had defaced the fair earth for generations you would no doubt have been encouraged—even subsidised, who knows—to get rid of it. This whole business of the conservation of buildings is one that needs to be looked at extremely closely and thought through much more carefully than has yet been done. Merely to clap a conservation order on a property does nothing to solve existing problems but only to create a few new ones.

CHAPTER 15

'*When in Rome . . .*'

'Europe, Israel and the Americas' must appear a queer collection of geographical bedfellows. Actually it refers to one of three divisions into which for administrative purposes the work of our Overseas Council is divided. Since the days of the great missionary outreach of last century we have had extensive fields of activity on the continent of Africa and on the sub-continent of India—they are all now grouped in two main divisions, Africa and India. For one historical reason or another we also carry responsibilities in Jamaica, Bermuda, the Bahamas, Argentina and other corners of the American continent; then the work of the former Jewish Mission Committee, centred largely in Israel, continues to provide us with an opportunity and a challenge; and for generations there have been outposts of the Scots Kirk in cities on the continent of Europe. All of these last-named bits and pieces are grouped together to form one administrative unit—'Europe, Israel and the Americas'.

The official list of the Moderator's engagements takes him each year to one of the three divisions in turn, the particular part of the field varying from one triennium to the next. As it happened, the 'miscellaneous' group fell to my lot, and since, three years before, Jim Longmuir had gone to the Caribbean it was thought proper that I might visit Israel and some at least of the stations on the Continent. The difficulty at the practical level was of course that of getting from one to another when the bunch is so scattered. I was personally responsible for the suggestion that I might take my own car and travel by road from point to point, resorting to a plane once we got so far as Rome to take us on to Israel and Cyprus, and then returning through Europe so as to take in a few more of our places on the way back. In this way we should be able to spend a few days at each of our stations and to have a few days 'off the hook' when journeying from one to the next. A period of eight weeks would, I thought, be adequate for us to complete the round trip. The idea commended itself to the Committee concerned and we got busy.

It was on Monday 13th March that we set off for our tour, and we did so in a car packed like the proverbial 'tinkers' flittin'.' At the time of departure it was bitterly cold—the roads were white with hoar (cranreuch, as we call it) on the morning we left, and in the late afternoon of that same day we had to abandon an attempt to enjoy a walk in London, it was so cold. Yet our journey was to take us steadily southward towards more temperate climes, and with the passing of the days one was entitled to expect warmer weather. A month later we were sweltering at just below a hundred degrees Fahrenheit at the Dead Sea. So every type of clothing had to be included. As there would be few opportunities for visiting laundries we had to take many changes of raiment. In fact there was little left at home. Luckily my car has an enormous boot, so we were not restricted in the number of cases. The Press indicated a desire to come and photograph us setting off, but on learning that this event was to occur at 5 o'clock on Monday morning they opted to come along on the Sunday evening and 'do some shots' of us packing the boot. I do not know whether they got a better picture that way; but they certainly got a better reception.

An uneventful drive brought us to London in the early afternoon. I'd hate to have to live in London, but I dearly love a walk in its streets—denied us this time by the intense cold. We were to attend a dinner in the evening in the Guard Room at Lambeth Palace, when the Archbishop of Canterbury along with the Lord Chamberlain entertained a party in connection with the launching of an appeal by the Ecumenical Institute for Advanced Theological Studies in Jerusalem—one of those bodies of which as Moderator I found myself a patron. Some time later, when in Israel, we had the opportunity of visiting the Institute which is situated at Tantur about four miles from Jerusalem on the road to Bethlehem, on a site with a most wonderful outlook.

Next day we set off for Dover, from which we were to sail in the late afternoon. I was glad we were able to spend a few hours in Canterbury, and glad too that though the weather was still very cold the sun shone during our time there. Canterbury is one of the few places that for me really invokes a feeling of

the past. Other places that have the same effect are Chester
and Rye and York—particularly York, where I always expect
to turn a corner and meet a coach trundling in or see a man in
top-boots leaping into the saddle. Were I to be sailing away
from this land never to return, the parting picture of England
I should want to take with me would be one of Canterbury
rather than of the white cliffs of Dover, which, when we came
to part from them an hour or two later, gave the impression
that a long steep in one of those detergents that remove bio-
logical stains would not have come amiss.

It was perhaps as well we had a couple of days wandering
gently through Western France before we were due to reach
Paris, for it gave me a chance of getting accustomed to continental driving before having to face the hazards of the capital.
We had been a few times to Scandinavia with the car and I
considered myself something of an authority on driving on the
wrong side. Not like the man in the story. 'Going to Bournemouth for your holiday again this year?' asked his friend. 'No,'
he replied, 'we thought we'd be a bit adventurous this year and
take the car over to the continent.' 'That will be an adventure.
You'll take a wee while to get accustomed to driving on the
right.' 'Driving on the right?' the timorous one enquired. 'Oh
yes, didn't you know, you always keep to the right on the
continent.' They met again some weeks later and the friend
enquired how the continental holiday had gone. 'We changed
our minds and just went back to Bournemouth. In fact it was
you who put us off with telling us about keeping to the right.
I tried it here for a day or two. It's positively dangerous.'

For anyone accustomed to observing even the most ele-
mentary rules of the road the experience of the traffic in Paris
is something to be reckoned with. At one point we saw a
gendarme waving his baton madly while cars fought their way
around him on every side, utterly regardless. Beyond adding
whistle-blowing to the baton-waving he could do nothing about
it. Admittedly Parisian traffic is orderly and well-conducted by
comparison with the Roman variety. At least in the French
capital they appeared to wait until they had some excuse, however trivial, before blaring their horns; in the Italian they
required none. Indeed it seemed to me that as the Parisian
speaks with his hands so the Roman drives with his horn. You

know the tale, perhaps, of the Frenchman who on a trip to England had been arrested and spent the night in the cells. In the morning on his appearance in court he easily persuaded the magistrate that the whole thing had arisen out of an unfortunate misunderstanding. 'But why', asked the sympathetic bench, 'why did you not explain all this to the policeman at the time?' ''ow could I?' retorted the Frenchman with a flourish of his arm, 'I vos 'an'cuffed.' I feel sure that a puncture would be less of a handicap to the Roman motorist than the loss of his horn.

But I must not anticipate and get to Italy before we're properly into France. A very generous invitation had come for us to stay at the British Embassy with Sir Christopher and Lady Soames, and it was thither that we were heading—or trying to head. Having, or so it seemed, much time in hand we spent a few hours at Versailles walking in the gardens, and from there we set off (at about eight miles an hour, it transpired) for Paris. Coming at length in sight of the Eiffel Tower and espying a motorway we decided our troubles were now at an end—an opinion we were to change radically when we discovered we were being borne relentlessly, if not very rapidly, away from the city. Contriving at length to detach ourselves from the motorway I was fortunate to find a taxi and with my limited knowledge of French I managed to persuade the driver to guide us to the Rue Fauburg St Honoré. All I could remember about 'following' in French was the picture postcard of the boy and the donkey and the statement, 'Je suis ce que je suis.' But just how to make it applicable to a taxi I was not very clear, and, in any case, I doubted whether the driver might appreciate the reference to a donkey.

It was on a later occasion, on the road between Paris and Genoa, as we were driving into a town in one of whose hotels we were booked for the night, I found myself thinking of all the man-hours I had spent at school wrestling, at times with *la plume de ma tante*, at others with irregular verbs. Surely, I thought, I should be able to pass myself off in a bit of friendly chatter with a hotel receptionist. I accordingly prepared a few suitable remarks about the state of the weather, leading in to an explanation that they had accommodation booked in our name. Arrived at the hotel my first disappointment was to

discover that instead of the charming mam'selle I had antici-
pated I was confronted by a stern-faced Frenchman exuding
that hard Gallic realism which is the other side of French
charm. Undaunted I unloaded my piece. Gazing at me with a
look of unbounded incredulity he enquired, 'You speak
Engleesh?' I spoke English.

It was many years ago during a holiday in Norway that my
wife and I drove up to the very grand hotel in the town of
Dombas. An elderly gentleman with a fair proficiency in
English was on duty at the reception desk. He produced the
usual form to be completed by aliens. Noticing that under
'Nationality' I had entered 'Scottish' he said to me, 'You are
not English?' 'Oh no,' I replied with some enthusiasm, 'we are
not English; we are Scottish. British, yes. English, no.' He
looked a bit puzzled. Anxious to clear up the point I said to
him, 'You are Norwegian?' Happily he smiled acknowledgment.
I went on, 'You are Scandinavian?' He admitted it, even if, I
thought, a trifle grudgingly. I persisted, 'You are Swedish?'
His hands flew up in the air and he denied the allegation in at
least three different languages simultaneously. 'You see, then,
what I mean when I say that I am Scottish?' He smiled complete and sympathetic comprehension. An hour or so later I
was passing his desk and he beckoned me over. 'You speak
English,' he said reprovingly. I gave up the attempt to explain
the point further. To tell the truth, I don't know that I could
have explained it further.

Unhappily from our point of view, President Pompidou chose
the very day of our arrival in Paris to announce his intention to
submit to a referendum of the French people the question of
Britain's entry into the European Community. This caused
quite a stir in diplomatic circles and led to our host having to
dash off to London to a Cabinet meeting. He left us, however,
in the care of his most charming wife, Mary Churchill, a very
wonderful hostess and a vitally radiant personality. We were
talking one day about her father and I said to her that on any
occasion when I found myself doubting the value of preaching
and wondering whether the spoken word any longer had any
influence I recalled Winston Churchill's wartime broadcasts and
realised that any inadequacy there might be lay not in the
spoken word but in my inability to speak it. It's hard—near

impossible in fact—to convey to a generation that didn't live through those days just how much the Churchill broadcasts meant to the whole nation. Phrases like 'Never was so much owed by so many to so few' and 'some chicken; some neck' have been adopted into the language, but they are poor, cold things when torn from their context, and they do nothing to bring alive the spirit of the talks. Properly to appreciate them one has to recapture the atmosphere of the blackout and the wailing sirens and the desperate stories of disaster in each day's paper; one has to hear again the tone of voice in which people said they were hurrying home—'We'll need to be in by 9 o'clock; Churchill's on'; one has to catch again the sound of the thick slurred voice (any police officer hearing him say 'British constitution' would instantly have whipped out a breathalyser); and to visualise the company sitting around the radio, hanging on to every word, imbibing fresh hope like a shrivelled plant sucking up water. Thinking of these broadcasts one can understand what the Psalmist had in mind when he said of a man that he may be 'as the shadow of a great rock in a thirsty land'.

Our Church in Paris today is a fairly modest affair in the Rue Bayard, serving Scots and others in the Presbyterian tradition, who for one reason or another, temporary or permanent, are in or near the French capital. The present building is a new one erected to replace the Church destroyed during the war. That Church and Manse of the war days gained considerable and deserved fame because of the part they played in assisting escaped prisoners and others. It has all been written down by the minister of those days, Donald C. Caskie, under the title of *The Tartan Pimpernel*. It is a much less exciting and dramatic but no less important task that is being undertaken by the present minister, W. M. Dempster, who for so long was Secretary of the Church's Huts and Canteens Committee, a Committee that did such a tremendous job throughout the war, and for years after in the days of conscription, serving Scots— and indeed men of every nationality—through its agencies in many parts of the world. It's an odd thing, perhaps, but our cause in Paris has suffered through the improvement in travel facilities in recent years. Not so long ago when a young chap or a girl was sent by their firm—it happened often to accountants, journalists and others—to work for a spell in Paris, then if they were Scots they probably found themselves drawn at the weekend to the Kirk where they met others of their own kind. Today they may well become commuters, flying home at least every second week-end.

From the moment we had crossed the channel the sun had shone brilliantly and relentlessly; so it was in something of a holiday spirit that on the Monday morning we set off from Paris with the knowledge that our next engagement was not until Thursday afternoon in Genoa. We had planned the trip in such a way as to keep us off motorways at least as far as Nice, and to have to cover no more than 250 miles in a day. This gave us time to relax a bit and to enjoy the beauties of the French countryside which in the valleys of the Loire and of the Rhone we found very pleasant.

In Genoa we were guests of the consul, William Lyle, and his wife, a delightful couple from Fife who were at great pains to ensure that we'd enjoy to the full the couple of days we had to spend with them in their home, which is part of a magnificent villa overlooking much of the heart of the city—a city I was deeply sorry we had neither time nor opportunity to explore. Genoa and Florence are the two places in Italy to which I feel we must return with time—and lire—to spend.

Our cause in Genoa might be more accurately described as a seaman's mission than as a Church. There is a small resident congregation, but the main part of the work is done among the sailors using the busy seaport. Our man has advance news of every arriving vessel and is always among the first on board. Our premises are at the very harbour gates, and are able to extend their welcome even before the army of prostitutes that of an evening lines the street. A new man had recently been appointed to take over from Alex M'Vicar who had spent the past twenty years in Genoa. At the Assembly I had had the pleasure of giving the official blessing to Dane Sherrard and his wife as, along with a group of others, they set off for their respective postings abroad. Since taking over, Dane and Rachel had been working tremendously hard to remodel the quite considerable premises, and in particular to create a proper Chapel for regular services to be held. In the past they have had to depend upon the goodness of the Anglican community for a monthly opportunity from October to June to worship in their Church. They had made a fine job (even if the paint was no more than dry) and it had been planned that I should dedicate the Chapel on the occasion of my visit—as I was most happy to do, in presence of a widely representative congregation, on the Friday evening. Personally I had been a bit worried when the hour of the service came round and less than a dozen of the lovely new chairs were occupied, but I was assured that at least half an hour had to be allowed before you were even entitled to think of a person as a late-comer. We started thirty minutes after the hour appointed and even at that there were many who dropped in right through the service.

A somewhat unusual, and to us most enjoyable, feature of our visit to Genoa was a lunch given in our honour on board the *Kinnaird Castle* by the Master, Captain Briggs. I gather the connection between the ship and the seaman's mission was a close one—the Chief Engineer, shaking hands as he welcomed us aboard, apologised for the paint on his hands as he had just been putting some finishing touches to the decoration of the Chapel, and quite a few of the officers we met again in the evening in the mission canteen where a tea-party was held after the dedication service.

We visited the International Evangelic Hospital, a small hospital perched on the edge of a hill where a job of rebuilding and extending is going on under circumstances of indescribable difficulty, owing to the nature of the land and of the crowded surroundings. But if ever I saw enthusiasm and dedication I saw them on the face of the Director (a Waldensian) who took us around. He had us leaping over concrete-mixers, balancing on planks far above the ground, leaning through holes in the wall, as he portrayed for us what the ultimate set-up was going to be and envisaged the great work they were going to be able to do once it was all complete. In an age when so many couldn't care less, it was a tonic to spend an hour in his company even if there were moments on the scaffolding when we feared we might end up as patients in his hospital.

From Genoa to Rome by motorway is about 350 miles, and except for the regular stops to part with a few hundred lire by way of toll there is nothing to keep you back. It can, though, be quite an expensive business this of motorway travel in Italy.

In the case of the road from Genoa there seemed less excuse for charges than on the road to Genoa round the coast from the French border. That road appealed to me as a positive master-piece of modern engineering. Following a coastline where bays alternate with great ribs of mountain running down and out into the sea, the road maintains an even level all the way round, tunnelling through the mountains and bridging over the great gullies—the *galleria* and the *viadotta* constantly alternat-ing. Scarcely a yard of the road seems to benefit from the natural contours of the terrain, and the cost of building must have been phenomenal. From the point of view of scenery it must be a poor show compared with the old road that wound around as near to the sea as possible, but there comes a time when the most romantic of us is prepared to sacrifice some of the scenery for the sake of getting there.

We arrived in Rome itself with a good map of the city and a clear idea of where we wanted to get to, but, unhappily, with-out the least clue as to where exactly we were. Our ignorance on this score appeared to be shared by a couple of policemen whom I confronted with the map. To tell the truth I was glad to get away from them without further complication, for I had a suspicion they were considering inviting me to accompany them to the station there to explain how I came to be in possession of such a document in the first place. Some time later (and some miles nearer the heart of the city) I espied another pair of very smartly uniformed officers of police, clearly of high rank, who, I felt sure, would be happy to help me, and who might even be able to read a map. I pulled the car into what I thought was a suitable corner and ran after them. Scarcely had I begun my story when the most frightful clanging of a bell aroused in my mind a feeling that I might have left the car in the path of a tramcar. The officers too were alerted to this fact and one of them courteously pointed to a spot to which I ought to move. Having done this and got out of the car I looked round for my two friends only to see their back view as they walked away from the scene, happy, obviously, in the consciousness of a job well done.

In the event it took as long from our arrival at the outskirts of the city until we finally pulled up at our hotel in the Via Quattre Fontanes, as it had taken us to cover the 350 miles from Genoa. From our hotel to the Church could be done very comfortably on foot in five minutes, walking the wrong way of the one-way streets; if you did it in twenty minutes in a car you were extremely lucky, and at the busy times it would take much longer. The ostensible reason for the one-way system and for the other restrictions is, I am told, to discourage traffic in the historic part of the city—all it seemed to me to achieve was to dislocate the traffic. I believe the phrase about 'hastening slowly' comes from the Latin, but I have never been in any city where the traffic drove so fast or took so long to get there. Leave a yard between yourself and the man in front and some-one would push into the space; leave three yards and someone would drive through the space; stop at the red lights and someone behind would blow his horn at you; and the end-product one vast snarl-up of honking cars. It was with a feeling of considerable relief that I finally drove our car into the area in front of our Church there to remain during our stay in the city and later while we were in Israel and Cyprus.

There was one matter regarding our visit, however, on which Alex Maclean, our man in Rome since 1956, had not taken the responsibility of reaching a decision—whether I was to visit the Pope. This was a question that I alone could decide. A few days before leaving home, at a Press conference regarding the forthcoming tour, one of the reporters hearing that Rome was on the itinerary had asked, 'Obvious question: will you be visiting the Pope?' To which, without thought, I had snapped back, 'Obvious answer: it's manners to wait till you're asked.' It seemed a good enough answer at the time and my inclination now was to think it was a fairly good answer at any time. Exactly ten years had elapsed since Dr A. C. Craig, the Moderator of that year, had made his historic call at the Vatican. Archie was going out to Rome to participate in a centenary celebration in Alex Maclean's congregation, and the question was raised whether during his stay in the city he might call upon Pope John, both of them being well known for their devotion to the ecumenical ideal. As so often happens in such cases, the Press saw the makings of a good story. The result was that what might have occurred naturally and spontaneously was given the appearance of a major issue of ecclesiastical policy. A complication arose from the fact that it was believed our people in Rome were not sympathetic to the idea. A further complication arose from a threat that some of the down-with-the-Pope organisations in Scotland would be represented by men with banners. In the event it was agreed that in certain circumstances the Moderator was to feel free to visit the Pope, and this in fact he did. Incidentally, Archie's reaction to Roman traffic must have been much akin to my own. The priest who acted as interpreter at his audience was telling me that when Pope John spoke of the Scots as having a deep faith the Moderator replied that he was sure the same must be true of the citizens of Rome. His Holiness had expressed some little surprise—he hadn't, apparently, noticed much evidence of this—and Archie explained that without such faith he didn't see how they could ever bring themselves to cross the street.

In the course of the Saturday evening of our arrival I had a phone call from Canon Purdy, the English Secretary of one of the Vatican Departments, who wondered whether I should want to seek an audience. I said I had come to visit our Scots people and felt I should not want to be doing so. In the end, however, I received a formal invitation to visit His Holiness on the Monday morning, and this, as I saw it, bare courtesy required me to accept—as I was happy and pleased to do. Arrived at the Vatican on the Monday morning we first of all spent some time with the members of the Secretariat for Christian Unity, and then I was taken by Father Hamer, the acting Benedictine head of the Secretariat (who was to act as interpreter when that was needed) into the private library where, for close on half an hour, the Pope and I discussed the desirability of closer unity and the desperate need of the present-day world for the Christian evangel. We spoke a little too about Northern Ireland. It was all very platitudinous; nothing was said that was either new or of world-shattering significance. But it did seem a sign of grace that we could thus converse together as representatives of two Churches in Scotland which have inclined overmuch to waste in strife and mutual recrimination resources sore needed in the struggle against our common foe. Later we were joined by my wife, the Macleans and Canon Purdy, and, at the Pope's suggestion, we stood in a semi-circle and repeated together each in his own tongue our Lord's own prayer—an experience which I found especially moving.

I had been warned that if I paid a visit to the Vatican it was usual for a small exchange of gifts to take place. I had been grateful for the warning, and in case the event should come off I had equipped myself with a copy of Principal Burleigh's *History of the Church of Scotland*—I scarcely expected His Holiness would read it but I felt it would considerably enrich the Vatican Library. I myself came away with a magnificent reproduction of the Codex B, a thing of surpassing beauty, and a fitting memento of a memorable occasion.

It was on the following day that we were visiting the Lateran Palace (the original Roman home of the Popes) and there saw hordes of pilgrims climbing on their knees the twenty-eight steps of the Holy Staircase, which according to tradition was the stairway in Pilate's palace that must have been climbed by our Lord on the day of His trial. From there we crossed over to the Lateran Church of St John (claimed to be the oldest place of Christian worship in the world) and as we were leaving my attention was attracted to a notice-board near the door on which it was stated that this same Pope Pius with whom I had conversed the previous day granted forgiveness and absolution to all who on certain specified Saints' days, and also on one further occasion of their own choosing, repeated a stated number of pater-nosters within this Church. And it occurred to me that while our two Churches may be quite a bit closer together than was once the case we are still a very long way apart. I am sure that some of the more 'superstitious' elements in Roman practice are an embarrassment to the more liberally-minded of the leaders of that Church, but not even the most advanced of them is prepared to condemn the practices. Indeed on a later occasion I was in a cathedral where the Canon was showing me a very chaste and lovely chapel—completely deserted. Just around the pillar was another chapel, richly endowed with stucco saints, candles and the like—thronging with people. With an air approaching one of apology my guide explained that 'some of our people seem to find a great deal of comfort in this kind of thing'.

Doubtless it has been no negligible part of the strength of the Roman Catholic Church that it has been able to embrace

within its fellowship people of such wide diversity of faith and
practice. We in the Scottish Kirk, on the other hand, have
inclined overmuch to conceive that what we hold on to with
such dogged tenacity is not the faith once delivered to the saints
but the one faith delivered to the saints. The City of God in
John's vision has twelve gates—it's a poor interpretation that
sees only one of them partially open for admissions, the others
being dedicated to dealing with ejections. A friend of mine
used to say, 'Had General Booth emerged in the Roman
Catholic Church the Salvation Army would have been em-
braced as an Order within that Church.'

Our departure from our hotel in Rome was almost the
occasion of an 'incident'. It arose simply enough, and the
amount at stake was trivial enough (even for a canny Scot);
but I felt that the principle involved was one of some importance. It appeared there was in our bedroom one of those little
refrigerators filled with miniature bottles of all kinds of liquor.
It was only on our last night that we had so much as discovered
the existence of this secret horde. Hearing a ticking noise
coming from the direction of this box, and thinking we might
be entertaining a time-bomb unawares, I opened the thing and
found what it was. When presented with our bill I noticed an
item marked 'Bar', and on my explaining that I had never
visited the Bar I was informed that a miniature bottle of
whisky had been consumed from the store in the bedroom. I
took a strong line; they took a strong line; in the end my line
proved the stronger and the offending entry was removed. As
we have travelled around I have noticed this 'fridge in the bedroom an increasingly common feature of hotel life. It seems to
me to raise an interesting legal question about the guest's
liability for the safe custody of what is in the 'fridge. Hotel
managements are always at pains to deny in advance any
responsibility for the safety of any of your goods that you may
leave in your bedroom, yet you are apparently to be responsible
for the safety of their goods left in that very place. It would
seem to me that the guest should be provided with a key to
the 'fridge and that a check of the contents should be made
before as well as after if liability is to be alleged.

But I'm travelling too fast—we're not yet taking farewell of
Rome. A large number of members of the staff of the World

Food and Agriculture Organisation are connected with our congregation, and they very generously invited us to lunch. The caterer was labouring under severe difficulties, since a strike of waiters was in progress that day, but he was master of the occasion and contrived a meal which he himself was able to serve single-handed (I tactfully refrained from asking how the dishes were to be washed) and a very delightful meal it proved. The chief of the organisation is a Dutchman with a most charming Irish wife, and many members of the staff are Scots—a legacy, perhaps, from the days of Lord Boyd Orr. Ultimately, I'm sure, the organisation has to do with hunger and want, but a visit to the premises would scarcely convey that impression, and the various conference rooms, furnished by separate nations (of which there seemed to be very many indeed) are most impressive, if a trifle terrifying in their magnificence.

A visit to the Scots College and a hilarious dinner with the staff there; a visit to the Waldensian School of Theology; a visit to the Vatican Library to see the breath-taking display of illustrated Bibles from many centuries; a lunch with the Canadian Ambassador, and another with our own Ambassador, Sir Pat Hancock—these and a dozen other events filled in our days in Rome and left us with but an hour or so out of four days in which to do any kind of private sight-seeing.

And then we found ourselves being driven to the airport to take flight for Tel Aviv and a spell in the Holy Land.

CHAPTER 16

Middle-Eastern Interlude

If you come out of the Jaffa Gate from the old City of Jerusalem and, keeping the Mount of Olives on your left, look straight across the Valley of Hinnom you will see standing on the hillside before you the Church and Hospice of St Andrew, built in 1930 as a memorial to the men from Scotland who fought and died under Lord Allenby in Palestine in the First World War. The choice of the site for this Scots memorial was a real stroke of genius—comparable, almost, to the choice of the rock in Edinburgh Castle—for it sets out to perfection the quiet, dignified white building with the sun shining upon it. It is once you are inside the Church itself, though, that the full beauty of the memorial reveals itself and you appreciate the skill of its architect. By contrast with the busy, fussy, over-elaborate, gaudily-decorated, brightly-painted sanctuaries of which the city has such a superabundance, the chaste dignity of this Church, whose whole effect depends upon simplicity of line and the clever use of light and shade, strikes you with real force. And, lest the visitor should still have failed to catch the atmosphere of Scotland, there is set in the floor behind the Table that piece of green-veined marble from Iona on which the minister stands as he gives the elements in Communion. The chairs in the Church were gifts from various towns and villages at home and bear the names of the donors, so that a walk down the aisle is a kind of mini-tour of Scotland. Most impressive of all, perhaps, is the plate set in the floor that states so simply: 'In Remembrance of the Pious Wish of King Robert the Bruce that His Heart Should be Buried in Jerusalem. Given by Citizens of Dunfermline and Melrose in Celebration of the 6th Centenary of his Death.' It was the Douglas, you remember, who was commanded by the dying King to take the heart from his body and carry it in battle against the infidel. But the farthest Douglas got was Spain where, with the King's heart hung round his neck in a silver casket, he met his end in an engagement with the Moors. It's generally believed

that the royal heart eventually found repose beneath the
arches of the Abbey of Melrose—his body lies at Dunfermline.
But what a splendid way for those who revere his memory
to honour his wish—albeit after the lapse of six hundred
years.

It was in this lovely sanctuary on Easter morning that I was
to be assisting the local minister, William Gardiner Scott, in
the conduct of Morning Worship and in the Communion
Service that was to follow it. As the congregation was gathering
I was reminded not so much of the first Easter as of the first
Whitsunday, when the streets of Jerusalem were thronged with
people of every nation and the air resounded with the clamour
of many tongues. For there were many parties of pilgrims in the
city this Easter day, and many of them seemed to be heading
for the Church of St Andrew. Ere long every place-named
chair had its occupant and more chairs were being carried
across from every room in the hospice. When there were no
more chairs to carry, corners were found where people could
stand—even out into the vestibules. And over all there hung a
great air of expectancy of the kind you could actually feel. Our
worship that day and in that place is an experience I shall not
readily forget. To know that it had all happened somewhere
over there—I should not for my part be unduly worried about
identifying the precise spot—that feeling gave a new meaning
to familiar words of Scripture, a new urgency to well-known
items of praise, a new cogency to much-worn phrases of prayer.
When at the close of public worship the minister, as is our
custom in the Kirk, extended a welcome 'to all who are in love
with the Lord Jesus Christ' to share with us in the Sacrament
I was amazed that not one single person left his seat. We must
have represented a highly inter-denominational company; I'm
sure there were among us many who in normal circumstances
would not have wished to be associated in such a celebration;
but the spirit of the occasion had laid hold upon us and together
we broke the bread and passed from hand to hand the cup.
I've never been an ecumenical enthusiast; but if this is ecu-
menism let us have more of it.

I've never really wanted to visit the Holy Land. For I've
always had a notion that it was better to go on enjoying my
own picture of what it had all been like in our Lord's time than

to have this picture shattered by a reality which, I suspected, might well be as grim as it was real. From what I had seen of what devotion can do to holy places I had no desire to examine them at closer quarters. It seemed to me that so often a misguided zeal for honouring some sacred spot had led to the destruction rather than to the preservation of it. And to see denominations in bitter competition as to which possesses the true spot where such-and-such an event occurred would not, I have always felt, prove a very edifying spectacle. No, I had no intention of visiting the Holy Land, a pilgrimage in the steps of the Master was not for me. And then they made me Moderator and to the Holy Land I had to go.

Coming from Rome it was already evening and quite dark when we touched down on the runway at Tel Aviv, so that we saw nothing of the countryside as we were driven to Jerusalem. We were lodged in the hospice in a bedroom that looked across the Valley of Hinnom to the walls of the old city. Awakened on the first morning by the crowing of the cocks, mingled with the horn-hooting of the Arab lorry-drivers, we saw the splendour of the view and felt already that it was good for us to be here. Later that morning we were put under the care of a pleasant young Coptic guide, with whom we spent a fair part of the day touring the old city, visiting many of its well-known historic places. Sure enough we learned about the competing claims of the Church of the Holy Sepulchre and that other place known as 'Gordon's Calvary' to be the true Golgotha, the Place of a Skull. It does seem strange that Calvary, about which the one thing certain is that it was 'without the city wall' should be found so near the centre of the city as is the Church of the Holy Sepulchre. On the other hand it seems even more strange that so obvious a howler should have been perpetrated in a tradition that can be traced back to those who must have been alive at the time of the Crucifixion. For me, on that Easter Sunday morning in St Andrew's Kirk as I took into my hands the cup that was the symbol of His suffering love, it was sufficient to think that somewhere over there in an upper room He sat with His disciples; for me as I sang 'Christ is risen' it was sufficient to think that somewhere across yonder was a tomb from which the stone had been rolled away. Now I had no regrets that I had been obliged to travel to the Holy Land, to walk the narrow streets of the Holy City, to see at first hand something of its life and ways.

We had had a service already that morning. At 4.30 a surprisingly large company met on the esplanade in front of the Church, and in the cold of the morning—it was bitterly cold— we welcomed the sunrise with praise and prayer. To be quite accurate we welcomed it also with a sermon; but this, with all respect to Gardiner Scott (it was not he who was preaching), I thought to have been a mistake. I'm all for preaching. But a sermon is something to be mentally enjoyed without the distraction of physical discomfort. And in any case the setting of such a service should be left to proclaim its own message, a message that can be clouded and confused rather than underlined by the intrusion of the spoken word. I myself was thinking of Peter and his denial—I was positively standing shivering at his side before the brazier of coals in the court-yard waiting for that cock to crow—and the preacher's words, however well chosen, were an irritation and an irrelevance.

This year of our visit, as it happened, the Jewish Passover and the Christian Easter coincided. For us this had two interesting results. The first was an embarrassing inability to get our hands on any money. Let me hasten to remark that shortage of funds was no new experience for me; but to have plenty of money and to be unable to get my hands on it, this was certainly something of a novelty. One day when business had more or less resumed its normal course I thought I had achieved success in a Jewish bank where, after a long wait, they agreed to recognise my Barclaycard and were prepared to honour my Scottish cheque. The notes were all counted out and I had my hand outstretched to accord them the right hand of fellowship, when the teller decided he'd better have a look at my passport. This, I need scarcely say, I did not have with me, and having already spent close on an hour in the bank I had no time to go for it. And so a hopeful exercise came to nothing. The overall situation was not helped by the fact that the following weekend, when we were in Cyprus, it was the Greek Easter so that the Greek banks were out for us, and it was also the occasion of a strike by Turkish bank-clerks, which shut the doors of the Turkish banks in our face. But for the generosity of our hosts on each occasion in advancing loans against no collateral we'd have been in sore straits.

The other effect of the Passover was to rule out any possibility of meeting with Israeli officials—normally a feature of our visit. Actually the Speaker of the Knesset died at that very time and all had to come together for the Funeral Service—but death, of course, recognises no public holidays. While we were naturally disappointed not to have the opportunity of meeting with the personalities of government in Israel in these critical days, we had the compensation of a lighter official programme and some time therefore to wander round the old city and elsewhere on our own, and this we much appreciated.

Authority had, however, before going on holiday, laid on a trip for us, providing us with a guide, a car, and a driver to take us around the new city to see some of the tourist attractions there. A most impressive record of planning and building and extending it certainly presents. In particular I was glad of the opportunity to visit the great museum built, literally, around the Dead Sea Scrolls, 'The Shrine of the Book', as it is called. We were later to have the chance to go down to Jericho and look across at the cave at Qumran beside the Dead Sea where the shepherd lad discovered the first of these priceless survivals. We were then under the care of Graeme Auld, one of our own probationers from Aberdeen, who was then 'digging' with the British School of Archaeology in Jerusalem under the leadership of Mrs Crystal M. Bennett. Our main visit this day, however, was to Yad Va'shem, the memorial of the holocaust, the tribute to the memory of the six million Jews who were murdered, shot, massacred, gassed in the days of the Nazi pogrom. It is a very simple shrine—sorrow of such magnitude must inevitably be mute—and there is nothing to harrow the feelings or to re-create the horror of those ghastly days. But once every year each Israeli schoolchild is brought to Yad Va'shem and is told the pitiful story. The attitude of our guide impressed and terrified me. He was a man in, I should say, his late thirties, cultured, well-educated, intelligent, and extremely charming. His father had been a solicitor in Germany who, seeing how things were shaping, had got out to Israel in time, so that his son had seen nothing and suffered nothing at first hand. Yet when he got out of the car at the memorial something happened to him. He became a man possessed. Not that he shouted and

raved—I'd have been much less worried of he had. Instead he
very quietly told me the story of David and the Amalakites and
of how the king was ordered to destroy them root and branch
because they had failed his people in the hour of their need;
with analytical care he drew the distinction between a war of
conquest and a war of extermination; he told me proudly of
how a new generation of Israelis is being indoctrinated—'Once
each year every child comes here and is told the story'. 'So,' I
said, 'this is your new passover. Only instead of being designed
as a thanksgiving for deliverance this is to be a call for vengeance.' He assured me that it had nothing at all to do with the
passover—which, of course, I clearly recognised. I don't
think he had even taken my point. I don't think he was in a
mood to think reasonably. I was immeasurably saddened.
Here, surely, in Jerusalem, within sight of Golgotha (wherever
precisely that may be) we should have learnt the lesson that if
there is to be a day of peace and goodwill among men somebody must break somehow into the chain of hatred and counter-
hatred, of vengeance and super-vengeance, and, even if it has
to be from a cross, proclaim a new doctrine.

Unhappily this old theory of reprisal and counter-reprisal
seems to characterise Israel's defence policy. Admittedly, whatever may be the rights and wrongs of the Arab-Jewish situation
—and that question is indeed a very complicated one—the
Israelis are being made the victims of frightful terrorism and
outrage. It's not obvious to me that reprisals in bombing raids
on Arab villages are any answer. I had the feeling in Israel that
people were acutely conscious that they were the objects of
criticism and that they were ready in consequence to take
offence and then to take the offensive. A display of strength
must surely impress their critics; it certainly reassures themselves. There's an old Scots proverb that assures us that a man
with a big nose is satisfied that everybody's speaking about it.
This kind of attitude seemed to me to characterise both sides
in Israel, where any remark you may make, however innocent,
is liable to be interpreted as a hostile (or laudatory) comment.
At one point, on our return to Jerusalem after a few days in
Galilee, my wife was asked how she had liked the northern land.
'It was lovely,' she said, 'everything was so green and fertile
compared with Jerusalem.' Her partner bridled, 'Oh but,' she

said, 'you must give the Arabs some credit for that—it's not all just because the Jews have taken over.' In so far as Queenie had been awarding credit it had been to the Almighty, but her innocent remark had been treated as a value-judgment in the Arab-Jewish controversy. I'm sure the Israelis have done a great deal to bring prosperity to the land; would they could do something to bring peace to it.

They are, too, a people of queer contradictions—as I suppose we all are. The name Ein Gev, the title of the great kibbutz on the east bank of the Sea of Galilee, will for me be for ever associated with two incidents that illustrate these two sides of the Israeli character. We had travelled on the Sunday afternoon from Jerusalem up through Samaria to Tiberias, where we have a Minister, a Church, and a Hospice (until the Israelis took over it was a hospital), and I was to be taking an Easter Service in the Church in the evening. We were therefore to stay for a few days in the Manse with Hugh Kerr, our young minister there. On the Monday morning Hugh suggested we might sail across the Sea of Galilee to Ein Gev on the farther shore, and to this end we armed ourselves with tickets and joined the milling crowd that was awaiting the arrival of the little ferry-boat. Immediately she had tied up there occurred what I can only describe as the Battle of the Gangway. There was, in fact, adequate room on board for everyone, and in any case there was another sailing in an hour's time; but the pushing and struggling, the kicking and the tearing could not have been exceeded had she been the last boat away from a condemned island. It occurred to me to wonder as we watched —for we stood aside and looked on and then quietly stepped aboard when the battle was over—whether a reaction of this sort could be some kind of carry-over handed down to the next generation from the experiences of the concentration-camps. The following evening we went again to Ein Gev, driving this time round the southern shore of the lake, to attend a symphony concert in the huge open-ended concert hall—seating about three thousand—built on the kibbutz. There we saw the same people who had fought in the Battle of the Gangway sitting rapt in the enjoyment of classical music. Culture and barbarism side by side. How far, I wonder, is it to be traced to Auschwitz and like places? I'm sure a generation doesn't eradicate the effect, even if it could eradicate the memory.

While staying at Tiberias we had the opportunity of visiting a kibbutz not far from Cana of Galilee. We were actually calling on a member of Hugh's congregation who had been at the service on the Sunday evening, a Dutch girl who had come out in the first place as a volunteer worker. She had married one of the Israeli team, a Jew born in London who had later moved with his parents to South Africa. I do not think he was a practising Jew and he made no difficulty about his wife following her Christian convictions although the children were not baptised. I was much interested in the agricultural programme. There are about three thousand acres on the kibbutz and they grow a great deal of citrus fruit, much of which was being harvested at that time. They also had cattle and sheep. They were busy cutting green barley and putting it into silage pits layer about with the orange and grapefruit pulp that returned from the juice factory. It looked mildly revolting, smelt distinctly so, but appeared to commend itself to the sheep at least—I didn't have the chance to observe how the cattle reacted. They had a flock of ewes in milk, they machine-milk them three times a day, and make cheese with the milk.

It was the human aspect of the development, however, that I found so intensely interesting. Originally here, it would seem, the team all lived in a kind of hostel in which each couple had a room, in which there was communal feeding, clothing, washing, and living generally, the children being taken care of by staff set apart for the purpose. One Saturday at the weekly policy-meeting the question was asked 'Are we all happy here?' To this somewhat unusual query the males to a man gave an affirmative answer while the women with equal unanimity gave a negative. Why was this? 'We want to see more of our children.' In consequence the policy was changed and small detached houses were built (very attractive ones at that) in which the separate families are together in the evenings and throughout the night. They still feed communally and the children, irrespective of age, are away from their parents right throughout the day. The main furnishing of the cottages comes out of the common pool, but a small sum is credited to each individual monthly and, from this, little items of a personal kind may be bought for the embellishment of the house. Major items are not allowed. You can't have a television or a motor-car no matter how much is in your bank account. But you can have a picture on your wall or an ornament on your mantel, and I suppose there's nothing to prevent the picture being an old master or the ornament being a precious curio. Once there's enough in the common kitty to put a set into every cottage then they may decide to have television. One exception has been made to the television rule, however, and that in the case of a couple whose daughter is house-bound as a result of polio. I think it will be interesting to watch further developments here. The separate houses, the claim to 'your' children, and the right to be different even in little things seems rather like capitalism raising its ugly head; and the one exception to the television rule could so easily become a second exception (our old grannie is never over the door), and a third exception, and then farewell to the rule. As an answer to a temporary situation of emergency the kibbutz idea seems an excellent one. It remains to be seen how it can stand up to the strains that will be put upon it when it has to be adopted as a permanent way of life.

Our stay in Tiberias ended with a visit to the Edinburgh Medical Missionary Society's hospital in Nazareth, where Israel seems perfectly content we should continue to serve the Arab population and where a quite remarkable service is being given by the Swiss doctor chief (who was on leave at the time of our visit), by his deputy, our own Scots lady, Dr Mackay, and by their international staff. That evening we were entertained at the home of our other man in Tiberias, Paul Re'emi. Paul is a Jew who was converted to Christianity, studied at Edinburgh University and New College, and qualified as a minister of the Church of Scotland. Life in Tiberias cannot be easy for him, for the Jews have never taken kindly to apostasy. He is, however, dedicated to the task of producing a Hebrew concordance to the Old Testament. It is said that Cruden lost his reason after producing his English concordance and I've always felt that the same would have happened to me. But what the effect of a Hebrew concordance!

Next morning we set off for Jaffa where we were to visit our famous Tabeetha School. But first we were entertained to lunch by the British Ambassador, Sir John Barnes, and Lady Cynthia, his wife. Sir John is a son of the famous Bishop of Birmingham who provided the Anglican communion of my young days with many anxious moments because of his adherence to 'advanced' ideas that today are accepted as commonplace. It seems to me that sometimes when we are taking a heroic stand on some point of principle we should pause and ask ourselves what the passage of the years is likely to do for our principle. So clearly I remember a day when a hatless girl wouldn't have been allowed over the porch into a cathedral, even on a weekday as a sightseer, until she had draped a handkerchief over her head. It was a matter of principle—basic, fundamental, incontrovertible principle at that. Recently I was present at a well-attended Anglican Sunday service at which I could detect only one solitary woman wearing a hat. Yet so far as I am aware nothing has happened to shake the foundations on which the principle was so securely founded; St Paul hasn't come back to add a postscript to his epistle; there has been no fresh revelation on the subject of women being covered in Church. Who knows but what in another twenty years Apostolic Succession will have gone the same way—and be equally unlamented.

Sir John's son, who appears to have inherited the family brilliance, was a pupil of the school at Tabeetha, so the Ambassador had been invited to take the chair at a meeting of parents in the school in the afternoon—the children of course being on holiday. I've forgotten just how many ambassadors I met that afternoon, their children being pupils, but I remember that it included the Turkish, and I'm pretty sure I'm right in saying that the total roll-call of the school contains representatives of no fewer than thirty-eight nations. The school is passing through a difficult time, though. It made its name under the headmistress-ship of Miss J. B. Rosie, a woman remarkable in every way. Unfortunately Miss Rosie has had, for reasons of health, to retire to her native Caithness, and the question of how she is to be replaced is proving a tricky one for the Overseas Council.

Back from Jaffa to Jerusalem to a very largely attended reception which Gardiner Scott had organised for us in the Hospice. There, oddly enough, I met a Jewish couple from Glasgow now settled in Israel, the man being a doctor, and discovered that his wife's young brother had been in my class at school. One last night in Jerusalem and then off next morning by plane to Nicosia for a few days in Cyprus. But not before a great deal of searching of luggage, emptying out of contents of brief-case and handbag, running us over with a mine-detector. The figure of a sentry with machine-gun on the roof of the air-port reception lounge reminded us—if all the searching hadn't already done so—that for all its appearance of prosperity and wellbeing the true promise of this Land of Promise is still to be fulfilled.

To move from Jerusalem to Nicosia was but to go from a divided country to a city still more obviously divided—for Nicosia has its Turkish quarter where Greeks are not allowed, and its Greek quarter where Turks are permitted but not exactly welcomed. At every second street-corner the forces of United Nations stand on guard—and incidentally bring a fair amount of money into the country. There are those who slyly tell you that when from time to time United Nations get around to squaring its accounts and discovers the exact cost of the Cyprus peace-keeping exercise, there is always a fresh out-break of violence somewhere on the island and the visitors remain—representative of four different armies.

Just before our arrival President Makarios had carried through a brilliant piece of political legerdemain, out-manœuvring with real genius a couple of bishops who were trying to dis-credit him in the eyes of the Church. At a dinner one even-ing when I was asked to sign my name in the Visitors' Book I did so in red (it happened to be the biro that first came to my hand) to the complete horror of my hostess who assured me that the Archbishop was the only person in Cyprus who signed all documents in red. For my own part I thought that for him the choice was singularly inappropriate but resolved that all my signing while there would be done in red.

Cyprus is a pleasant island with a fine climate, as trips to Army and Air Force units at Dhekelia, Akrotiri, Episkopi, Limassol and Berengaria convinced us. James Morrison, a retired Army Chaplain, was acting as minister of the Com-munity Church at the time of our visit but was leaving for Rotterdam in the summer. The congregation at Nicosia is small but enthusiastic, and contains representatives of many nationalities. It is hard to think of them as being without a minister.

It is not possible, apparently, to fly direct from Nicosia to Rome—you have to go via Athens. On the first draft of our tour I had noticed we were to have three hours between planes in the Greek capital. Three hours is just long enough to take a taxi from the airport to the city, and then search for another taxi for the return trip. So I suggested we wait for the next connection. This too appeared to present difficulties, so it was arranged that we spend the whole day in Athens, stay over-night, and set off first thing in the morning. In this way we were able to see something of the city—barely enough to entitle us to say we've been there. Of all the places we have visited it appealed to me—probably quite wrongly—as the one most efficiently geared to glean the last ears out of the harvest of the tourist trade. I was amused at the efforts of one touting guide who seemed to me to say, 'You Amaireecan, I do you in dollars; you Engleesh, I do you in sterling.' I was tempted to reply, 'No, I Scottish; I do you in bawbees.' It would have been an idle boast.

This I discovered in the morning. We had been booked in at the Hotel Bretagne, a very magnificent establishment on the corner of the main city square. I ascertained that we had to present ourselves next morning at the offices of TWA, at the diametrically opposite corner of the square, about a hundred yards distant. Had it been possible to sneak unobserved out of the Hotel Bretagne, Queenie and I could, without either in-convenience or exhaustion, have conveyed ourselves and our cases across to the said offices. But even at six in the morning the reception hall bristled with uniforms and gold braid. I thought one of the porters might be prepared, for a suitable considera-tion, to relieve us of the indignity of the case-carrying. Having picked a suitable model I put the proposition to him. ''ow many valise?' On hearing there were three he felt a taxi was called for, but by a fortuitous chance his cousin was at hand with his vehicle and would find great satisfaction in affording us this little service. The three valises, my brief-case, my wife and myself were got into the cab and we had just got the door shut when we pulled up outside the offices of TWA. The meter showed a reading of five drachmae and I was smiling to myself at the incongruity of the five drachmae fare and the fifteen drachmae tip which I was proposing to offer. Until I learned that my bill was twenty-three drachmae—without the tip. I paid up with a smile suited for that hour of the morning. An American lady who arrived a few moments later in someone else's cousin's taxi was, however, made of sterner stuff, and she marched her driver into the office, demanding that the girl at the counter there act as interpreter and explain to this thieving scoundrel that she, from the land of Abraham Lincoln . . . The girl, having exchanged a few words with the driver, said patiently to the infuriated niece of Uncle Sam, 'Let me explain. It says five drachmae on the meter; right? It is now between 11 o'clock at night and 7 in the morning, so there is a surcharge of five drachmae; right? It is not yet ten days after Easter so there is a holiday bonus of five drachmae; right? You have four valises at two drachmae each, eight drachmae; right? Total 23 drachmae; right?' The whole thing sounded so incontrovertibly right that even my American friend paid up—but without the smile.

And on that happy note we said Farewell to this very interesting section of our tour.

CHAPTER 17

Headed for Home

For some reason best known to himself the Weather Clerk frowned upon our visit to Northern Europe. It was now the second half of April and we drove into the Great St Bernard Tunnel in real summer conditions such as we had enjoyed ever since landing in France just over a month before. A few miles away we had sat at a hillside café in brilliant sunshine, enjoying our elevenses, having climbed up out of Aosta where we had had a walk in very pleasant conditions. When we emerged from the tunnel at the northern end it had become grey and overcast and cold—a totally different world from the one we had left. It was quite distinctly worse when we parked the car in Martigny and went to get ourselves some lunch. The meal was good and we lingered over it, only to step out of the hotel into cold, sleety rain. This, it is true, lasted for only a few hours but the dull, cold, grey weather persisted right through Switzerland, France, Belgium and most of our time in Holland. Indeed, during nearly a week in Geneva and Lausanne we never once saw the mountains.

We had had, I suppose, a premonition of what was to come. For the rain had begun on 'the morning of the drachmae' as we drove from Athens to the airport, and the plane rose into grey cloud—so different from the previous day when we had admired the sun-drenched islands of Greece lying there beneath us in the glorious blue of the sea. We arrived in Rome to a warm welcome from the Macleans but to a cold one from the Weather Clerk—a heavy, relentless, steady downpour and a solid kind of rain to which we're not accustomed—we get plenty of wet weather but it's a soft kind that we 'enjoy' at home. We had quite a job of repacking and reorganising and it was long past lunch when we got away from Rome. We had been advised to take the coast road to Florence and this we did, though we found it a long, dreary drive in rain that never let up and that did not allow us to see anything of the country-side. From Florence next day we had only a short trip to

Parma, and this allowed us long enough in Florence to locate exactly where were situated the galleries and so on that we should have wanted to visit if time had permitted! Then next day away from Parma by Cremona and Como to Aosta, the weather being now completely recovered. On the last lap of that magnificent trip we disdained the motorway and found the old road provided a unique feeling of the mountains.

Throughout the trip generally, when we were on our own, we had quite a bit of fun over menus, but in Aosta that evening we had a particularly entertaining time ordering our evening meal. It transpired that the hotel in which we had been booked didn't have a dining-room and after some searching around we found a modest little place which was able to provide us with a splendid repast. The boy who acted as waiter was most obliging, but, as he knew no English and we no Italian, we had our problems. At length we got round to identifying a steak for main course, but our efforts to convey 'very well done' produced bottles of sauce, ash-trays, a wine-list, and many other strange things. Then I had a brainwave and said 'bien cuit' and all was well. Another illusion shattered, for I had always believed that every continental waiter had at least three words of English—rare, medium and well-done.

It brought back to my mind an incident during a holiday in Norway. For miles before we reached the town of Dale we had noticed that every flag-pole carried the national flag at half-mast, and as we were actually driving into the town itself I had to nip smartly into a side street out of the way of a great funeral procession that was marching down the main thorough-fare, while at the head of the village a kirk bell solemnly tolled. After a bit of a walk we went into a tea-room. The Italian proprietor was balancing masses of jam on the most out-rageously delicious waffles when my wife asked about the funeral—it had been a person of much importance in the com-munity who had died? He was utterly mystified. Queenie's efforts at depicting death and burial in mime didn't help noticeably. I have often felt that I possess considerable theatrical gifts which have never been given an outlet, so I took over at this point and gave a—to me—convincing impersonation of a corpse, repeating the while the word 'kaput'. 'Ah,' he said with a happy smile, 'toilets straight through that door'. We'd really be better to learn the language, but it would be so much less entertaining.

We awoke in Aosta to a lovely day, but, as I have said, it was not to last long, and we arrived in Geneva in cold, grey conditions that continued throughout the whole of our stay. It's not so long since John Hood went from Auchterarder to be our man in Geneva—indeed I had many messages to convey to him and to his delightful wife from some of their former members with whom I had been in contact during our time in that Presbytery. The day after our arrival was Sunday and I found it a great thrill to be taking part in a service in the Calvin Auditoire, to sit on Calvin's own chair, and to preach to a large congregation in that city so closely associated also with our own John Knox. In the evening we drove along Lake Leman to Lausanne, where again I preached to a fully international congregation.

When in Geneva one naturally pays one's respects at the offices of the World Council of Churches. This is an institution which has mushroomed since, so recently as 1948, it was formed by the fusion of two world ecumenical movements, that of Faith and Order and that of Life and Work. There are now over two hundred member Churches, and in 1961 the Council went on record in a statement of its common purpose—'The World Council of Churches is a fellowship of Christians who confess the Lord Jesus Christ as God and Saviour and therefore seek to fulfil together their common calling to the glory of the one God, Father, Son and Holy Spirit.' I've never understood how the word 'therefore' came to be there. It seems designed to convey the idea that what is merely a statement of fact carries the force of a logical argument. And in my opinion the reference to 'their common calling' is a begging of the question, as I would have thought the object of such a statement was to tell us what that common calling was. The set-up at Geneva is most impressive—a kind of cross between United Nations and the Vatican (albeit on a more modest scale). I am sometimes tempted to wonder whether it is in somewhat similar terms that the officials envisage their functions.

The issue of what exactly the powers and functions of the World Council ought to be came to occupy a good deal of attention lately because of a decision taken at Geneva to make

grants to certain bodies in the emergent countries which are
committed to the use of violence in the achievement of their
political ends. It was made clear that the money was not to be
used directly in the pursuit of violence, but this reservation
carried little weight—understandably, I think—with those who
were opposed to the policy generally. In a realm where little
is certain one thing at least seems clear to me—that the World
Council is not itself a super-Church but merely a piece of
machinery designed to make easier and more effective the work
of its constituent member-Churches. If then such a body does
the necessary study and research that will enable it to say that
in the view of its experts such-and-such an organisation is
engaged in a truly Christian exercise, however much appearances may be to the contrary, and that it is deserving of all the
support the Churches can give to it, this, as I see it, is the
Council fulfilling its proper function. I should still have no
complaint if it went further and said that it was setting up a
piece of organisational machinery to get to the people concerned any help which the member Churches cared to provide,
and that contributions should therefore be forwarded to
Geneva. But when I hear that grants have been made by the
World Council I instantly react by wanting to know where the
money came from and whether it was subscribed for this
purpose. The only money we in the Church of Scotland ever
give to the Council is either for ordinary administrative expenses
or for the erection and maintenance of their offices, and is given
as a definite proportion of these costs allocated to us and to all
the other Churches on some sort of per capita basis. The
money to meet this charge comes, in our Church, from what is
called the General Purposes Fund, the income of which, in turn,
is subscribed by congregations in the form of a tax that is a
first charge on income. That is to say, money contributed by the
ordinary Church member for congregational purposes was finding its way to a highly controversial objective without the
consent of the member, of his congregation, or even of the
General Assembly of his Church. I am glad to learn that this
method of supporting these organisations has now been departed
from.

As I see it the World Council is constantly confronted with
two very real dangers. One is that it inclines to be dealing with

international issues and to be doing so at the highest level, and it is therefore tempted to see itself as having to reach decisions that are to be the Church's decisions—and that at the highest level. If it had been given power by the constituent bodies this would be all right. But in fact it's got no authority to speak for anybody. Its job is to speak to the Churches—not for them. The other danger arises from the fact that it operates at a level so very far removed from the man-in-the-pew as almost to be in an ecclesiastical vacuum. Hence it is easy for it to forget this man-in-the-pew, or at least to think that his views are of little significance—after all what can he be expected to know of these intricate matters. Yet it is this very man-in-the-pew and none other who is providing the wherewithal to make the efforts of the World Council possible, to make the splendid offices and considerable staff at Geneva a reality; and it's the man-in-the-pew who in the long run can alone make any of the decisions of the Council effective.

I did not, I admit, discuss these reservations of mine with the retiring Secretary of the Council, Dr Eugene Carson Blake, when he gave a lunch in our honour on the occasion of our visit. Had that visit occurred some months later I should certainly have felt impelled to challenge him on the subject of a telegram he sent to the Israeli President immediately after the tragedy of Munich, when a number of Israeli athletes were held hostage by a group of Arab terrorists and in a shoot-up at the airfield all of the Jews and two of the Arabs lost their lives. In this telegram the Secretary expressed the horror of the Council and its sympathy with the Israeli people in this terrible thing that had happened to them. Perfectly right and proper. But then the Secretary went on, in a quite gratuitous fashion, to pass a hostile judgment upon the way in which the West German police had dealt with the emergency. Now I am in no position to say that the Munich police acted rightly or wisely; but neither was Carson Blake when he wrote the telegram in any position to say that they acted wrongly or foolishly; and, in any case, he was under no obligation to make any comment upon their conduct. If my tinkering with law has taught me anything it has taught me to withhold judgment until I have heard the evidence—all the evidence. There are those, I know, who feel it's terribly important that the Church should be heard to be speaking on every significant occasion; my own view is that when the Church is heard to be speaking on any kind of occasion it must be heard to be speaking the truth. If I'm right in this it follows that the Church must at all costs eschew snap judgments. It's nice to be in first: it's often wise to be in last. A man who speaks in a representative capacity just daren't let himself go.

The first part of our journey away from Lausanne was through impressive scenery and this we much enjoyed, in spite of a continuance of the grey weather. The first night we spent in a very interesting little town in France called Langres. From there to Brussels was through pretty dreich undulating country, on none too good French roads. In sunny conditions it could have been pleasant enough, but in the prevailing greyness it was a disappointment. Unhappily this state of affairs persisted during the four days we spent in the Belgian capital.

It would certainly be premature, but it might well be prophetic, to describe Brussels today not as the Belgian capital but as the Capital of Europe, since the development of the Common Market and of the Community which it is creating seems likely to bring that about. We Scots have had a Church in Brussels for a long time, and I'm sure it's of supreme importance that we should be developing our activities there. Alister Macleod, our man on the spot for the past dozen years or so, is very acutely conscious of the possibilities of the situation and will, I am convinced, see that we are kept abreast of things. We met many people in the congregation whom we knew, or of whom we knew—I even met a third cousin of my own of whom I had often heard but whom I did not expect to meet— least of all there. A particularly large representation of Americans in the congregation—in spite of the presence of two American causes in the city—seems to indicate again what we had seen so often on the continent, that the traditional type of worship of the Presbyterian Church has something to offer which still is of inestimable worth.

While in Brussels I had the chance of meeting, at a luncheon given by the Ambassador, the famous Cardinal Suenens, Archbishop of Malines-Brussels and Primate of Belgium, probably the most liberal-minded of all the upper hierarchy

of Rome, leader of the Second Vatican Council, mentioned
freely as possible successor for the chair of St Peter. The following
afternoon Alister and I visited him at his palace at Malines,
at which he lives very simply. He presented me with an
autographed copy of the little book on *The Future of the Christian
Church* which is the text of a series of lectures given in New York
in 1970 by himself and Michael Ramsey. I was much impressed
by and attracted to Cardinal Suenens, but I could not echo
the words of the Archbishop of Canterbury, 'I think it is daft—
absolutely daft—that we should have to belong to separate
ecclesiastical establishments.' Unfortunate it may be, deplorable
some would even say, but to any student of history it can
surely not appear as 'daft'. I am not at all sure in my own mind
—and my various encounters in the course of my year have
done nothing to reassure me—that the Roman Catholic Church
sees reunion in any other shape than as a gathering in of the
separated brethren—probably on more gracious and more
generous terms than might at one time have been the case. The
various subdivisions of Protestantism seem to be dedicated as
never before to the search for one Church. 'Right,' say the
Romans, 'we've got the very thing they're looking for.' While
that is said it must, I feel, be added that the gulf separating us
from Rome is a narrowing one these days, and it is so because
of the changes that Rome has made and is still making since
the Second Vatican Council. Of this at least I feel certain, that
if the changes of the last ten years had been effected within the
Church of Rome in the first half of the sixteenth century there
never would have been a Reformation. Whether or not it
would have been a good thing for the fruits of the Reformation
to have been gathered without the pain and struggle and
anguish is a question on which I should not wish to venture an
opinion.

Our Dutch congregations are the oldest of our causes in
Europe—it was in the Scots Kirk in Rotterdam that in the
Killing Times many Scots ministers, including James Renwick,
were ordained. Before the Union of the Parliaments in 1707
opened up the colonial markets to Scottish trade our people
had their own ideas about the European Economic Community, and maintained the closest trading links with the
continent and in particular with the Low Countries, in which

at one time or another we had no fewer than ten congregations. Due to some extent to the fact that both Rotterdam and Amsterdam were vacant at the time, our programme in Holland was a comparatively light one, involving only evening functions in one or other of the two cities; and so we had been planning to treat ourselves to a bit of a holiday before returning at the beginning of May to fulfil the remaining engagements at home and then to face the Assembly. The cold weather rather played havoc with this plan, though we had one magnificent day when we went to Keukenhof, that huge garden of bulbs—such a mass of colour was never seen. It was the Queen's Birthday holiday in Holland, and many thousands had fallen upon the same idea of how to spend it. I don't think I ever milled about among such crowds.

The two most recent ministers of our Scots kirk in Rotterdam had been pupils of Glasgow High School, and the school and its Former Pupils' Association had decided to instal two little stained glass windows in the Church to celebrate this fact. To this end Dr David Lees, the rector, along with a couple of masters, two representatives of the Former Pupils, and about a score of boys had come over for a long weekend. Among us we dedicated and unveiled the windows. A dinner in a Rotterdam hotel attended by the consistories of the two congregations (the first time in all their long history they had ever met as one) brought our stay in Holland to a close and the next evening we set sail for Hull.

We disembarked early, got straight through Customs and made splendid time through Yorkshire, Cumberland and Dumfriesshire. We had got into Lanarkshire and over Beattock Summit and I was calculating that with luck another hour would see us home and we'd not bother stopping for lunch, when a strange noise came from under the bonnet and I was fortunate to be able to freewheel to a layby. It transpired that a piston had broken. By the time we got towed into Abington and had managed to arrange for a hired car to be got out from Lanark, and had transferred to it not only the mass of luggage with which we set out in the first place but also the mementoes of our visits which we had collected en route, and then continued the interrupted journey home, ours was indeed a mighty late lunch that day. I was impressed not so much by the misfortune of a breakdown like this within fifty miles of home but by the good fortune that it had not occurred say fifty miles from Rotterdam—which could have landed us in real trouble.

I had still to attend the Assembly of the Presbyterian Church of England in London's City Temple, and then my period as Moderator was as good as complete. But on the way south I was to be speaking to the students at Westminster College, Cambridge, and preaching in the Presbyterian Church of England charge there, where my friend Ronnie Spiers is minister—Ronnie was a student under my care at one time in the Presbytery of Paisley. And even before that I had meetings of one kind and another to address each day—often twice a day—so there would be no danger of slacking off on the final furlong.

And all of that takes us round to the opening day of the 1972 Assembly and the Officer shouting, 'Moderator'—and, as we used to say in the days when we still went to the pictures, 'This is where we came in'.

Epilogue

'What has been your most memorable experience?' is a question I'm constantly asked. I find it an exceedingly difficult question to answer. As anyone who has persevered thus far through these pages will realise I've managed to remember a great many of our experiences—they've all been memorable to that extent. And there are whole tracts that I haven't even got round to mentioning—our entire spell in London, my visit to Balmoral, the foundation-stones I have laid (I was always expecting a demand that I take out a union card I was getting so proficient in the use of a trowel), the new Churches and Halls and redecorated and refurnished Churches I have dedicated, the countless schools and hospitals we've visited— it's not that they have been forgotten, or ever will be. But I should need the advantage of that perspective that comes only when you are far enough away from the events to sort them out ere I could even begin to range them in any kind of order of importance or significance, or say which was 'the most memorable'.

Nobody, oddly enough, has yet asked me what was the most embarrassing moment of my year. We have had our moments, though none of them, I'm glad to say, has been serious. There was the time, for example, when I travelled on the overnight train with Roy Tuton, my chaplain, to attend an important function in the Metropolis, and when in the morning I came to change into full regalia I discovered that I had left my stud-box at home. Having travelled in a shirt with collar attached, the question how I was to get my 'dog-collar' fixed was more than I could figure. Mercifully my chaplain—who is invariably better organised than I (otherwise why have a chaplain)—had both a front and a back stud, so we were able to effect a kind of 'stud transplant' and function for the rest of the day on a single stud apiece. It would have been a sad thing if the Church of Scotland had had to go unrepresented on an important occasion for want of a stud. They used to tell of how for want of a nail for a horseshoe a battle was lost. So I've taken a

mental note that wherever I go I should take a spare stud as
well as a spare horse-shoe nail.

One thing which I did carry about with me wherever we
went was a huge autograph book in which I now have a quite
unique collection of signatures of people in high places and in
humble. The authenticity of the signatures of the boys of the
Fourth Tank Regiment is borne out by the oily thumb-marks
all over the page. We had been touring a hospital and were
drinking tea with the matron and some members of the staff
and I passed my book round for signatures. A sweet little
nurse enquired whether I'd like her to put in her phone-
number as well—and then blushed to the roots of her hair.

It was a nice mixture of anxiety and amusement that
characterised the situation in which we found ourselves on the
morning of our departure from Nicosia. We were to be at the
airport somewhere about 9 o'clock, but we were up and packed
and ready very early, and Jim Morrison suggested he might
fill in the hour by taking us into town to see the cathedral
turned mosque—as he had earlier promised to do. It took us a
long time in the warren of streets in the Turkish quarter to get
to the spot, but once having got there we just could not find
the road away. Wherever we went we turned a few corners,
along a few twisted lanes, and so back to the point of com-
mencement. There seemed a real chance that we'd miss the
plane while touring the maze. And then a Turkish policeman
came to our rescue and guided us out. I'm sure poor Jim
Morrison was thoroughly embarrassed that morning.

Then there was the day when I was telling a group of very
small school-children someting about my outfit, and I had got
as far as the ring, the signet ring with the crest of the Church
of Scotland engraved on it 'backside foremost'. To help them
with the 'signet' business I enquired happily, 'Now when
you've written a letter what do you put at the very end?' A
little hand shot up. 'Yes, my dear?' I said. 'Kisses' she replied.
It's a long mental hop from kisses to the burning bush in
reverse.

That same ring brought not so much a moment of embarrassment as rather a few hours of anxiety. Apparently I have
thick fingers and I had great difficulty forcing the ring on
when Hugh Douglas placed it on my finger on the opening

day. The crushing must have damaged something, for the finger swelled enormously and the ring had to be enlarged to a tremendous extent. Within a couple of days the swelling subsided and the ring was now far too slack so that I had to be constantly on the alert not to let it fall off my finger. One evening it went missing. Alarm and despondency on every hand. The bedroom was searched, as was the bathroom. The Moderatorial car was practically dismembered. The next morning at 8 o'clock Edward Marr was at the Assembly Hall learning from the chief cleaner that the Moderator's room had been swept and dusted with minute particularity and there was no ring there. Breakfast was eaten in an atmosphere of deep gloom. When we all got up to the Hall Roy Tuton spied something behind the leg of the huge Moderatorial armchair and it was none other than the missing ring. The bush burned again and the Kirk took fresh heart.

And, of course, there was the night when I arrived at Balmoral. One of the things which the Moderator always does is to take a service at Crathie one Sunday in the autumn when the Royal Family are in residence; and there is a tradition dating from the days of Queen Victoria that the preacher at Crathie is invited to spend the weekend as a guest at the Castle. I was there the last Sunday in August, had arrived at the appointed door at the appointed hour, and was welcomed by the equerry, Jock Slater, who introduced me to a young man in livery who, he said, would look after me during my sojourn—as in fact he did and that with the utmost efficiency. The young man indicated that if I'd give him the car keys he would take up my things out of the boot and the car would be taken care of till I required it again for my departure on Monday. The taking up of my things from the boot to the bedroom he carried through with terrifying thoroughness; he didn't actually take up the spare wheel; but everything else, including an old mud-splashed, oil-stained waterproof coat which I keep stuffed in a corner in case of a puncture on a dirty night. An embarrassing moment, surely, for the poor garment which must have felt intensely self-conscious draped over a hanger in the royal wardrobe.

Embarrassing moments? Oh yes, we've had not a few.

And what am I most grateful for in my whole year? I don't

know what the order should be; but I am most deeply grateful for the good health and vitality that never failed me during a pretty heavy spell of many and varied demands; I am most deeply grateful for the constant comfort and companionship and good cheer—not to mention occasional reprimand—which my wife supplied and without which I just could not have gone on as I did; I am most deeply grateful for the prayerful support of the whole Kirk which I felt was constantly with us in all our labours and on all our journeyings. And last of all I'm very thankful now to have got it all off my chest—even if it's only in a Record Apart.